THE POLITICS TODAY COMPANION TO
WEST EUROPEAN POLITICS

MANCHESTER
UNIVERSITY PRESS

Ideology and politics in Britain today
Ian Adams

Political ideology, 2nd edition
Ian Adams

Scandinavian politics today
David Arter

American society today
Edward Ashbee

US politics today
Edward Ashbee and Nigel Ashford

Pressure groups today
Rob Baggot

French politics today, new edition
David S. Bell

Local government today, 3rd edition
J. A. Chandler

Political issues in Ireland today,
2nd edition
Neil Collins (editor)

Irish politics today, 4th edition
Neil Collins and Terry Cradden

General Elections today, 2nd edition
Frank Conley

East Central European politics today
Keith Crawford

US elections today (*Elections USA*,
2nd edition)
Philip John Davies

Political issues in America today
Philip John Davies and
Fredric A. Waldstein (editors)

British political parties today, 2nd edition
Robert Garner and Richard Kelly

Spanish politics today
John Gibbons

*The Politics Today companion to American
government*
Alan Grant and Edward Ashbee

Political issues in Britain today, 5th edition
Bill Jones (editor)

British politics today, 6th edition
Bill Jones and Dennis Kavanagh

Trade unions in Britain today, 2nd edition
John McIlroy

Italian politics today
Hilary Partridge

Britain in the European Union today, 2nd
edition
Colin Pilkington

The Civil Service in Britain today
Colin Pilkington

Devolution in Britain today
Colin Pilkington

*The Politics Today companion to the British
Constitution*
Colin Pilkington

Representative democracy in Britain today
Colin Pilkington

German politics today
Geoffrey Roberts

European politics today
Geoffrey Roberts and Patricia Hogwood

Debates in British politics today
Lynton Robins and Bill Jones (editors)

Government and the economy today
Graham P. Thomas

Prime Minister and Cabinet today
Graham P. Thomas

Political communication today
Duncan Watts

THE POLITICS TODAY COMPANION TO
WEST EUROPEAN POLITICS

Geoffrey K. Roberts
and Patricia Hogwood

Manchester University Press
Manchester and New York

distributed exclusively in the USA by Palgrave

Published by Manchester University Press
Oxford Road, Manchester M13 9NR, UK
and Room 400, 175 Fifth Avenue, New York,
NY 10010, USA
www.manchesteruniversitypress.co.uk

Distributed exclusively in the USA by
Palgrave, 175 Fifth Avenue, New York,
NY 10010, USA

Distributed exclusively in Canada by
UBC Press, University of British Columbia,
2029 West Mall, Vancouver, BC, Canada V6T 1Z2

British Library Cataloguing-in-Publication Data
A catalogue record for this book is available
from the British Library

*Library of Congress Cataloging-in-Publication
Data applied for*

ISBN 0 7190 5420 6 *hardback*
     0 7190 5421 4 *paperback*

First published 2003

10 09 08 07 06 05 04 03   10 9 8 7 6 5 4 3 2 1

Typeset by Carnegie Publishing Ltd, Lancaster
Printed in Great Britain by Biddles Ltd,
Guildford and King's Lynn

Contents

Preface

Generally politics textbooks lack sufficient space to provide full details of important political actors or of particular political events or crises. They may well refer to political leaders or events, such as Konrad Adenauer or Olaf Palme, the Suez crisis or Poujadism, but usually only in passing and not in sufficient detail to inform the reader adequately about the political careers of these politicians, or the origins, course and consequences of the events. As co-authors of the textbook: *European Politics Today*, we are aware that students need a background in the contemporary history of European countries in order to understand the significance of the political developments which we trace in that textbook. We have therefore endeavoured to write an accessible and relevant guide to the kind of background information which students will need in order to get to grips with the political systems of Western European countries and the changes taking place in those political systems.

This *Companion to West European Politics* has five sections. Sections 1 and 2 provide, in the style of a dictionary, (a) explanations of significant political events, groupings and developments, and (b) details of the political careers of significant West European politicians, especially those who have been head of their country's government or head of state. Entries in both sections contain, where appropriate, cross-references to other entries in those two sections: for instance, the entry for *Mitterrand* has a cross-reference to *cohabitation*, and that for the *Suez crisis* has cross-references to *Eden* and *Macmillan*. The third section consists of lists of abbreviations (or short names) of political parties and

other important organisations which play (or have played in the recent past) a significant political role, together with the names of those organisations. Where appropriate these are given in English translation and in their 'home' language. The fourth section is a set of chronologies, divided into groups based on particular countries or groups of countries. As well as a general chronology for each country or group of countries, specialised chronologies of major developments are supplied, which cover, for example, the reunification of Germany and the transition to democracy in Spain. The fifth section is a set of political data relating to the political system of each country in Western Europe.

Of course difficult choices had to be made concerning what to include and what to leave out. Generally speaking, the time-frame is from the start of the Second World War onwards (with December 2001 as the 'closing date'). We have selected the Second World War as a starting point, as this turned out to be an important watershed in the development of societies and political and economic systems in most Western European countries. We have, though, included occasional references to some earlier developments and events where these have been especially relevant to post-war developments, such as the Spanish civil war and nazism. Geographically, the book is confined to Western Europe. Special emphasis has been placed on the United Kingdom, France, Germany, Italy, Spain and the political system of the European Union, to reflect the relative size and political importance of those political systems, as well as the fact that they constitute the focus of most courses in West

European politics in universities and colleges. We have, though, been careful to include politicians and events which have proved decisive for smaller and less familiar European democracies, and which have often impacted upon larger countries and the European Union. In the first section, covering events and developments, no attempt has been made to provide coverage of general political science concepts, such as *presidentialism* or *opposition*. Only where a concept has special relevance to Western Europe has it been included. Examples are: *cohabitation*, *consociationalism*, *grand coalition* and *new politics*.

The authors hope that students will find this book useful as a supplement to their textbooks, and that teachers and other readers will make use of the book as a reliable source of information and reference.

The authors wish to express their thanks to Ian Gillan, Jill Lovecy, Elisa Roller and Alasdair Young for their valuable advice and suggestions. Full responsibility for the work remains, of course, with its authors.

Geoffrey K. Roberts, Manchester
Patricia Hogwood, Glasgow

Section 1
Events, groups and developments

Events, groups and developments

Related entries are listed at the end of an entry by '[See also: ...]'. An asterisk indicates a cross-reference to Section 2, 'Biographies'. For example, the entry for **Colonels' coup (Greece)** has at the end '[See also: Enosis; Papandreou*]'. The entry for Enosis is in this section; that for Papandreou is in Section 2.

acquis communitaire

The French term: acquis communitaire (sometimes called Community patrimony) refers to the constantly evolving rights and obligations deriving from European Union (EU) treaty agreements, laws and regulations concluded by member states since the Treaties of Rome establishing the European Economic Community entered into force in 1958. Together, these agreements are held to represent the constitutional basis of the EU. Amongst other aims, the Single European Act (1987), the Treaty on European Union (TEU: the Maastricht Treaty) (1993) and the Treaty of Amsterdam (1997) have attempted to revise and rationalise the acquis communitaire by simplifying and consolidating the existing Treaties of the Union. The acquis is now understood to comprise not only a strict definition of Community law, but also all acts adopted under the second and third pillars of the European Union and, more importantly, the common objectives laid down in the treaties. The acquis can therefore be understood to cover both the judicial decisions and the policy programme of the EU. The concept has played a major role in discussions concerning the enlargement of the EU to countries of Central and Eastern Europe. These countries are expected to accept the acquis communitaire and, to some extent, to have restructured their national legal, policy and administrative frameworks to accommodate it prior to entry.

[See also: Amsterdam Treaty; Maastricht Treaty; Single European Act; Treaties of Rome; Treaty of Nice]

Action Directe

A French anarchist/Maoist terrorist group founded in 1979, Action Directe played an active role in European terrorist networks until it was neutralised by a police operation in 1988. It had links with the Basque separatist movement ETA and with Middle Eastern pro-Palestinian groups. The group attacked public and government buildings. Two prominent members, Jean-Marc Rouillan and Nathalie Ménigon, were arrested in Paris in September 1980, but were controversially released under an amnesty declared by Mitterrand when he took office as President. Action Directe then began a bombing campaign against US and Israeli targets and was banned by the French government. The now illegal group split into factions. In January 1985 the 'internationalist' section led by Rouillan began a joint action with the West German Red Army Faction (RAF), announcing the formation of a united urban politico-military front in Western Europe, with NATO as its main target. That month Action Directe shot dead General Audran, the government minister responsible for French arms sales, and in April 1986 tried to kill Guy Brana, Deputy President of the employers' federation CNPF. In July 1986 the group bombed the offices of the French police anti-terrorist unit and in November killed the Chairman of Renault. Four founder leaders of the group were arrested in February 1987 and sentenced to life imprisonment in January 1989, by which time the other members had been arrested and the group had collapsed.

[See also: ETA; Red Army Faction]

additionality

The European Union's (EU) cohesion policy is a regional policy which sets out to reduce economic and social disparities between richer and poorer regions of the EU. The financial instruments used to effect cohesion policy are termed the structural funds. The additionality rule was introduced during a major reform of the structural funds of 1988 and maintains that EU funds for regional development must be allocated in addition to, rather than instead of, member state funds. The European Commission monitors member state compliance with additionality rules when structural funds are implemented.

[See also: Economic and Social Cohesion]

Additional Member System (AMS)

An electoral system based on the principle of proportional representation, but which combines election of candidates from (usually single-member) constituencies with some form of reserve or 'top-up' list, in order to produce an overall result that is more closely proportional to the percentages of votes which parties have received than if constituency-based election were used alone. The electoral system in use to elect the Bundestag in the Federal Republic of Germany since 1949 has been based on the 'additional member' system, at first using a single vote to count for election of the candidate and for the party list of that candidate, but since 1953 using two,

separate, votes: one for the candidate in a constituency contest, one for a party list, with that party list vote used to determine overall allocations of seats. Many of the German Länder also use AMS in some form to elect their Land legislatures. Italy combines election of three-quarters of its lower chamber of the legislature with election of the remainder from party lists. The Scottish Parliament and Welsh Assembly were both elected by means of versions of the Additional Member System in 1999, using two votes. The overall degree of proportionality attained in AMS elections depends to a large extent on the ratio of directly elected legislators to those chosen from top-up lists, and whether a national, regional or only a more local top-up list procedure is utilised.

[See also: Grabenwahlsystem (Germany)]

adversary politics

A political process in which two opposed political parties, or blocs of parties, debate and decide upon political issues by presenting competing arguments, representing radically opposed positions or derived from opposed ideologies, and the issue is settled by majority adoption of one of these arguments. Adversary politics contrasts with consensus politics, in which controversies concerning political issues are resolved by adoption of generally acceptable compromises. The term 'adversary politics' was applied particularly to the British House of Commons in the post-Second World War period, where the Labour and Conservative parties opposed each other on issues such as state control of industry, comprehensive education and housing policy (e.g. the iron and steel industry was twice nationalised and twice returned to private ownership). Adversary politics has been regarded as a product of the 'first-past-the-post' electoral system, which encourages the more extreme proponents of a policy to gain power in a party and thus in governments, leading to sub-optimal policy outcomes, lacking continuity and consistency. The term was publicised by S. Finer in the book edited by him: *Adversary Politics and Electoral Reform* (London, Antony Wigram, 1975), in which he advocated electoral reform in Britain as the way to avoid the negative consequences of adversary politics.

[See also: First-past-the-post system]

Aegean Sea dispute

Greece and Turkey have been in dispute over the rights to territorial waters and the continental shelf in the Aegean Sea since the early 1970s. While Greece has traditionally argued for the resolution of the matter by the International Court of Justice, Turkey has argued for the bilateral negotiation of a fair solution. In February 1974, the conflict escalated when oil was discovered within Greek territorial waters off the island of Thassos. In May 1974, Turkey underlined its counter-claim to these waters by sending a survey ship and 32 warships to patrol the western limits of the area. At this time, the dispute became entangled with a similar one over airspace jurisdiction in the Aegean and with a controversy over arrangements for Greek reintegration within the military structure of NATO. An agreement between Turkey and Greece to establish a commission to investigate the sea dispute lapsed during the Turkish military dictatorship of 1980–83. When the Turkish government recognised the newly declared Turkish Republic of Northern Cyprus, Greece suspended all direct negotiations with Turkey. In 1987 the Greek Socialist government took steps to nationalise the North Aegean Petroleum Company (NAPC) and to have the state-owned Public Petroleum Corporation extend

explorations of the area. Turkey again sent a research ship and warships to the area and a conflict was only avoided through NATO calls for restraint. The seriousness of the crisis led the then Greek and Turkish Prime Ministers, Papandreou and Özal, to conduct a number of secret negotiations in Davos, Switzerland, in 1988, in which they agreed to avoid hostilities and to pursue confidence-building measures between their two countries.

Algerian conflict (1954–62)

The Algerian conflict brought about the transition from the French Fourth Republic to the Fifth Republic under de Gaulle, the former leader of the Free French during the Second World War. The Algerian conflict began in November 1954 with the anti-colonial struggle of the Algerian nationalist movement, the National Liberation Front (FLN), founded by Ben Bella. The French Algerian territories had a population of some nine million indigenous Muslim Algerians who were subordinate to a colonial population of one million French settlers, the 'pieds noir'. The FLN started anti-French riots and launched a spate of co-ordinated attacks on French soldiers and police. As the violent conflict escalated to involve atrocities against activists and civilians alike, the French army developed strong sympathies for the French settlers and were enraged by the French government's apparent inability to bring the situation under control. On 12 May 1956 a new government was formed under Pflimlin, who made known his intention to negotiate a cease-fire with the FLN. The following day, the army in Algiers took power, set up a military government, the Committee of Public Safety under General Massu, and called for de Gaulle to form a national government capable of maintaining a French Algeria. On 17 May, the French Parliament awarded

5 EVENTS, GROUPS AND DEVELOPMENTS

the Pflimlin government emergency powers to try to resolve the conflict. Meanwhile, a rival government was established in Algiers and on 24 May a Committee of Public Safety took power in Corsica. On 28 May the French President, Coty, intervened by asking de Gaulle to form a 'government of national safety'. De Gaulle was confirmed as Prime Minister by Parliament on 1 June and proceeded to erode the army's political power by a combination of institutional reforms and key appointments. Between 1958 and 1962, reciprocal terror campaigns were conducted by the FLN and the rival pro-French Algerian Secret Army Organisation (OAS) led by General Jouhaud and General Salan. In 1959 de Gaulle granted self-determination to Algeria, a measure which was roundly approved by referenda both in France and Algeria. The Évian Agreements of March 1962 gave full independence to Algeria in exchange for guarantees to protect the rights of the pieds noir. However, resentment by extremist Algerian Europeans fuelled widespread violent conflict with militant Muslims and by the end of 1962 some 800,000 European settlers had fled to France.

[See also: Évian Agreements; Secret Army Organisation; Coty*; de Gaulle*; Pflimlin*]

Alternative Vote System (AV)

An electoral system using single-member constituencies, where voters place the candidates in order of preference, using the numbers 1, 2, 3 ... etc., rather than place a cross by the name of one candidate. A candidate securing more than 50 per cent of 'first preference' votes is elected. In constituencies where no candidate has obtained that absolute majority of first preferences, the candidate with the lowest number of first preference votes is eliminated, and the second preference votes of that candidate are distributed among the other candidates. This elimination and redistribution procedure, using second, third and later preferences if necessary, continues until one candidate secures an absolute majority. No West European state uses this system, though it has been proposed as a replacement for the simple-majority first-past-the-post British system, either by itself or – as the Jenkins Commission on the Electoral System proposed – in conjunction with local 'top-up' lists.

[See also: Additional Member System; Single Transferable Vote]

Amsterdam Treaty

The Amsterdam Treaty of the European Union (EU) was signed on 2 October 1997. The Treaty had two central aims: to revive popular interest in the EU by making it appear more relevant and accountable; and to prepare the EU for the planned enlargement to incorporate new members from Central and Eastern Europe. The Treaty encompasses six main areas: freedom, security and justice; the Union and its citizens; external policy; the Union's institutions; co-operation and flexibility; and the simplification and consolidation of the existing Treaties of the Union: the acquis communitaire. The Treaty negotiations were marred by a general unwillingness by member state governments to make concessions to the Union; growing divisions between large and small member states; and a rocky period in the Franco-German relationship. As a result, the Treaty is an unwieldy document which experts fear will not serve its stated aims well.

[See also: acquis communitaire; democratic deficit; Maastricht Treaty; Treaty of Nice]

animal rights

In Western European countries, campaigners for animal rights have formed organisations to protect animals from abuse and to promote their welfare. Ongoing animal rights campaigns have included calls for a ban on the use of animals in scientific experimentation, particularly in medical research and in the production of toiletries, where the concept of 'cruelty-free beauty' has attained mass popularity in recent years. Similarly, animal rights campaigns against intensive and inhumane farming methods have dovetailed with environmentalist and consumer concerns for 'safe' foods to reach a mass public. Animal rights campaigners have also regularly targeted blood sports. Although most groups campaign peacefully, extremist movements such as the UK's Animal Liberation Front (ALF) have been active since the early 1970s. These engage in more militant protests, even terrorist activity, including attacks on animal testing sites, on staff of companies engaged in animal testing, and on shops selling luxury animal products, particularly furs.

anti-capitalist riots

Between 30 November and 3 December 1999, demonstrations against the World Trade Organisation (WTO) brought the retail centre of Seattle to a standstill. Militant, non-violent protesters tried to block access to the meeting. Over 40,000 workers, students and environmental activists took part in a legal march organised by the AFL-CIO. These peaceful demonstrations were usurped by small groups of self-proclaimed anarchists, who, dressed in black, smashed windows. The police responded with anti-riot measures and running battles took place between police and protesters on the street. Those arrested in the police action became known as the Seattle 580. Such protests were then emulated in Western European countries, for example during the European Union summit in Nice in

December 2000 and in Genoa, where the G-8 was meeting in July 2001. These riots followed a number of earlier instances of violent demonstrations in London and elsewhere by anti-capitalist groups.

[See also: Group of Eight]

antifa groups [See: anti-fascism]

anti-fascism

A general term denoting opposition to fascism, including nazism. More particularly, it has been employed as a legitimising principle and integrative idea by communist organisations and regimes, including the Soviet occupation regime in Germany and the GDR, based on the idea that fascism had been defeated primarily by the USSR and communist resisters elsewhere. In the GDR, non-communist political parties and social organisations such as the trade union and youth associations were linked to the SED (the communist party) through membership of an 'anti-fascist bloc'.

A number of 'anti-fascist' ('antifa') groups were formed throughout Germany at the end of the Second World War, to act as organisations for the purging of Nazis from public life and to provide an organisational basis for the regeneration of political and social life in devastated German towns and cities. These were chiefly made up of socialists and other trade unionists. In the Soviet zone of occupation, the autonomy of these groups was perceived as potentially dangerous to the claims of the Communists to be the 'leading party', and they were swiftly disbanded by the Soviet authorities.

[See also: fascism]

anti-Semitism

The term in its literal sense means hostility towards 'Semites': people from the Middle East defined by their use of the Semitic language. It has, since the nineteenth century, come to refer to hostility towards the Jews, though such hostility predates the use of the term, since anti-Jewish rhetoric and persecution date back to the first century AD. Such anti-Jewish sentiment has been based on two main strands: the biological – that the Jews were an inferior race and had the capacity by inter-breeding with non-Jewish races to harm the qualities of other races, and a socio-economic and cultural strand – that Jews sought domination in areas of finance and commerce, that they sought to constitute themselves as a social elite and that they posed a threat to indigenous culture. Both strands contributed to anti-Semitism as defined and fostered by the Nazi regime, and which culminated in the Holocaust. Since the Second World War anti-Semitism has been evident in other countries, especially the former USSR and, since the downfall of communism, in Russia and some other former communist states.

[See also: final solution; Holocaust; nazism; xenophobia]

Armed Forces Movement (Portugal)

A right-wing dictatorship had been established in Portugal by Salazar in 1932, led by Caetano from 1968. On 24–25 April 1974, this regime was overthrown by a military group, the Armed Forces Movement (MFA), in a bloodless coup known as the 'revolution of carnations'. A military administration led by General de Spínola, the Committee of National Salvation, was established as a temporary measure pending a return to democracy. Although democratic reforms were introduced, there followed a period of uncertainty as the MFA split into left and right factions. Spínola resigned in September 1974 and was succeeded by General da Costa Gomes. An unsuccessful counter-coup led by senior

military officers in March 1975 prompted a shift to the left in government policy. The organs of the MFA were dissolved and a Supreme Revolutionary Council was created. The promised constitutional democracy was introduced in 1976, and, after free elections, the army Chief of Staff General Eanes was selected as President by the Parliament. In 1982, a substantial constitutional review removed the direct political influence of the army by effectively replacing the Council of the Revolution with an explicitly civilian Council of State; it also reduced the powers of the presidency, still occupied at this time by Eanes. A further revision of 1989 removed Portugal's constitutional commitment to Marxist principles.

[See also: Eanes*; Salazar*]

asylum

The countries of Western Europe allow individuals who claim political persecution in their own country to cross their national borders and apply for political asylum. While the asylum principle is upheld in the Geneva Convention of 1949, asylum entitlement is regulated by each country's national laws or constitution. Belgium, Sweden, Switzerland and West Germany were popular destinations for asylum seekers because of their generous asylum policies and good employment prospects. Since the 1980s, claims for asylum have rapidly escalated to a scale which causes problems for Western European governments. Between 1981 and 1991 the annual number of asylum applications to European countries increased five-fold, exceeding half a million in 1991. Numbers have risen because of continued population growth, economic weakness, and unrest in the developing countries of Africa and Asia. Also, in the late 1980s, the political transitions from communism in Central and Eastern Europe created widespread economic uncertainty and a rise in nationalist feeling, spilling over into civil war in the former Yugoslavia. These pressures sent thousands of asylum seekers and illegal immigrants to nearby western borders, particularly to Germany and, to a lesser extent, to Austria and Sweden. Many asylum claims are ruled by the authorities to be unfounded and 'false' asylum seekers are increasingly used as scapegoats for social problems in Western European countries. Western European countries have begun to amend their asylum legislation to restrict applicants to those who genuinely face political persecution in their home countries, rather than those who are looking for better employment prospects and a better standard of living.

[See also: immigration]

Atlanticists and Gaullists

Terms used to designate groups within the West German CDU which differed regarding the priority which the Adenauer and Erhard governments should give to relations with the USA (the Atlanticists) or relations with France and other West European allies (the Gaullists). The Atlanticists warned against following French policy concerning especially security and trade too slavishly, while the Gaullists played on fears of American dominance in military and foreign policy, and wished to further the 'European integration project', building on the Franco-German Treaty. Neither group went as far as proposing disregard of the policies of the USA or France. The Atlanticists included Erhard and his Foreign Minister, Schröder, and were supported by most of the CDU, the SPD, the FDP, the trade unions and economic elites and most of the mass media. The Gaullists had the support of Adenauer, Strauss (leader of the CSU) and Gerstenmaier, a prominent and respected 'elder statesman' in the CDU,

as well as the CSU and some in the CDU.

[See also: Adenauer*; Strauss*]

ausserparlamentarische Opposition

(APO) [See: extra-parliamentary opposition]

Aussiedler

A German term meaning: a person who is resettled. It is a technical term within German law relating to immigrants, referring to those migrating into the Federal Republic who can claim German nationality by virtue of former residence in German territory or in certain other states (mainly of Eastern Europe) before 1945. It especially applied to ethnic Germans deported from former German territories in Poland, Czechoslovakia and the Soviet Union. Such persons had privileged status in the Federal Republic with regard to the right to reside there and receive social benefits, compared with other immigrants or asylum seekers.

[See also: immigration]

Austrian State Treaty

Following the Second World War, although democracy was restored in Austria in 1945, that country remained under the occupation of the four victorious Allied Powers: the USA, the Soviet Union, Britain and France, each with its own zone of occupation. The capital, Vienna, was subject to four-power control. As the Cold War developed, there were fears that Austria might be lastingly divided into pro-Western and pro-Soviet part-states in the same way as post-war Germany. However, on 15 May 1955 the Allied Powers signed the State Treaty with Austria, ending the occupation. The Treaty recognised Austria as a sovereign, independent and democratic state. Moreover, it recognised the regime of the second Austrian Republic.

It banned political or economic union between Austria and Germany and also required Austrian neutrality by banning the country from aligning itself with either of the two Cold War alliances which formed around the USA and the Soviet Union. In a constitutional law of 26 October 1955, Austria declared its permanent neutrality, but chose to interpret this stance actively rather than passively. Austria joined the UN in December 1955 and has frequently participated in UN peace-keeping operations. In 1956, the country allowed refugees from the Hungarian uprising to cross its borders to safety.

[See also: Cold War]

Autonomen (the Autonomous)

The German Autonomen are an alienated group of anarchists who take part in demonstrations (irrespective of the specific aims of these) to confront their enemy, the police. While they appear to have no links with terrorists, in the late 1980s, the federal office for the protection of the constitution estimated that of the 6,500 active Autonomen, some 1,500–2,000 were militants prepared to use force. They made a sinister impression in their 'uniform' of masks, black helmets and black clothes. In June 1985, the federal Parliament passed a bill to prohibit the wearing of masks (except during the annual Carnival). The bill also made it a criminal offence to carry 'protective' weapons, or to refuse a police order to disperse if a demonstration turned violent. In November 1987, two policemen were killed by an unidentified perpetrator at a small demonstration at Frankfurt airport, at which Autonomen were present.

Baader-Meinhof group

The Baader-Meinhof group was an extreme left-wing terrorist organisation active in West Germany in the early 1970s. On 14 May 1970 the members of the Baader-Meinhof group founded their political organisation, the Red Army Faction (RAF), as an urban guerrilla liberation group. The ideology of the Baader-Meinhof group was set out in four papers written in 1971 and 1972, one by Horst Mahler and three by Ulrike Meinhof. These papers identified the RAF as anti-imperialist and anti-fascist, and sought to justify the need for an 'armed struggle' against what they perceived as the oppressive political system of the FRG. The authorities' handling of the Baader-Meinhof trials and conditions of imprisonment was criticised by some as heavy-handed. The deaths of Holger Meins following a hunger strike and Meinhof through suicide appear to have been the catalyst for the 'Offensive '77' launched by the 'second generation' of the RAF. When the Offensive failed to secure the release of the original RAF members from prison, they attempted suicide. Andreas Baader, Gudrun Ensslin and Jan-Carl Raspe succeeded. The fourth member, Irmgard Möller, survived her suicide attempt and was eventually released from prison on 1 December 1994.

[See also: Red Army Faction; Schleyer Affair]

Bad Godesberg Programme [See: Godesberg Programme]

Barschel Affair

Barschel, the leader of the Schleswig-Holstein Christian Democrats, was accused of initiating a series of 'dirty tricks' against his Social Democrat opponent, Engholm, in the 1987 Land election campaign. These included investigation of Engholm's private life, and spreading rumours about Engholm's evasion of taxes. Barschel insisted at a press conference that he had nothing to do with such improper actions. However, when evidence was offered

that seemed to implicate him,
Barschel resigned as Prime Minister
of the Land government, and days
later was found dead in a Swiss hotel
room, apparently having committed
suicide, though this has been the topic
of speculation. In May 1988 the SPD
won an overwhelming victory in a new
Land election. Engholm was later
damaged by admissions that he had not
revealed everything he knew about the
affair when questioned by an
investigatory committee. He resigned as
SPD leader and Land Prime Minister in
1993.

[See also: Engholm*]

Basic Law

The name given to the constitution of
the Federal Republic of Germany drawn
up by the Parliamentary Council in
1948–49 and promulgated in May 1949.
This name (*Grundgesetz* in German)
was deliberately chosen rather than the
term: constitution (*Verfassung*) to
emphasise the expectation of the
Parliamentary Council that Germany
would soon be reunited, and that
therefore this constitutional provision
was temporary until such time as all
Germans could freely choose their own
constitution: an expectation embodied
in the Preamble to the Basic Law
and in its concluding Article (Art. 146),
which provided for its termination when
such a constitution for a unified
Germany came into force. In fact the
Basic Law not only lasted for 41 years
until the reunification of Germany; it
was then retained as the constitution for
reunified Germany (with only minor
revisions and adjustments) by decisions
of the legislatures of the two German
states. A Joint Commission of the two
chambers of the legislature of the
Federal Republic to consider whether
further changes were desirable
following reunification reported in 1993.
As a result, a small number of changes
were adopted in 1994.

Basic Treaty (1972)

An important part of the Ostpolitik of
the Brandt government, the Basic Treaty
was a treaty-like agreement between
the Federal Republic of Germany and
the German Democratic Republic. It
was deliberately not given the status of
an international treaty because the
Federal Republic of Germany would not
recognise the German Democratic
Republic as a foreign state. The Basic
Treaty, ratified and taking effect from
1973, bound the partners to promote
good relations between the two German
states, recognised the inviolability of the
border between them, and renounced
the use or threat of force in their
mutual relations. Both states accepted
the restriction of their claim of
sovereignty to their territories within their
own borders, and explicitly stated
their mutual respect for the internal and
external independence of both German
states (which paved the way for their
admission to the United Nations
Organisation and other international
organisations). Supplementary protocols
regulated free access for journalists
within both German states, easier travel
between the two states, better
conditions for reuniting families and
other such measures.

An attempt by refugee organisations
and the Christian Democrats in the
Federal Republic to have this treaty
declared unconstitutional (on the
grounds that it improperly diluted the
constitutional principle of national unity)
failed. The Constitutional Court rejected
a case brought by Bavaria, and stated
that the treaty fell within the obligations
of the state to promote German
reunification.

[See also: Ostpolitik]

Basque separatism

The Basques are a distinct ethnic,
cultural and linguistic group found in a
cross-border area of Spain and France

equated by Basques with 'Euskadi', the historic Basque homeland. Although an independent Basque state has never existed, the Spanish Basque provinces had a semi-autonomous relationship with the Spanish Kingdom until the nineteenth century. After the Spanish civil war most of the Basque regions were harshly treated by the victorious nationalist forces as punishment for their support for the republicans. However, government policy to stamp out the distinctive Basque language and culture backfired. The existing regional identity was consolidated by a new sense of grievance over the community's treatment as an alienated minority. The traditional nationalist political groups and movements were supplemented by new radical and militant separatist forces, of which the group Basque Nation and Liberty (ETA) is the most notorious. The containment of tensions in the Basque region was one of the main challenges facing Spain in its transition to democracy in the late 1970s and early 1980s. In 1980 the Basque region was granted its own autonomous government with potentially more far-reaching powers than any other region of Spain. However, there have been constant disagreements between the region and successive central governments about the interpretation and implementation of Basque autonomy. Local Basque nationalist parties compete alongside Spanish parties in elections and include the traditional Christian Democratic PNV, founded in 1895; the Basque Left (EE), a workers' movement founded in 1976 to work peacefully for independence; and Herri Batasuna (HB), founded in 1978 as ETA's political wing.

[See also: ETA; Spanish civil war]

Belgrano Affair [See: Falklands War]

Benelux

In 1956, to help promote economic recovery after the Second World War, Belgium, Luxembourg and the Netherlands formed a treaty community known as the Benelux economic union. In fact, the treaty was a formal recognition of an existing arrangement. Plans for a customs union between the three countries had been drawn up in 1944 and had come into operation in 1948. By 1956 practically all trade between the countries was tariff-free. The Benelux union provided for free movement of persons, goods, services and capital between the member states; the co-ordination of national economic policies; and a common trade policy towards other countries. The Benelux model strongly influenced the European Economic Community (1958), of which Belgium, Luxembourg and the Netherlands were founder members.

Berlin airlift [See: Berlin blockade]

Berlin blockade

The closure by the USSR occupying power of the road, rail and inland waterway access from the western zones of occupation to West Berlin. This commenced in June 1948, after a period since April 1948 of harassment of military and civilian transport to and from West Berlin. The reasons for the blockade were the steps being taken by the Western occupation powers (a) to introduce a new, more stable currency to their zones (a currency which had been offered to the Soviet zone also, but refused because of conditions attached to that offer) and (b) to promote the founding of a – temporary – West German state pending a peace treaty and the reunification of Germany. The USSR sought in this way to force West Berlin to accept USSR control in return for food, fuel and other necessities. The blockade was broken by the Berlin airlift, by means of which the basic necessities were flown into West Berlin from West Germany, and gradually stockpiles were built up and the West Berlin economy enabled to operate reasonably effectively. Air corridors from West Germany to West Berlin had been guaranteed by four-power agreements, unlike surface transport routes. The success of the airlift and thus the failure of the blockade constituted a propaganda defeat for the USSR, and strengthened the determination of West Berliners to reject any negotiations or compromises with the Soviet occupying power. The blockade was lifted in May 1949, and the airlift concluded in September 1949.

[See also: Cold War]

Berlin uprising 1953

A general strike and public street protest against policies imposed by the communist government of the GDR which involved longer hours and increased production by workers but without compensating increased wages. A strike by East Berlin construction workers on 16 June was followed by a general strike which spread from East Berlin to nearly 400 other localities in the GDR. Economic demands of the protesters were soon supplemented by demands for political reforms, such as free elections, the release of political prisoners and the reunification of Germany. A state of emergency was declared by the Soviet military command, and martial law was imposed. Demonstrations were prohibited; ringleaders were arrested; Soviet tanks and troops occupied the streets. The communist leadership of the GDR explained the uprising as 'fascist provocation' engineered by West German leaders. Critics of the repressive policies of the USSR military leadership and the GDR government were punished. The uprising did show clearly that without the support of Soviet

military forces, the GDR regime would not survive. It also provoked a harsher regime of surveillance and control of the population in the GDR than existed in many other states of the Soviet bloc.

Berlin Wall

A wall erected in August 1961 by the German Democratic Republic, with the encouragement of the USSR. It was intended to control more absolutely movement of individuals from one part of Berlin to the other, following a period in which increasing numbers of East Germans were migrating from the GDR to the Federal Republic through Berlin (where border controls were more lax than elsewhere between the two parts of Germany). The Berlin Wall came to consist of the concrete wall itself, and a cleared area on the East Berlin side of the wall which was floodlit, mined and patrolled. Many East Germans, wishing to escape to West Berlin by crossing the Wall, lost their lives or were wounded by gunfire from the border guards. Controls were relaxed on 9 November 1989 in the period of crisis leading to the collapse of the communist regime in the GDR a few weeks later, and soon afterwards the Berlin Wall was physically demolished by individuals on both sides of the Wall and by the GDR government. Only a few remnants have been preserved in situ, though other sections are in various museums.

[See also: Cold War; reunification of Germany]

Beveridge Report (UK)

A government report on the social services produced in 1942, whose author was Sir William Beveridge, an economist, a former Director of the London School of Economics and at the time the master of University College, Oxford. The Report recommended a comprehensive and universal system of social insurance, a national health

13 EVENTS, GROUPS AND DEVELOPMENTS

service and family allowances. It became the source of ideas for policies relating to the welfare state, especially those of the Labour government which came to power in 1945. Beveridge was given a peerage in 1946.

Bizonia

The term applied to the merged British and US zones of occupation from 1 January 1947, formally known as the United Economic Area (*Vereinigtes Wirtschaftsgebiet*). A set of institutions was developed to bring West Germans themselves into the decision-making process, including initially an indirectly elected Economic Council, an Executive Committee (a kind of cabinet) consisting of one representative from each Land in the two zones, and a set of Directors, to manage policy sectors such as transport and agriculture. These institutions were revised in 1948, to give more political freedom to the West Germans, especially the Länder. These institutions served as models upon which the Parliamentary Council which drafted the Basic Law could draw in constructing a political system for the Federal Republic of Germany.

Bizonia improved the economic situation of the two zones of occupation, and was used as the instrument for the introduction of the Deutschmark in the currency reform of 1948 and for the groundwork for the 'economic miracle': the rapid growth of the economy of the Federal Republic in the 1950s and 1960s. The French zone of occupation joined the Bizonia scheme (which then became 'Trizonia') in April 1949, a few weeks before the Federal Republic came into being.

[See also: Basic Law; economic miracle]

Bonn Republic–Berlin Republic transition

The reunification of Germany involved decisions concerning the seat of

government of the enlarged Federal Republic. Prior to reunification, Bonn was the seat of government, though Berlin was always regarded as the capital of the German state, a fact that was confirmed in the Treaty of Reunification.

The issue of whether to retain Bonn as the seat of government or to move most or all of the governing institutions located in Bonn to Berlin was settled in principle by a vote in the Bundestag on 20 June 1991. 338 Members of the Bundestag voted for Berlin, 320 for Bonn. Those in favour of the move to Berlin emphasised the advantages which Berlin could offer because of its size and status, and its role in fostering the integration of Germany because of its more easterly location, close to the 'new Länder'. Those arguing that Bonn should remain the seat of government stressed the role which Bonn had played in the development of a peaceful, prosperous Federal Republic and its proximity to places such as Brussels and Luxembourg, symbolic of European integration. The costs and disruption involved in moving to an already crowded Berlin were also emphasised. On 26 June 1991 the government instituted a working group of senior civil servants to prepare for the move to Berlin. On 5 July 1991 the Bundesrat decided to remain in Bonn, though retaining the right to reconsider that decision in the light of circumstances. In December 1991, the federal government announced that some ministries would remain in Bonn, while others would have parts of their organisation in Bonn though their main activities would be located in Berlin. The year 2000 was taken as the target date for completing most of the move to Berlin. Certain federal institutions would move from other parts of Germany to Bonn, and the government would make efforts to attract European Community and other international organisations to Bonn. Bonn would also receive subsidies to off-set the loss of income and employment until the year 2004. On 23 November 1998, the first institutional transfer took place when the office of Federal President Herzog moved to Berlin. The former Reichstag was renovated and is now used as the location of the Bundestag. In recognition of this institutional transfer and of other subtle changes in the FRG regime since reunification, commentators refer to the post-unification FRG as the Berlin Republic.

[See also: reunification of Germany; Herzog*]

Bundesbank

The central bank of the Federal Republic of Germany, located in Frankfurt (Main). It was created in 1957 on the basis of a Law implementing provisions of Art. 88 of the Basic Law, and replaced the Bank of the German Länder, which from 1949 had co-ordinated banking activity in the Federal Republic. The Bundesbank acted independently of the federal government to protect the value of the currency of the Federal Republic, using interest rates, intervention in currency markets and control over the money supply as instruments to this end. This independence sometimes led to conflicts between the government and the bank. A notable example concerned the proper rate of exchange of East German Marks for Deutschmarks when currency union was introduced between the two German states in July 1990. An amendment to Art. 88 of the Basic Law in 1992 provided for the Bundesbank to transfer its duties to a European Central Bank, once such a bank was created and in position to act independently to protect the value of the currency.

[See also: Pöhl*]

Campaign for Nuclear Disarmament (CND)

Founded in 1958 to promote the cause of unilateral nuclear disarmament by the United Kingdom, CND developed into a large and influential movement in the 1960s, of which prominent Labour Party politicians such as Foot, Kinnock and Blair (all future party leaders) were members at some time. Briefly, the Labour Party officially adopted unilateral nuclear disarmament as official policy following a party conference resolution in 1960, but the government of Harold Wilson refused to implement such a policy. In opposition after the Conservative election victory of 1979, CND again developed influence within the Labour Party. Electoral defeat in 1983 under Foot's leadership led many in the Labour Party to blame CND for the Party's unpopularity. CND has become politically impotent since the downfall of communism and the end of the Cold War, though it did sponsor demonstrations following the terrorist attack on the USA in September 2001.

[See also: Blair*; Foot*; Kinnock*]

'cash for questions' affair

A parliamentary scandal arising from accusations that certain MPs had accepted payments from private interests in return for them tabling questions (whose answers would be beneficial to those who made the payments) to be raised in the House of Commons at Question Time. The *Sunday Times* in 1994 used subterfuge to demonstrate that two MPs were in fact prepared to accept payment for this activity. Another MP, Neil Hamilton, was accused later of this same practice, and threatened to sue the *Guardian* for reporting that accusation. Hamilton decided not to go through with the court case, and in the 1998 general election was defeated by an Independent candidate, the former television news reporter Martin Bell. The Labour and Liberal parties declined to present their own candidates to enhance Bell's chances of victory. The affair contributed to the creation of a Commission under Lord Nolan to inquire into 'Standards in Public Life'. The Nolan Report in 1995 made several recommendations designed to reduce the likelihood of improper links between MPs and private interests.

chancellor democracy

A term applied at first to describe Adenauer's interpretation and utilisation of the office of chancellor in the Federal Republic of Germany, then by extension used to refer either to the system of government of the Federal Republic of Germany generally, or to the assertive style of certain chancellors in particular.

Adenauer used the constitutional powers afforded the chancellor by the Basic Law to exert his supremacy over his own cabinet, the whole of the government and the political system more generally. These powers included the authority to set general guidelines for the government (*Richtlinienkompetenz*: Article 65), the power of the chancellor to nominate and remove ministers, the lack of political powers of the federal president and the inability of the Bundestag to remove the chancellor except by a constructive vote of no confidence which provided a majority for a named successor. The fact that at first the Federal Republic did not have foreign or defence policy competence also buttressed the authority of the chancellor. Indeed, in 1951 Adenauer became his own Foreign Minister when the restrictions imposed by the occupation authorities were removed, retaining that post until 1955. Thus Adenauer was able to impose his authority in any and all the policy areas in which he had an interest, often taking key political decisions without

formal consultation in the cabinet or with his parliamentary party group. The development of the Chancellor's Office (bearing some resemblance to the US White House staff) also was a factor in the growth of 'chancellor democracy', as has been the general trend for the mass media to personalise the reporting of politics. Adenauer's control of government meant that he was able to restrict the independent powers of his Party (the Christian Democratic Union: CDU), which anyway in those early days of the Federal Republic was little more than an organisation to elect the chancellor. His electoral victories, especially the absolute majority he obtained in 1957, reinforced his personal authority.

His successors could, on the one hand, draw on the precedents set by Adenauer, but several, on the other hand, lacked his personal qualities or a desire to govern in the dominating style adopted by Adenauer. The growth in the power of the Party (particularly of the CDU after it went into opposition in 1969) and the increasing assertiveness of the Free Democrats (FDP) as a coalition partner – already apparent in the Adenauer period: e.g. the 'Young Turks' revolt' in 1956 and the Spiegel Affair in 1962 – also restricted the autonomy of the chancellor. Erhard could not escape from the shadow of Adenauer, who remained as party Chairman for much of Erhard's period as chancellor; Kiesinger was limited by the special constraints of the grand coalition; Brandt, though a very assertive chancellor, did not seek to mimic Adenauer's patrician style; Schmidt was hampered by his own left wing and by the fact that he was not party leader. Only Kohl came close to reinventing the style of Adenauer in terms of most of its attributes, and he had to accept to a considerable degree the autonomy of Genscher (FDP) as Foreign Minister. However, Kohl did dominate his party, was able to resist challenges to his authority from Strauss and the Christian Social Union, was personally responsible for key decisions concerning German reunification and European integration, and, like Adenauer, was the party's chief electoral asset. Schröder, now that he is also party leader, may also come to exert a very personal and dominant style of government, though his coalition partners, the Greens, act as a constraint in some policy areas.

[See also: constructive vote of no confidence; Spiegel Affair; Young Turks' revolt; Adenauer*; Brandt*; Erhard*; Genscher*; Kiesinger*; Kohl*; Schmidt*]

church tax

A supplementary income tax imposed in the Federal German Republic to help to finance religious organisations. After the income tax of a person is assessed, a supplement of between 8 and 10 per cent of the tax payable is added, and that extra tax is passed on to the church to which the taxpayer belongs (if only nominally). This form of taxation was found in the constitution of the Weimar Republic, and is now based on Art. 140 of the Basic Law of the Federal Republic. The product of the church tax is very high, and means that the main denominations in the FRG are very wealthy. Taxpayers can 'opt out' of the church tax, but have to take action to do so. Such opting-out may have consequences if the taxpayer then wishes to have church ceremonies for weddings, christenings or funerals.

citizen initiative groups

Citizen initiative groups emerged in Western Europe in the late 1960s as informal, voluntary and usually temporary associations of citizens outside the established political parties and interest groups, whose aim was to influence policy makers on a specific issue. Initially they were largely preoccupied with planning decisions affecting a local community, especially decisions relating to environmental issues. Citizen initiatives were common in the Federal Republic of Germany in the 1970s and many of their members were later active in the Green Party.

[See also: green movement]

citizens in uniform

The concept at the heart of the revived post-war armed forces of the German Federal Republic. There was considerable conflict within the Federal Republic concerning the decision of the Adenauer government, in association with the USA and its West European partners, to revive the military. Those who did support such a decision (in the context of the Cold War) were aware of the criticisms which had been made of German armies before 1945: especially the unthinking obedience and strong military discipline which characterised the armed forces. Consequently, it was decided that a democratic state should possess a democratic military, and that in future members of the military should be regarded as 'citizens in uniform', which meant two things. First, they were still in possession of all the rights of other citizens of the Federal Republic, including those fundamental rights listed in the Basic Law. Such rights could only be modified or restricted by explicit legislative provision, when necessary for the effective operation of the armed services. Examples of such restrictions are: freedom of speech and expression within barracks and overt support for political parties or causes in certain situations. Second, members of the armed forces were personally responsible for their actions with regard to their morality and legality. They could not abandon responsibility behind the excuse of 'only obeying orders'. Of course, disputes about interpretation of these principles have occurred, involving for example the rights of soldiers to join

17 EVENTS, GROUPS AND DEVELOPMENTS

trade unions and the extent of freedom of speech in the Military College. But these have not called into question the principles themselves.

An important constitutional innovation is the creation of an Inspector-General of the Armed Services (*Wehrbeauftragter*) who is appointed by the Bundestag and reports to the Bundestag on matters relating to the armed forces. Any member of the armed forces can direct a complaint directly to this official, by-passing the normal 'chain of command' and the Inspector-General has unconditional rights (subject only to requirements of state security) to information from the Ministry of Defence and the armed services. This official is sometimes referred to as the 'military Ombudsman' in Germany.

civil society

The term: civil society is used in many different ways. At its loosest, it means simply 'the citizenry' or even 'the public'. In democratic theory there is a tension between the state as the source of authority and civil society as the embodiment of popular sovereignty. The concept of a civil society distinct from that of the state first emerged with the Enlightenment, when civil society was viewed as a guardian against the authoritarian potential of the state. Major structural economic upheavals in European life brought about a reversal in the way philosophers conceptualised the state–citizen relationship. With the progressive differentiation of society which accompanied the transition to market economies, civil society came to be seen as consisting of competing, selfish interests. Thinkers such as Hegel looked to the state to regulate civil society. De Toqueville identified a sphere of civil organisation between economy and state, now referred to as 'political society'. For de Toqueville, the function of political society was to

counteract both the egotism of private interests and the tyrannical potential of the modern state. In practice, this mediating sphere is the associational activity comprising local self-government, parties, churches, the media and public opinion. Work of sociologists such as Durkheim and Simmel developed the notion of civil society as associational activity founded on social infrastructures. However, during the twentieth century, previously apparently stable social and economic structures in Western European countries began to change under pressures such as globalisation, technological change and post-Fordism. In response, political scientists and sociologists have continued to reconceptualise the state–citizen relationship. They tend to present a picture of an educated and self-aware civil society progressively disenchanted with traditional forms of representative government.

Clause Four

Clause Four of the constitution of the Labour Party in its 1918 version committed the party to the pursuit of policies which would lead to the common ownership of 'the means of production, distribution and exchange'. All members of the party had to agree to accept this pledge as a condition of joining the party. It tied the party to radical policies of extensive nationalisation, in theory far beyond the nationalisation policies implemented by the Attlee government of 1945–51. Such policies were not acceptable to moderate social democrats such as Gaitskell nor likely to be supported by the electorate if brought forward in a Labour Party electoral manifesto, so Gaitskell sought to remove that clause from the party's constitution, but was defeated by his party's left wing. Though the proposed policies were never included in party election programmes, Clause Four was considered to be symbolic of the Labour Party's commitment to socialism. However, Blair, once elected as party leader, undertook as part of his campaign to modernise the party an intensive and skilful campaign to substitute a new statement of party principles for the old Clause Four, and succeeded in doing this in 1995 whilst still retaining the support of most of his party.

[See also: Blair*; Gaitskell*]

'clean hands' operation [See: Mani pulite]

clientelism

The term refers to the practice of offering favours to groups and individuals in return for political support. In democratic countries, there are laws to restrict or prohibit clientelistic practices as these are seen to distort the democratic process. Clientelism is both informal and particularistic: these characteristics conflict with democratic principles of equality and regulated access to the political system. In some Western European countries, though, clientelism – legal or otherwise – remains a significant feature of political life. The worst affected has been Italy, particularly the southern regions of the Mezzogiorno. The Italian term *partitocrazia* ('partyocracy') refers to the way in which the country's political parties have not remained separate from other social and economic institutions as is desirable in a democracy, but have come to penetrate and influence all areas of state and social life. The parties have used clientelism to build up power networks, and, in the process, corruption has become endemic. Moreover, collusion between the parties in maintaining their networks of relationships and in ensuring the free flow of favours had, by the early 1990s, seriously

undermined the development of an effective democratic opposition in Italy.

[See also: Mani pulite; Mezzogiorno; Tangentopoli]

co-determination

Arrangements in industrial policy whereby employees (or their representatives) are provided with institutionalised means of participating in decision-making by a firm or other employing organisation (such as a school or hospital), on topics which directly affect employee interests, such as mergers, personnel policies or safety issues. Such arrangements were developed in the Federal Republic of Germany, first in the coal and steel industries, then in other industries; the detailed arrangements depend upon the size and legal status of the firm. It is to be found in other countries in Western Europe (such as Austria), and it has been proposed that the system should be extended to member states of the EU under social policy arrangements.

'cod wars'

The conflicts between the United Kingdom and Iceland in the period 1972–76 concerning the territorial limits for fishing in the Atlantic ocean claimed by Iceland. Fearful that fishing boats from other countries were depleting stocks of cod and other fish, upon which much of the Icelandic economy depended, Iceland unilaterally declared a 50-mile limit within which no foreign vessels would be permitted to fish. A series of clashes involving fishing boats from the United Kingdom and naval vessels from Iceland and the UK led to a negotiated settlement in 1976, which largely accepted Iceland's claims.

cohabitation

A term applied to the pattern of executive government in the French

Fifth Republic where the president and the prime minister come from opposed party blocks. It has occurred so far three times: twice when Mitterrand (Socialist Party) had to appoint a Gaullist prime minister (Chirac in 1986 and Balladur in 1983), and once when Chirac (a Gaullist president) in 1997 had to appoint Jospin (Socialist Party) as Prime Minister. The situation arises because the constitution of the Fifth Republic allows the president to appoint the prime minister, but the prime minister still needs the confidence of a parliamentary majority in order to pass legislation and a budget. The constitution also – if at times slightly ambiguously – provides the president and prime minister with separate and autonomous spheres of responsibility. When the president and prime minister are from the same party or party block there is no problem, but, because the president and National Assembly are elected at different times (and until 2001 the president has been elected for seven years, the National Assembly for a five-year term), it can happen that changes in the mood of the electorate produce a parliamentary majority opposed to the president. The president has powers of dissolution, so if a president is elected at a time when the National Assembly has a majority opposed to the president, a dissolution can be arranged immediately after the president takes office.

Cohesion Fund [See: Economic and Social Cohesion]

Cold War

A 'Cold War' was so called because a state of armed conflict had not yet arisen. The term is applied to the situation whereby the Western powers on the one side (in particular the USA and its NATO allies) and the USSR and its satellite states on the other side, regarded each other with hostility. They therefore directed military

and foreign policy under the assumption that war with the other side was a likely future event. They engaged in a competitive arms race, and sought through cultural, economic and diplomatic means to influence other countries in their favour, especially countries whose geographic location or natural resources (such as oil) could be of crucial significance in affecting the outcome of such a future war.

The Cold War was based on each side's perceptions of the other as ideological enemies whose intentions, whether declared or denied, would be to expand territorially and to weaken and eventually overcome the other side. The West could point to the USSR's hegemony in Eastern Europe after the Second World War, its communisation of its zone of occupation in Germany and its support for communist groups in Western countries and for anti-Western groups in third world states such as Egypt and Cuba. The USSR regarded the West as a group of countries which had failed to eradicate fascist and imperialist tendencies in their countries, whose reliance on capitalism protected the propertied classes and exploited the working class, and which, because of imperialism, sought to retain or extend its powers in Africa, Asia and Latin America. The failure of the USSR and the Western occupying powers in Germany to agree on policies for the treatment of Germany after the war both exacerbated the situation of mutual distrust and provided each side with propaganda to use against the other side. Some would include Asian communism and the reaction of the West to the crises in Korea, Vietnam and Afghanistan within their definition of the 'Cold War'.

It is difficult to put a precise date on the commencement of the Cold War. Some date it to the 1920s or the 1930s when Stalin came to rule the USSR. Others consider the start of the Cold War to date from the Potsdam conference, the Berlin blockade or the creation of two separate states in Germany in 1949. Most would agree that it ended – at least in its European version – in or around 1990, with the reunification of Germany and the commencement of transitions to democracy in the USSR and its former satellite states. This termination owed much to the reform policies of Gorbachev, but also to the realisation in communist states that economic and technological backwardness and a failure to afford to keep pace with Western developments in armaments meant that the communist camp had 'lost' the Cold War.

[See also: Berlin blockade; glasnost; perestroika; Potsdam conference; reunification of Germany]

collaboration

The term: collaboration is applied to those governments, groups and individuals who actively co-operated with Nazi occupying forces in European countries during the Second World War. The term originated in France, where General Pétain of the Vichy government announced that he would 'enter into the way of collaboration' in October 1940. After the liberation of France in 1944 the tide turned against collaborators. It was rumoured that over 100,000 were executed, although estimates now suggest a figure of some 10,000. There was no thorough purge of public officials needed to lead France's reconstruction after the war, nor of commerce and business. In spite of the anti-collaborator policy, some Vichy officials were even elected to Parliament after 1945.

[See also: Resistance groups; Vichy regime]

Colonels' coup (Greece)

Following a series of centre-left governments in Greece in the 1960s, a military coup was carried out in Greece in April 1967 by a group of officers, led by Colonel Papadopoulos. This military junta – which claimed, falsely, to have the support of King Constantine (who had come to the throne on the death of his father, King Paul, in 1964) – declared a state of emergency, suspending the constitution and abolishing civil liberties. Parties were persecuted, and many politicians imprisoned. The failure later that year of a counter-coup instigated by King Constantine led to the King going into exile. In 1973 an attempt to develop a more democratic form of regime was crushed by the military. In 1974 a failed attempt to secure the union of Cyprus with Greece, which provoked an invasion of northern Cyprus by the Turkish military, led to withdrawal of the military from government and the transfer of political power to a government of national unity. Free elections took place in November 1974. In December 1974 a referendum voted by a large majority to abolish the monarchy.

[See also: Enosis; Papandreou*]

Common Agricultural Policy (CAP)

The Common Agricultural Policy played a key role in the negotiations between the founder members of the European Economic Community (EEC) which came into being in 1958. At this time some 20 per cent of the workforce was engaged in agricultural production and France in particular wanted to establish a scheme for agricultural co-operation which would protect its smaller-scale farmers. The principles of the CAP were established in Articles 38–47 of the EEC's founding Treaty of Rome. The fundamental objectives of the policy are (originally Article 39, now Article 33, EC Treaty) to increase agricultural productivity, thereby ensuring a fair standard of living for workers in agriculture; to stabilise

21 EVENTS, GROUPS AND DEVELOPMENTS

markets; and to ensure the availability of food supplies at reasonable prices. The CAP proved to be an enormous drain on the resources of the EU – in 2002 it cost about 42 per cent of the EU's budget. The policy's intervention mechanisms tended to encourage over-production, resulting in the scandals of the EC 'wine lake' and 'butter mountain'. Reforms in 1992 on beef and cereals did little to alleviate the problem. Further reforms were proposed by the Commission in Agenda 2000 (July 1997) to enable EU enlargement to countries of Central and Eastern Europe, which have large agricultural sectors. In response, a reform package was adopted in 1999 for the period 2000–06. The reforms reinforce the 1992 measures, moving away slightly from the CAP's traditional focus on pricing policy towards an emphasis on food safety; environmental directives; sustainable agriculture; greater price competitiveness; direct income support for farmers; and a genuine integrated rural development policy.

[See also: Treaties of Rome]

consociationalism

Consociationalism is a principle for governance designed for 'segmented' societies: that is, societies which are deeply divided according to sectional loyalties such as religion, language, culture, etc. There are four main principles behind consociationalism: executive power-sharing by the sectors in a grand coalition; a high degree of autonomy for each sector in the management of its own concerns; the proportional representation of the sectors in representative and policy-making institutions; and veto rights for each sector over policy-making. Elements of consociationalism can be found in the political systems of Austria, Belgium, the Netherlands and Switzerland.

constitutionalism

Constitutionalism is a liberal democratic doctrine. It dates from the bourgeois revolutions in European countries which brought absolutist government under legal control. Designed to prevent arbitrary government, it encompasses principles such as commitment to the rule of law; standard procedures of government; and 'balanced' government, where institutions of government check each other's authority so as to avoid a concentration of power. Constitutionalism requires that governments and legislatures defer to a body of superior rules, in practice codified in a constitution. A constitution upholds the legality of the state and guarantees the individual citizen respect for his or her liberties. Constitutionalism implies that respect for the constitutional order is the foundation of a country's political consensus and stability. The fascist regimes in Italy and Germany during the inter-war period revealed the vulnerability of European political systems to non-liberal, arbitrary government. Following the Second World War, political elites have looked to constitutionalism as a means of strengthening their democratic systems. There is a growing belief that all government acts must conform to constitutional law to be considered legitimate. Western democracies have taken steps to standardise individual liberties and civil rights through international treaties and implement them through national and international courts. The Charter of the United Nations of 1945 and the 1948 Universal Declaration of Human Rights were followed in 1953 by the European Convention for the Protection of Human Rights and Fundamental Freedoms. At a domestic level, there has been a 'judicialisation' of politics, in many countries promoted by the work of a constitutional court.

[See also: judicialisation]

constructive vote of no confidence

A device included in the Basic Law of the Federal Republic of Germany (Art. 67) which restricts the power of the Bundestag to remove a chancellor from office to cases where it can simultaneously provide a different chancellor with a majority. The constructive vote of no confidence requires that a vote of no confidence in the chancellor be combined with the nomination of a successor chancellor. If this motion receives a majority, the chancellor is compelled to resign in favour of the named successor. It has been employed twice in the history of the Federal Republic: without success in 1972, when the Brandt government had lost its majority due to defections to the opposition by some Members of the Bundestag, and successfully in 1982 when the liberal Free Democratic Party had abandoned their coalition with the SPD and promised to support the nomination of Kohl, the Christian Democratic nomination for chancellor. The device is a deliberate scheme to improve on the 'simple' vote of no confidence which was frequently used – or was threatened to be used – against chancellors in the Weimar Republic. This would bring about the downfall of a government without imposing on those who voted in favour any requirement to ensure that a majority for an alternative government was available.

[See also: chancellor democracy]

corporatism [See: neo-corporatism]

Crichel Down

An area in southern England which was compulsorily acquired by the state, but later returned to private ownership. It is famous as an apparent case of a ministerial resignation on grounds of civil service errors, though this is not clear, and some commentators view it as a case of ministerial resignation on grounds of policy disagreement with the cabinet.

When the Crichel Down land was returned to private ownership, it was done by invitation, rather than the required tendering process. This was criticised by the opposition, and an inquiry was held which exonerated the minister and civil servants from any charges of corrupt behaviour, but which did confirm the failure to abide by agreed rules. The then Minister of Agriculture, Sir Thomas Dugdale, made a speech on 20 July 1954 in Parliament outlining the situation, but announced his resignation at the end of that speech.

cumul des mandats

A French term, meaning 'cumulation of offices', which refers to the practice in France of politicians holding several elected offices (e.g. being simultaneously a member of the National Assembly and a local mayor or town councillor). Though there have been some advantages from this practice, such as strengthening representation of local interests at national level, it has also been criticised for its potentially corrupting effects and its inefficiency. Since a law was passed in April 2000, legally politicians may not hold more than two public elected offices.

democratic deficit

The term reflects concerns about the institutions and operation of the European Community, now the European Union (EU), concerns which have been mounting since the 1980s. It is suggested that powers of decision-making which are binding on European populations are being transferred from the member state national Parliaments to EU institutions which are not sufficiently democratically accountable. One aspect of the problem is that institutional checks on EU decision-making are seen as inadequate. Within the EU, executive and legislative functions are not divided between a government and a Parliament respectively, as is the case in national politics in most European countries. Instead, they are largely shared between three EU institutions: the Commission, the Council of Ministers and the European Parliament. As the EU has no single 'executive', it is difficult to control by the traditional means of parliamentary scrutiny or a constitutional court. Many decisions are made behind closed doors and it has been left to the media to expose major problems of fraud, mismanagement and corruption. This view is encouraged by the complexity of decision-making processes within the EU. Further, there is a widespread public perception of EU politicians and bureaucrats as being elitist and out of touch with the realities of life in the member states. The Amsterdam Treaty (1997) attempts to address part of the problem by providing for an extension of the powers of the European Parliament and for providing a regular flow of information to national Parliaments.

[See also: Amsterdam Treaty]

denazification

One of the core policies agreed upon by the Allied powers at the Potsdam conference in July–August 1945. It came to involve the total dissolution of the Nazi Party and all its auxiliary and associated organisations and the removal of members of the Nazi Party from public office. It also required the capture and trial of suspected war criminals and the process of investigation of all citizens (for example, by means of questionnaires) as a means of determining what, if any, sanctions should be imposed on them before they could resume a normal existence as citizens. In fact many of

the intended measures had to be abandoned or diluted. The occupation authorities in West Germany found that they could not administer their zones or local areas without the assistance of Germans, most of whom had – of necessity or by choice – been members of the Nazi Party, and the questionnaire procedure proved too much of an administrative burden to carry out in a comprehensive and equitable manner. One adjunct to denazification was the policy of 'education for democracy', involving the reshaping of the German educational system to emphasise democratic values. Others included the political resocialisation of the citizenry to develop a democratic electorate, and the process of licensing of political parties, trade unions and other associations, and the mass media, to ensure that they were free from any taint of nazism.

In the Soviet zone of occupation, denazification was pursued very vigorously, and became combined with the policy of creating a communist society in that zone. Consequently many persons were imprisoned or even executed, often without any proper judicial process, and the Soviet occupation authority was able to proclaim in February 1948 that denazification had officially been successfully completed in that zone.

[See also: fascism; nazism; Nuremberg tribunal; Potsdam conference; Vergangenheitsbewältigung]

détente

A term generally applied to relations between the Western nations and communist states in the Cold War. It refers to the condition of decreased international tension, resulting from foreign and defence policy decisions. It can be applied to various periods in the Cold War (and there is no logical reason why the term should not be applied to periods in relations between other sides in a situation of international tension, such as between India and Pakistan concerning Kashmir, or Western powers and post-Shah Iran). However, it is more commonly applied to the period in the 1970s when the USA and West European states deliberately sought to develop improved relations with the USSR and China. This involved steps such as Nixon's visit to China and formal diplomatic relations between the USA and China in President Carter's term of office. Germany's Ostpolitik (policy towards Eastern Europe) developed especially by the government of Chancellor Brandt, and the Helsinki accords (1975), also made a contribution, though the failure of the USSR and its bloc partner states to observe the human rights provisions of those accords and renewed international interventions (for example in Angola and Afghanistan) by the USSR led to a deterioration in relations with the West. The accession to power of Gorbachev in the USSR produced another period of détente which lasted until the replacement of communism by democracies in the USSR and Eastern European states.

[See also: Helsinki Agreement; Ostpolitik; Brandt*]

economic miracle

A term applied to the rapid growth of the post-Second World War economy in West Germany. The Germans used the word *Wirtschaftswunder* to refer to this growth period, which resulted especially from a reform of the currency, by which the new Deutschmark was exchanged for the old occupation currency, and the stimulus of aid supplied through the Marshall Plan (officially known as the European Recovery Programme), which received the approval of the US Congress in 1948. The 'economic miracle' owed much to the social market economy policies developed by the Economic Council of Bizonia, and

by the first government of the Federal Republic, under Chancellor Adenauer and his Economics Minister, Erhard, from 1949 onwards. Production, exports and personal incomes grew rapidly for several years, and the Deutschmark became the strongest currency in Europe.

The term has also, by extension, been applied to rapid economic expansion in some other countries, such as Italy, whose *miracolo economico* between 1958 and 1963 produced an annual average growth rate of 6.6 per cent.

[See also: Bizonia; Marshall Plan; Adenauer*; Erhard*]

Economic and Monetary Union (EMU)

Economic and Monetary Union was the process of transition from existing national currency areas to a single currency area encompassing 12 member states of the European Union (EU). Under EMU, the 12 member states come under the authority of the independent European Central Bank (ECB), whose main task is to maintain price stability. EMU is provided for in the Treaty on European Union (TEU: the Maastricht Treaty), which came into force in November 1993. Steps towards EMU took place in three stages. Stage one (1 July 1990–31 December 1993) concerned the free movement of capital between member states, closer co-ordination of economic policies and closer co-operation between national central banks. Stage two (1 January 1994–31 December 1998) involved the convergence of the economic and monetary policies of the member states. Stage three (from 1 January 1999) required the establishment of the European Central Bank, the fixing of exchange rates and the introduction of a single currency. The single currency, the Euro, became the participants' sole legal tender on 28 February 2002. The TEU established entry criteria for prospective members of EMU to ensure the system's credibility: (i) an inflation rate not to exceed that of the three best performing member states by more than 1.5 per cent; (ii) an interest rate not to exceed the average of the three best performing member states by more than 2 per cent; (iii) a two-year membership of the ERM, without a devaluation, is to precede entry into EMU; (iv) the deficit-to-GDP ratio must not exceed 3 per cent; (v) the debt-to-GDP ratio of all levels of government must not exceed 60 per cent. The Stability and Growth Pact agreed at the European Council in Dublin in 1995 aims to ensure that member states continue to exercise budgetary discipline now that the single currency has been introduced. The Pact offers the Council the potential to sanction member states which fail to take appropriate action to reduce a large budgetary deficit. EMU is now considered part of the EU's acquis communitaire (existing body of law) and applicant states must be prepared to accept its terms on joining the Union. Nevertheless, some existing member states have qualms about exchanging their traditional currencies and independent monetary control for a common scheme, and it remains uncertain whether the UK, Denmark and Sweden will subscribe to EMU at all.

[See also: acquis communitaire; European Central Bank]

Economic and social cohesion

Economic and social cohesion became a Communities objective with the Single European Act (1986). It aims to create a balanced and sustainable development, reducing structural disparities between regions and member states and thereby securing equal opportunities for all European citizens. Cohesion policy is implemented through a variety of funding processes, principally through the Structural Funds. The Cohesion Fund of the European Union (EU) was established in 1994 under the terms of the Treaty on European Union (Maastricht Treaty). This fund is used to part-finance environmental and transport infrastructure projects in economically underdeveloped member states to help them meet the convergence criteria for Economic and Monetary Union (EMU). The Cohesion Fund was negotiated to persuade the poorer member states – Greece, Ireland, Portugal and Spain – to support EMU during the negotiations of the Maastricht Treaty. From 1994 to 1999, the funding of economic and social cohesion was the Community's second largest budget item (after the CAP), costing around 35 per cent of the budget. With the prospect of EU enlargement, expected to bring in new and relatively poor countries in Central and Eastern Europe, the Community's structural policy was reformed in 1999 to improve its effectiveness. Its budgetary allocation was increased from EUR 208 billion to EUR 213 billion for 2000–2006, including EUR 195 billion for the Structural Funds and EUR 18 billion for the Cohesion Fund.

[See also: additionality; Common Agricultural Policy; Economic and Monetary Union; Single European Act]

empty chair crisis

In July 1965, France precipitated a crisis in the European Economic Community by walking out of the Council of Ministers and the Committee of Permanent Representatives. This blocked the decision-making processes of the Community until the crisis was resolved with the Luxembourg compromise in January 1966. The French delegation had objected to a Commission proposal: to link a financial provision for the Common Agricultural Policy (CAP) with an institutional reform which would increase its own power and that of the European Parliament. France was in favour of supporting the CAP, but not of increasing the power of the 'supranational' institutions of the Community. The French also objected to the introduction of majority voting in the Council of Ministers, which, according to the terms of the Treaty of Rome, was due to come into effect in January 1966. The final outcome was as follows: a temporary funding scheme for the CAP was adopted; the proposed institutional reform was deferred; and the Luxembourg compromise adopted the principle of majority voting in the Council of Ministers, but acknowledged the right of any member state to require unanimous decision-making on issues concerning its own special interests.

[See also: Common Agricultural Policy; Luxembourg compromise; Treaties of Rome]

Enosis

A movement originating in the 1930s in Cyprus to bring about union between Cyprus and Greece. It attracted much support in the 1950s, especially the EOKA (the underground organisation of Cypriot nationalists) and the religious leader, Archbishop Makarios. Terrorist outrages against the British colonial government of the island became frequent. The United Kingdom gave Cyprus its independence in 1960, but the demand of Greek Cypriots for union with Greece continued. An attempt to declare unilateral union with Greece led to the partition of Cyprus, because the Turkish minority invited the Turkish military to come to their aid as protection against such union.

[See also: Makarios*]

ETA (Euskadi ta Askatasuna; Basque Nation and Liberty)

ETA was formed in the late 1950s as a radical and militant breakaway movement from the traditional Basque nationalist party, the PNV. The movement was formed in the context of the active repression of the Basque culture and language by the Spanish state, and of regional autonomy in general, under the Franco regime. Although heavily factionalised and prone to divisions over tactics, the movement shares a rationale of armed struggle with the Spanish state. ETA has carried out kidnappings, assassinations and bombings. It has targeted individuals it sees as representative of the Spanish state and has also engaged in more indiscriminate violence, such as the bombing of tourist areas in Spain. In December 1973 the group killed Franco's appointed Prime Minister, Admiral Luis Carrero Blanco. In 1978 the political party Herri Batasuna (HB) was founded as ETA's political wing. Governments of democratic Spain have attempted to negotiate a cease-fire with ETA leaders, but, although temporary cessations of violence have been achieved, the movement remains an active terrorist threat. By 1988 the main parties of the Spanish Parliament had signed an anti-terrorist pact with all of the Basque parties except HB. In 1992 police operations managed to prevent ETA from disrupting the Barcelona Olympic Games and tensions began to emerge between ETA and HB as the political wing believed that continued ETA terrorism would damage their electoral base. Several of ETA's leaders were captured in 1994, but the violence continued. In April 1995 Aznar, leader of the christian democratic People's Party (PP), narrowly avoided death in a car bomb attributed to ETA; in July 1997 the group kidnapped and later shot dead a local PP councillor, Miguel Angel Blanco, when the government refused to meet demands that ETA prisoners be transferred to the Basque country to serve their sentences. This incident provoked massive popular demonstrations against ETA. In 1998 ETA declared an end to its military

EVENTS, GROUPS AND DEVELOPMENTS

activity, but has since resumed the armed struggle.

[See also: Basque separatism; Aznar*; Carrero Blanco*; Franco*]

eurocommunism

A term applied to the reformist strategies pursued by several West European communist parties (especially those of Spain and Italy) in the 1970s, and given formal expression in a joint statement by the leaderships of the Spanish and Italian Communist parties in 1975. This strategy emphasised independence from the ideological leadership of the Communist Party of the Soviet Union, acceptance of parliamentary multi-party political procedures and emphasis on legislative reform at the expense of revolution as a method of promoting communist goals. Democracy, pluralism and tolerance were accepted as features of the political system within which communist parties should function, and the existing constitutional arrangements were respected. However, relatively little electoral benefit resulted from adoption of eurocommunist principles, and the significance of this development tended to fade away, until the reforms of Gorbachev in the USSR made the notion superfluous.

[See also: historic compromise]

European Central Bank (ECB)

The European Central Bank of the European Union came into operation during stage three of the plans outlined in the Maastricht Treaty on Economic and Monetary Union on 1 January 1998. It took over from the European Monetary Institute (EMI). The ECB is an independent body with sole responsibility for formulating and implementing the EU's single monetary policy. It pursues price stability, ensuring noninflationary money supply and monetary growth and conducting

monetary policy for the single currency area. Now that the ECB has come into operation, the member states' existing central banks will function as 'regional' central banks. Together with the ECB, they form the European System of Central Banks (ESCB). The ECB makes policy through its Governing Council, composed of the governors of the member state central banks and the ECB's six-member executive board. The ECB is accountable to the European Parliament, and is based in Frankfurt, Germany.

[See also: Economic and Monetary Union]

European Coal and Steel Community (ECSC)

The first supranational institution in Europe after the Second World War, and a forerunner of the European Union. The ECSC was formed as a response to the unresolved problem posed by West Germany's coal and steel industries, which were to be controlled by some form of international authority as a guarantee that they would not be a resource for future German aggression. The Schuman Plan (1950) set out a proposal to combine the coal and steel productive resources of several states under international control. The intention was to ensure that France and Germany would not be able to go to war with each other in the future, because of this mingling of their coal and steel resources, and to promote European co-operation more generally. Germany and France were joined by Italy and the Benelux countries to form a six-state group, which signed the Treaty of Paris in 1951 to initiate the ECSC in 1952. A Council of Ministers supervised a supranational executive (the High Authority), and both a legislative assembly consisting of a selection of members of national parliaments, and a court to adjudicate on disputes, were included in the

Treaty. A levy on sales of coal and iron and steel products provided the ECSC with its financial resources. The success of this scheme and the pattern of institutions which had been devised led directly to the Treaties of Rome, creating for the same six states a European Economic Community (EEC) and EURATOM. Together with EURATOM (the supranational atomic energy authority) the ECSC and EEC were merged into the European Community (EC) in 1967.

[See also: Monnet*; Schuman*]

European Currency Unit (ECU)

The European Currency Unit (ECU) functioned as the currency of the European Communities (EC) prior to the introduction of the Euro. It was used to calculate the Communities' accounts, replacing the European Unit of Account (EUA) when the European Monetary System (EMS) was established in 1979. The EC budget was represented in ECU, as were grants received from the EC or fines levied by the European Court of Justice. Also, each member state participating in the Exchange Rate Mechanism (ERM) had a bilateral exchange rate against the ECU. On 1 January 1999, the ECU was replaced by the Euro on a one-for-one basis in all contracts.

[See also: Economic and Monetary Union]

European Defence Community (EDC): Pleven Plan

Shortly after the Second World War, there was an attempt to create the European Defence Community as a Western European defence structure with a common army and a common European political authority, the European Political Community (EPC). The scheme was first proposed by the French Prime Minister, René Pleven, on 24 October 1950 as a way of meeting

the threat of Soviet conventional military superiority in Europe. The EDC was launched by a treaty signed on 27 May 1952 in Paris by Belgium, France, Italy, Luxembourg, the Netherlands and West Germany. The UK supported the EDC but refused to join on account of conflicting commitments outside Europe; Denmark and Norway opposed the project. By this time, though, Western European leaders were growing less convinced of the need for full political and defence integration and conflicts over the creation of a common army prevented the further development of the EDC. The EDC collapsed when the French Parliament refused to ratify the Paris Treaty in August 1954. By this time, the Soviet threat in Europe appeared to have receded. Stalin had died, the Korean war had ended and the Soviet Union seemed content to consolidate its hold on its existing satellites. In 1955 a number of European countries formed the Western European Union (WEU), a defence organisation based on a far less integrated model of co-operation than the EDC. West German military forces were incorporated into NATO.

European enlargement

Enlargement refers to the four successive waves of new membership acceding to the European Communities in addition to the six founder members: Belgium, France, (West) Germany, Luxembourg, Italy and the Netherlands. The first enlargement took place in 1973 and brought in Denmark, Ireland and the UK as members. In 1981, Greece joined, and, in 1986, Portugal and Spain. Austria, Finland and Sweden joined in 1995. Countries applying to join the EU include Turkey, Cyprus, Malta and many of the countries of Central and Eastern Europe (CEEC). In June 1993 the European Council in Copenhagen recognised the right of the CEEC to join the EU on condition that they met political and economic criteria set down by the EU and incorporated the acquis communitaire. This demand was later detailed in the 'accession partnerships' set out in the Commission's document: Agenda 2000. These are pre-accession framework agreements made bilaterally between the EU and each applicant country setting out priorities and a timetable for the adoption of the Community acquis. With the opening of membership to CEEC, the European Union faces its most ambitious phase of enlargement. It is widely acknowledged that further enlargement on the scale now proposed must be accompanied by institutional reform if the EU is to function effectively in future. Institutional reform with respect to enlargement was addressed in the Amsterdam Treaty (1997), the document: Agenda 2000 adopted by the Commission in 1997 and in the Treaty of Nice (signed 2001).

[See also: Amsterdam Treaty; Treaty of Nice]

European Free Trade Association (EFTA)

An organisation created as an alternative to the European Economic Community by seven countries which had not become members of the EEC. It was initiated under the Treaty of Stockholm in 1960, signed by the UK, Austria, Denmark, Norway, Sweden, Switzerland and Portugal. Finland and Iceland joined later. It was an arrangement to promote free trade among its member states, but without the common external tariff or the supranational institutional arrangements which were to be found in the EEC. However, changes of policy direction especially by the British government under Macmillan and Wilson meant that the UK and Denmark, two of the most important EFTA member states, left to join the EEC in 1972, and Portugal also joined the EEC in 1985. Despite closer trading arrangements with the EC, EFTA

soon became almost irrelevant to its member states, and Austria, Finland and Sweden also joined the EU (as it had become) in 1995. EFTA is now a very small and relatively insignificant trading organisation.

European Unit of Account (EUA) [See: European Currency Unit (ECU)]

euro-sceptic

A term applied to those – principally in Britain, Denmark, Sweden and some of the applicant countries – who support the idea of European integration in general terms, but who question either specific key policies of the EU (such as the common currency enterprise), or the degree of detailed control exercised by the European Commission in areas such as weights and measures, norms and standards, social and cultural policies or civil rights, or the extension of harmonisation to new areas of policy. Euro-sceptics challenge the economic, political and social assumptions made by those who favour greater integration, especially with regard to the effects this would have on national economies. However, euro-sceptics do not support British withdrawal from the EU.

Eurosclerosis

During the 1970s, the European Community (EC) was afflicted by a period of 'Eurosclerosis' when it seemed incapable of effective management and decision-making. At a procedural level, an increasing workload and the need for unanimity in the Council of Ministers slowed the decision-making processes of the EC and contributed to a serious loss of confidence in its institutions. Between 1973 and 1974 the European economy came under intense pressure from the first oil crisis, in which the price of oil quadrupled. Unable to reach agreement on a joint EC response to the energy crisis, they became increasingly protectionist. Alarmed by the lack of political leadership within the EC, President Giscard d'Estaing of France and Chancellor Schmidt of West Germany proposed regular summit meetings between the heads of government of the member states. The summits were intended to provide a forum for economic planning and policy development within the EC. In 1974 this forum became known as the European Council and in 1987 it gained formal recognition under the Single European Act (SEA).

[See also: Luxembourg compromise; Single European Act; Giscard d'Estaing*; Schmidt*]

Events of May (1968) [See: May Events]

Évian Agreements

A set of agreements signed in Évian in March 1962 between the French government and representatives of the Algerian independence fighters, which brought an end to the state of war between the independence movement and France in Algeria, and paved the way for Algerian independence, following referenda in France. These referenda produced majorities supporting Algerian independence, though the OAS (the 'secret army') continued by violent means to oppose independence.

[See also: Algerian conflict; Secret Army Organisation; de Gaulle*; Soustelle*]

Exchange Rate Mechanism (ERM)

The Exchange Rate Mechanism was the central tool of the European Community's European Monetary System (EMS). The EMS, in operation from March 1979 to the introduction of the Euro, was a scheme designed to preserve a reasonable level of price

stability between the member states in the context of fluctuating national exchange rates. The ERM allowed the member states' currencies to shift in value in relation to one another only within predetermined parameters. The UK joined the ERM in 1990, but was forced out on 17 September 1992, along with Italy. Similar to the original ERM (ERM I), ERM II regulates the valuation of the Euro in relation to other (non-EMU) member state currencies.

[See also: Economic and Monetary Union]

extra-parliamentary opposition (APO)

The German term APO (*Ausserparlamentarische Opposition*) referred to a loose alliance of radical democrats and Marxists in the Federal Republic of Germany (FRG), which had a strong influence on the development of radical politics in the FRG. From 1966 to 1969, the government coalition in the FRG comprised the two main parties, the christian democratic CDU/CSU and the social-democratic SPD, which had previously opposed one another. The only parliamentary party left outside the coalition was the small, liberal FDP, too marginal a force to act as an effective parliamentary opposition. In this context, the APO emerged, arguing that opposition had to be exercised from outside Parliament. The APO saw itself as part of a world revolutionary movement. It opposed the USA's involvement in Vietnam and supported the protests comprising the May Events in France (1968). The APO was dominated by the Socialist German Student Association (SDS), a group debarred from the SPD because of its radical extremism. The APO pressed for reforms to the outmoded system of higher education and also for radical reforms to the state institutions. It was particularly opposed to the use of emergency laws and anti-radical loyalty tests for state employees. It found support from university students and from some of the citizen initiative groups, but its failure to secure much support amongst the working class and trade unions led to the fragmentation of the movement from 1969. It collapsed after the government introduced reforms in higher education. Some APO members decided to work within the system, joining the SPD or the civil service: an approach termed the 'long march through the institutions'. Others retained a radical approach, turning to environmentalism or even terrorism – the Baader-Meinhof group had its roots in the APO.

[See also: Baader-Meinhof group; May Events]

Falklands War

The military conflict in 1982 in the Falkland Islands, a British colony in the south Atlantic, provoked by the Argentinean invasion. Argentina had long disputed the right of the British to exert sovereignty over the islands, and negotiations concerning the islands had taken place under United Nations auspices for some years, without result. The British military force sent to the islands by sea and air eventually compelled the surrender and withdrawal of the Argentinean invasion force. Mrs Thatcher and her Conservative government benefited from popular support for her actions, and her party won a resounding victory at the general election the following year, due, according to many experts, in large measure to 'the Falklands factor'. Currently the Falkland Islands remain under British sovereignty, in conformity with the wishes of the inhabitants.

A long-running controversy concerned the circumstances under which the Argentine cruiser 'Belgrano' was sunk by a British submarine. Claims were made that, when sunk, it was outside the exclusion zone (an area of the sea surrounding the Falkland Islands) imposed by Britain.

fascism

A name first used by Mussolini for his nationalist and authoritarian movement which later took power in Italy. It was then applied to other movements or political parties whose ideologies shared many of the principal characteristics of Italian fascism, especially the Nazis in Germany, but also Franco's Falange movement and radical right-wing parties in France, Britain and several other European countries in the 1930s.

There remain deep disputes concerning the definition and the applicability of the term: fascism. For communists, it is equivalent almost to anti-communism, and anti-fascism has been used – by the USSR in its zone of occupation in Germany and in the Eastern European states over which the USSR exercised hegemony – to mobilise the population in favour of communism and against perceived enemies of communism. Definitions focus upon several distinguishing features of fascist ideology. These include belief in a charismatic leader, such as Franco, Hitler and Mussolini; active promotion of nationalism, in defence against alien immigration or racial integration, and perhaps involving territorial expansion and military strength; and hostility to liberal democracy as a political system based on divisive pluralism and effete tolerance of views and interests hostile to the nation or race. Fascism also often includes acceptance of ideological pronouncements, especially from the leader, as scientifically irrefutable. However, the variations found in Nazi Germany, Franco's Spain and Mussolini's Italy, as well as among fascist parties and movements in countries where fascism has not been the ideology of the government, and the necessary differences in details of policy to be found among parties and movements which emphasise – different – nationalisms mean that it is difficult to form a generally accepted definition of fascism. It is unhelpful to apply the term indiscriminately to all radical right-wing or nationalist political parties, some of which are little more than populist in their doctrines and policies.

[See also: anti-fascism; anti-Semitism; nazism; populism; Spanish civil war; xenophobia; Franco*; Haider*; Hitler*; Le Pen*; Mussolini*; Schönhuber*]

Felipeism (Felipismo)

A term applied in Spanish politics to refer to the style and approach of the PSOE and its leader, Felipe Gonzalez. This approach to party politics involved the abandonment of class-based politics by the party, with emphasis placed on the dominant leadership style of Gonzalez and a modernised, centrally directed and professionally managed party organisation. The term was applied as criticism by the opponents of the PSOE, to emphasise the tendency of Gonzalez and his government to by-pass Parliament and the lack of transparency of that government in its policy-making. Some of the characteristics of 'Felipismo' match the defining features of 'catch-all' parties, as analysed by Kirchheimer.

[See also: Gonzalez*]

final solution

The term used to refer to the policy of Hitler's Third Reich to eliminate the Jewish population from Europe. The specifics of this policy were presented to the 'Wannsee conference' on 20 January 1942 by Heydrich, Himmler's closest associate, to participants which included Adolf Eichmann. The measures involved the deportation and murder of Jews in a systematic fashion, and this conference is regarded as the signal for the commencement of the Holocaust.

[See also: Holocaust; Eichmann*]

Finlandisation

A polemical term describing those policies of Finland which were adjusted to take account of the interests of its dominant neighbour, the USSR, especially in relation to foreign affairs and security policy. By extension, the term is sometimes applied to other small, independent states, when these appear to be arranging their policies, particularly concerning security matters, to accommodate the interests of a more powerful neighbour. In the case of Finland, defeat in war against the USSR and threat of occupation by the USSR encouraged such a policy stance. A treaty between Finland and the USSR in 1948 seemed to give formal expression to this stance. After the collapse of the USSR, Finland declared itself to be no longer bound by that treaty, and negotiated a treaty with Russia signed in 1992 which contained no terms that could deserve any continued application of the term: Finlandisation.

First-past-the-post system (FPTP)

An electoral system, usually but not necessarily based on single-member constituencies, in which the candidate with the most votes is elected. Variants of the system, such as that used in France, may require that a candidate secure an absolute majority (more votes than all other candidates) to be elected on the first ballot; if that condition is not fulfilled, a second ballot, with a limited number of candidates, is then held, in which a simple majority is required for election. Elections to the British House of Commons use the FPTP system, as do British local council elections. Most 'Additional Member Systems' utilise FPTP voting to elect a part of the legislature (the Federal Republic of Germany and Italy, for instance, as well as in elections to the Scottish and Welsh devolved assemblies). Used without the election of additional members, the FPTP system is likely to provide a very disproportional result in terms of the percentage of seats a party obtains and the percentage of votes it has secured. The FPTP system does have advantages of simplicity and transparency, and enables elected representatives to develop close links with their constituencies.

[See also: Additional Member System]

Flick Affair

A scandal concerning party financing in the Federal Republic of Germany. The Flick concern, a large industrial company, had sold a large holding of shares in the Daimler-Benz company in 1975, reinvesting most of the proceeds. The Ministers of Economics (Friderichs, then later Lambsdorff) certified as required by law that the reinvestment was beneficial to the country's economy, and so these funds escaped profits tax. It later came to light that a series of secret donations by the Flick company to political parties (including the Free Democrats, to which Friderichs and Lambsdorff belonged) could have influenced the decisions of these ministers. Lambsdorff resigned as minister in 1984 when charges were brought against him. Charges of bribery were not pursued due to lack of sufficient evidence, but in 1987 Lambsdorff, Friderichs and the agent of Flick, von Brauchitsch, were found guilty of tax evasion (since the donations had improperly escaped taxation) and fines were imposed. A series of constitutional court cases on party financing and reforms of the Party Law relating to donations were direct consequences of the Flick Affair.

floating voter

Voters who do not admit to long-term identification with a particular political party, and who are prepared to assess their likely voting decision at every election, sometimes switching from one party to another at successive elections. It is generally accepted that over the past two decades the proportion of floating voters has increased (even if in fact some do vote for the same party as at the previous election).

Fundis [See: Realos and Fundis]

G-7 [See: Group of Eight]

G-8 [See: Group of Eight]

Gang of Four

The name associated in British politics with four former Labour Party ministers: Roy Jenkins, David Owen, Bill Rodgers and Shirley Williams, who resigned from the party in 1981 to form the Social Democratic Party (SDP). They did so because of concern about the leftward direction of the party under its new leader, Foot, and its hostility to British participation in the progress of European integration. The SDP had hoped to attract a substantial number of Labour MPs and peers, but few others joined the 'gang of four'. To avoid splitting the centre-left vote at the general election of 1983, the SDP formed an electoral alliance with the Liberal Party, and in that election the Alliance secured the highest third-party share of the vote since the Second World War (25.4 per cent, just over 2 per cent behind the Labour Party) and for a time in late 1981 and early 1982 the Alliance was more popular than the Conservatives or the Labour Party in opinion polls. The SDP had over 55,000 members for most of its existence. Though the Alliance did moderately well in the 1987 general election (22.5 per cent), it had failed to displace the Labour Party as the chief opposition party in Britain. A decision was therefore made by the two Alliance parties to merge into a single party. Though Owen and a small number of

SDP politicians remained outside this merged party (as did a small number of Liberals), the merger, supported by membership ballots following decisions by each party's delegate conference, took place in early 1988. Owen and his small group of supporters continued as an independent political force for two years, but with no success.

Gastarbeiter

A German term (meaning 'guest-worker') which refers to the foreign employees brought to the Federal Republic of Germany, originally on the basis of a short period of residence, to be followed by a return to the home country and the entry of replacement workers on a kind of rotation system. However, large numbers of such workers stayed on in the Federal Republic, many of whom have married and had children in Germany, which leads to issues concerning naturalisation. Originally brought to the Federal Republic to meet labour shortages, guest-workers are the target in times of unemployment of racial abuse and campaigns for their repatriation.

GCHQ case

In 1984, the Government Communications Headquarters (GCHQ) case established an important precedent: that the UK government could no longer be considered immune from a legal challenge on the grounds of the ancient prerogatives of the Crown. The UK government had debarred staff of GCHQ, who dealt with highly confidential government matters, from trade-union membership. GCHQ staff challenged the ban on the grounds that it had been made without consultation. In defending its action, the UK government claimed that prerogative powers could not be reviewed by the courts and that their decision was therefore unchallengeable.

The staff lost their case as it was deemed to be against the interests of national security for them to be unionised. Nevertheless, it was ruled that a decision taken under prerogative powers may be the subject of judicial review.

[See also: judicialisation]

German question

In general terms, the 'German question' has referred to issues of Germany's identity as a nation and boundaries as a state, and thus also to its status in international politics and its relations with other states, especially its neighbours. Thus even prior to German unification in 1871, the 'German question' arose in the diplomatic settlements following the Napoleonic wars and in the debates in the Frankfurt Parliament (1848–49), for example. Following the creation of the Second Empire by Bismarck in 1871, the 'German question' was a factor in the causes of the First World War and the peace settlement that followed its conclusion. The territorial losses and humiliating terms of the Versailles Treaty (1919) provided political ammunition for Hitler and contributed to his rise to power and to the expansionist policies of Germany leading to the Second World War. Since 1945, the Potsdam conference, the occupation of Germany, Germany's division, the Oder–Neisse and Saarland issues, and the diplomacy which led to the reunification of Germany were all caused by, or affected, the 'German question'. If ever it could be claimed that the 'German question' has been resolved, it would appear to be so now, following the treaties in 1990 which established the diplomatic and territorial status of reunified Germany.

[See also: Cold War; Hallstein Doctrine; Oder–Neisse line; Ostpolitik; Potsdam conference; reunification of Germany; Saarland question; 'Two plus Four' talks]

Gibraltar

Gibraltar forms a peninsula on the Spanish coast. It is of strategic importance as it allows control of the Gibraltar straits which link the Atlantic and the Mediterranean seas. Under Spanish control since 1462, it was taken by the British navy in 1704, became a British possession in 1713 and a Crown Colony in 1830. After a counter-claim by Spain, Gibraltar was awarded self-government in 1964. Negotiations between Britain and Spain followed, but broke down in 1966. In a referendum in 1967, a 95 per cent majority voted against becoming part of Spain. In response, General Franco closed the border in 1969. The issue resurfaced in the 1980s with Spain's application to join the EC. In order to gain the UK's support for its membership, Spain allowed some border traffic from 1982 and reopened the border in 1985.

glasnost

Glasnost (openness) was one of the innovative principles adopted by Gorbachev after his appointment as General Secretary of the Communist Party of the Soviet Union in 1985. Gorbachev believed that the Soviet Union was stagnating as a superpower because of the decline of discipline, order and morality. He saw greater openness as both a desirable end in itself and as a means of reviving an inert society. Problems should be faced openly and honestly and not denied as had been the practice under past Soviet leaderships. Debate began on formerly 'closed' issues such as the role of women in Soviet society, the environment (particularly after the accident at the Chernobyl nuclear power station in Kiev on 26 April 1986) and the problem of crime in the Soviet Union. The notion of glasnost widened to encompass freedom of speech and of publication. Criticism was tolerated,

first of Stalin, then even of Lenin, the main founder of the Soviet state. Previously banned works by authors such as Solzhenitsyn, Shalamov and Koestler were openly published for the first time. Together with perestroika (reconstruction), the term glasnost entered into common currency also in Western Europe, symbolising the new approach to government and international relations promoted by Gorbachev. The two concepts galvanised a reform process throughout Central and Eastern Europe and eventually helped to overthrow Communist rule in these countries and in the Soviet Union itself.

[See also: perestroika]

Godesberg Programme

The new basic programme of the West German Social Democratic Party, approved in 1959 at the party's congress in Bad Godesberg (near Bonn). It replaced the then-valid Heidelberg Programme (1925), which still bound the SPD to a Marxist, class-based collection of policies and attitudes, out of place in the rapidly modernising post-war society of the Federal Republic of Germany. The Godesberg Programme accepted the market economy, whilst emphasising the continuing role of the state in regulating the economy. It abandoned phraseology which seemed to attack the churches. It accepted the need for German contributions to its own defence and membership of regional defence organisations such as NATO. The party in fact had already been operating as a more modern and less class-related party, and this Programme, the product of a long period of discussion within the party, was as much a means of bringing the programmatic basis of the SPD in line with its actual attitudes and policies as it was a significant reformist document. Following the acceptance of the Godesberg Programme, the SPD gained

2–3 per cent at every federal election until in 1972 it overtook the Christian Democrats for the first time and became the largest single party in the Bundestag. This was largely due to the extension of its electoral appeal to groups beyond the working class and trade union members. It thus became, like the Christian Democrats, a 'catch-all party'.

Good Friday Agreement

The Treaty of 22 May 1998 which formed the basis for a peaceful settlement in Northern Ireland. Following nearly two years of talks involving the various parties and political groups in Northern Ireland, as well as the British and Irish governments, an agreement was reached on 10 April 1998. The core of the Treaty resulting from that agreement was a consensus that 'reaffirms total and absolute commitment to exclusively democratic and peaceful means of resolving differences on political issues'. It involved changes to British law and the Irish constitution to ensure that the future status of Northern Ireland could only be settled by the consent of the people of Northern Ireland. It provided a basis for the creation of a legislative assembly with devolved powers which would represent proportionally the various Northern Irish parties, and a power-sharing executive government based on that assembly. Cross-border structures would provide for co-operation between Northern Ireland and the Irish Republic, and a British–Irish Council would link the Irish government to the government of the United Kingdom and the devolved Scottish, Welsh and Northern Irish authorities. Prisoners with paramilitary status would be released over a 3-year period, and there was a commitment to decommission armaments held by non-state organisations.
The Good Friday Agreement was confirmed by referenda in Northern

Ireland (where 94 per cent voted in favour on a 56 per cent turnout) and in the Irish Republic (71 per cent in favour on an 81 per cent turnout). Implementation of the Treaty has proved problematic, mainly because of disagreements concerning the timing and modalities of decommissioning of armaments. A number of brief suspensions of the Assembly have been imposed by the British government to allow time for talks to be held to resolve such disputes. Conflicts concerning traditional parades and terrorist activity by paramilitary organisations which were not parties to the agreement have also proved disruptive to the 'peace process' since 1998.

[See also: Irish Republican Army; Adams*; Paisley*; Trimble*]

Grabenwahlsystem (Germany)

An electoral system which institutes a 'ditch' ('Graben') between seats won under a first-past-the-post electoral system and those awarded through proportional representation. The name was applied to the proposed revision in 1956 of the two-vote proportional representation system of election used in the Federal Republic of Germany, under which the allocation of seats on a proportional basis would be confined to the 50 per cent of Bundestag seats drawn from party lists, and would not (as the Electoral Law of 1953 had provided) take into account in such allocation any constituency seats won by a party. Since small parties tend in Germany not to win constituency seats, this would have, in effect, halved their Bundestag representation compared to the existing two-vote system. For example, if the Free Democratic Party (FDP) secured 10 per cent of list votes, they would expect to win about 50 seats in the pre-reunification Bundestag (10 per cent of 496 seats). The fact that the party won no constituencies would be irrelevant. Under the

Grabenwahlsystem, the 10 per cent would be calculated only for the 248 list seats available, giving the party only about 25 seats. The larger parties would win their proportional share of list seats, plus the constituency seats they had won. Thus the Christian Democrats, with, say, 47 per cent of list votes (their vote-share in the 1965 Bundestag election) would get about 116 list seats (47 per cent of 248); since they also won 154 constituency seats, they would have had 270 seats, providing an absolute majority, rather than the 242 seats which they were in fact allocated. Though the idea was floated by Christian Democratic politicians in 1956, it was soon abandoned, especially after strong opposition from the FDP.

[See also: Young Turks' Revolt]

grand coalition

A coalition composed of the two largest parties in a party system, usually parties which would normally be in direct opposition to each other. A grand coalition could also include one or more smaller parties, though this would not normally be necessary to provide a majority, so such a coalition would be over-sized. Austria was governed by grand coalitions consisting of the christian democratic People's Party and the Social Democrats from the end of the post-war occupation regime until 1966, and from 1986 until 1999, and the Federal Republic of Germany was governed by a grand coalition of the Christian Democrats and Social Democrats from 1966 until 1969. Grand coalitions have also sometimes been formed at Land level in the Federal Republic of Germany. They are generally criticised for removing effective opposition in Parliament.

green card system (of immigration)

The term 'green card' refers to a controversial new policy trend in Western European countries, based on practices in the USA. Amongst would-be immigrants, highly skilled and well-qualified individuals are selected by host state immigration procedures for special 'fast-track' entry. In March 2000, Chancellor Schröder of Germany proposed to meet a shortfall of specialists in Germany's industrial technology sector by giving temporary work permits to as many as 30,000 foreign computer experts. In March 2002 a law was passed to allow up to 1.5 million skilled workers to migrate to Germany. The proposal met with criticism from trade unions and opposition christian democrats. In a report of February 2001, EU Commission President Romano Prodi distinguished between mass immigration and a programme of co-ordinated admission of skilled workers, arguing that the EU would need at least 1.6 million new 'qualified immigrants' to achieve its goal of becoming the world's most competitive economic area by 2010.

[See also: immigration]

green movement

The green movement was one of the new social movements which, from the 1960s to the 1980s, challenged the post-war consensus in Western European countries. The green movement began with specific ecologist or environmentalist campaigns at the local level. It then extended its organisation to the national level in order to strengthen its political impact, beginning with the formation of umbrella organisations of green activists in the early 1970s. Concern over the use of nuclear energy helped to consolidate the green movement. After the 1970s oil crisis, many European governments decided to expand their civil nuclear energy programmes. Green activists found this alarming, both because of the potential for accidents and the chance that civil nuclear capacity might later be diverted to military uses. In the late 1970s, these concerns were compounded by the NATO twin-track decision on intermediate nuclear forces and the eventual stationing of cruise missiles and Pershing II in Western Europe. In many countries, peace activists and environmentalists joined forces over the issue of nuclear power, creating a broad-based movement with links with other countries. In the early 1980s, most green movements tried to persuade the socialists or social democrats in their national Parliaments to take up their proposals. Whereas some socialist factions were prepared to promote anti-nuclear or environmentalist issues, they could not support the greens' more radical demands, particularly calls for limits to economic growth to secure sustainable development. The established political parties have always seen constant economic growth as the key to improving the quality of life of the population and thereby to maintaining their support at elections. Finding their efforts blocked, many of the European green movements decided to set up their own parties to pursue their specific interests.

[See also: NATO twin-track decision; new social movements; Fischer*; Kelly*]

Group of Eight (G-8)

The name given to meetings of finance ministers and heads of central banks of the economically most important states and the EU. These meetings are to settle issues relating to the state of the global economy, exchange rates and financial issues affecting particular countries. The countries involved are: Canada, France, Germany, Italy, Japan, the United Kingdom, the USA (the 'Group of Seven': G-7), and, since 1991, Russia. It can also be applied to summit meetings of the heads of government of those states. Depending on the agenda, at meetings of the finance ministers the

EU is represented by the Economics Commissioner, the president of the European Central Bank and the finance minister of the country holding the presidency of the EU at the time (who might also be attending as a national representative, if that country is one of the G-8 states). At meetings of heads of governments, the president of the EU will attend.

Guillaume Affair

In April 1974 it was discovered by the German secret service that Günter Guillaume, a member of Chancellor Brandt's personal staff, was in fact an agent of the GDR Stasi, who had entered the FRG as a refugee and had acquired employment on the staff of the Social Democratic Party. He had been promoted in 1970 to a position on Brandt's staff in the Chancellor's Office, and had then used this opportunity to pass secret government information to the GDR. Brandt took personal responsibility for this embarrassing scandal, and resigned as Chancellor (though he retained his post as party leader). Guillaume was sentenced to thirteen years' imprisonment, but was released in 1981 as part of an exchange of prisoners, and returned to the GDR, where he was decorated for his espionage achievements.
[See also: Brandt*]

Gulf War

The war between military forces of the UN and Iraq, following Iraq's attempted forceful annexation of Kuwait in August 1990. Iraq had long claimed that Kuwait really belonged to the territory of Iraq, and disputes concerning oil production levels, as well as Saddam Hussein's territorial ambitions, led to the Iraqi invasion. A UN resolution requiring Iraqi withdrawal and the imposition of economic and diplomatic sanctions failed to produce an Iraqi withdrawal, so a military invasion of Iraq took place in January and February 1991 from bases in Saudi Arabia and from ships in the Gulf. British and French military forces were involved; Germany supplied only non-military resources. Iraq accepted UN resolutions and withdrew from Kuwait, but Iraqi refusal to destroy chemical and nuclear weapons resulted in the imposition of sanctions by the UN and a long-running dispute concerning UN inspection of suspected weapons facilities.

Hallstein Doctrine

Arising from the claim by the FRG that it alone was the legitimate representative of Germany, since, unlike the government of the GDR, its government had been freely elected, the Hallstein Doctrine (named after its author, Walter Hallstein) was included in Adenauer's 'Government declaration' on 23 September 1955. It stated that the FRG would not have diplomatic relations with any state (the USSR excepted) which gave diplomatic recognition to the GDR. The dilemma for many states, especially those which were neutral in the Cold War, was that the trade and development aid which the FRG could supply were often very advantageous, and the gains from diplomatic relations with the GDR were limited, so it proved an effective diplomatic instrument for the Adenauer government. The Hallstein Doctrine lost its validity with the onset of the Ostpolitik, which produced a degree of détente between the FRG and the GDR and other communist states.

[See also: Cold War; Ostpolitik; Hallstein*]

Helsinki Agreement

The Helsinki Agreement (also called the Helsinki Final Act) was drawn up by 35 nations which took part in the Helsinki Conference of 1975, on European

security, East–West economic co-operation and human rights. It did not have the status of an international treaty, but was rather a statement of joint commitment and political intent. The signatories included all the European states (except Albania), the USA and Canada. The Helsinki Conference also established the Conference on Security and Co-operation in Europe (CSCE), which until 1990 was the only forum in which both the capitalist and communist European states, together with the USA and Canada, met to discuss common concerns. In working towards the Helsinki Agreement, the member states of the European Communities co-ordinated their foreign policies through the mechanism of European Political Co-operation (EPC) for the first time. The human rights provisions of the Helsinki Agreement were used both in dialogue between the superpowers and increasingly within the Soviet Union to legitimise protest against the system. President Carter of the USA used the Helsinki Final Act to spotlight human rights abuses in the Soviet Union, particularly those concerning the treatment of dissidents. Throughout the late 1970s and early 1980s, those Russian dissidents who attempted to monitor the Soviet Union's fulfilment of the human rights clauses in the Helsinki Agreement were jailed.

historic compromise (Italy)

The historic compromise refers to the decision of the Italian Communist Party (PCI) to try to enter effective parliamentary politics through collaboration with other political parties. Since the Second World War, the PCI had been marginalised in Italian politics through the successful tactics of its rival, the christian democratic DC. The PCI had retreated into a stance of fundamental opposition and alignment with the Soviet Union. After the Soviet invasion of Hungary in 1956, though, the party adopted an independent, Eurocommunist position which aimed to achieve socialism within the existing democratic framework. The party's leader, Berlinguer, established the strategy of historic compromise in 1973. His efforts established the PCI as a mainstream party and eventually as a de facto party of government. In 1976 the PCI tolerated DC Prime Minister Andreotti's coalition government, abstaining from parliamentary votes to preserve the government. After the murder of Aldo Moro, the PCI even voted with the coalition, although it was never formally a part of the government. The strategy failed through the opposition of other parties who objected to the collaboration of the country's two largest political forces, the DC and the PCI. PCI leaders became disillusioned with the strategy when it failed to bring added electoral support, and Berlinguer dropped it in 1980.

[See also: eurocommunism; Andreotti*; Berlinguer*; Moro*]

Historikerstreit (historians' dispute)

The bitter dispute which erupted between rival schools of historians in West Germany between 1986 and 1987 centred around the question of whether it is admissible to relativise the atrocities of the Third Reich (as suggested by the historian Ernst Nolte), or whether these must be set apart as incomparable in historical experience (as argued by the historians Ernst Jäckel and Hagen Schulze and by the philosopher Jürgen Habermas). This debate was perceived as having a direct bearing on questions of German identity and moral integrity as a nation. In short, it posed the question as to whether the Germans could ever recover from the taint of nazism. The debate developed from an academic dispute to a nationwide concern. It took on a party political slant, with representatives of parties on the

centre-right arguing for relativisation and those of the centre-left arguing against.

[See also: nazism]

Holocaust

A term applied to the actions taken by the Nazi government in the Third Reich to physically eliminate the Jewish population, first in Germany, then in territories occupied by Germany during the war, by processes of mass killings, especially in concentration camps such as Auschwitz and Treblinka. It has been estimated that as many as 6 million Jews were killed by the policy of genocide adopted by the Hitler government. There has been a long and continuing debate concerning whether the Holocaust should be regarded as a unique event in history, unable to be compared to any other occurrence in any country of the world, or whether it can be classed alongside policies of mass extermination instigated in Stalin's Soviet union, Pol Pot's Cambodia or, more recently, in parts of Africa such as Rwanda.

[See also: anti-Semitism; Historikerstreit; nazism; Nuremberg tribunal]

immigration

Immigration concerns the entry of foreign-born people into a 'host' state, with the intention of living and/or working in that state on a temporary or permanent basis. Since the Second World War, long-term immigration has been steadily changing the national, ethnic and cultural balance of Western European populations. European states differ in their attitudes to and policies on immigration, but since the mid-1970s all popular host countries have tried to restrict immigration. Legal entry falls into the following main categories: temporary labour migrants, family reunion (e.g. of spouses and children of immigrants already working in the host country), asylum-seekers claiming political persecution in their own country, and refugees seeking entry on humanitarian grounds. With increasing restrictions on legal labour entry, host countries have experienced an increase in the 'abuse' of asylum provision, with many asylum claimants suspected of entering the country not primarily out of fear of political persecution, but in the hope of finding work. There has also been an increase in illegal immigration, often supported by 'trafficking' in immigrants by criminal gangs.

[See also: asylum]

informateur

A politician, often an elder statesman, appointed by a head of state to make inquiries concerning which coalition of parties might most probably command a majority and be able to form a coherent and stable government. Informateurs are employed, for example, in Belgium and the Netherlands. This procedure enables the head of state to be detached from the political process of coalition formation.

International Brigades

The International Brigades were composed of volunteers who supported the Republican cause in the Spanish civil war of 1936–39. The volunteers were communist and republican sympathisers from Europe and the United States who viewed the Spanish struggle against General Franco's Nationalist forces as part of a more general battle against European fascism. In 1996, the surviving members of the International Brigades were awarded Spanish citizenship.

[See also: fascism; Spanish civil war]

Irish Republican Army (IRA)

An organisation which was formed in 1919, to take action first in relation to

the struggle for Irish independence, then in protest at the 1922 partition of Ireland. It did this by raids on arms depots and bomb attacks, in Northern Ireland and on the British mainland. It was proscribed as an illegal organisation by the Irish government on several occasions before the Second World War. During the war it engaged in pro-German actions. After a period in the immediate post-war years when it was more or less dormant, from the mid-1950s it initiated sporadic raids on military targets in Northern Ireland and the British mainland. The commencement of civil rights protests in Northern Ireland gave the IRA a new opportunity to engage in terrorist activities, though a split concerning strategy led to the formation of an Official IRA and a Provisional IRA: the latter became the terrorist organisation which focused on securing a withdrawal by British troops from Northern Ireland. A series of bomb attacks in Britain led to the Irish government again denouncing the organisation. The IRA consented to a cease-fire agreement in 1994, and, following the 1998 Good Friday Agreement, its political arm (Sinn Féin) became a partner in the all-party government formed by Trimble in 1998. However, the refusal of the IRA to give up its arsenal of weapons has been a sticking-point in the promotion of a system of peaceful and democratic politics for Northern Ireland. A breakaway group, the 'Real IRA', continued terrorist bombings in 2000 and 2001.

[See also: Good Friday Agreement; Adams*; Paisley*; Trimble*]

judicialisation

Western European countries have experienced a 'judicialisation' of politics: a development in which political debate and decision-making are becoming more strongly influenced by legal norms and court rulings. A process linked to constitutionalism, judicialisation has in many countries been promoted by the work of a constitutional court. Constitutional courts have begun to exert a significant influence over legislation and policy-making. Their rulings can set a precedent not only for future court rulings, but also for decisions of the legislative and executive branches of government. For example, a court ruling may incorporate detailed guidelines regarding the implementation of a piece of legislation which in practice channel future legislative and executive decisions in a particular direction. This role of the courts as 'policy makers' is a controversial one.

[See also: constitutionalism]

Kiessling Affair

General Kiessling was a senior officer in NATO headquarters. On the basis of intelligence reports accusing him of homosexuality and thus indicating that he would be a security risk, he was sent into compulsory retirement in 1983 by the Defence Minister of the Federal Republic of Germany, Wörner. When these reports were shown to have been erroneous, Wörner offered Chancellor Kohl his resignation, but Kohl refused to accept it. Kiessling was unconditionally reinstated in 1984.

[See also: Wörner*]

Kopp Affair

A scandal in Switzerland, involving the first woman ever appointed as a minister in the Swiss federal government. Elisabeth Kopp was accused of using her position to inform her husband about possible links between a company with which he was concerned and investigations into laundering of drug money. She was acquitted on all charges in 1990. Repercussions from this affair included a commission of inquiry which criticised the state security services for partiality in its investigations.

Lib–Lab pact

The pact between the Labour government headed by Callaghan and the Liberal Party from March 1977 to May 1978. It resulted from the loss by the Labour government of its overall majority through by-election defeats. Steel, on behalf of the Liberal parliamentary party, offered to support the government in return for being consulted on key policies and obtaining a promise of a free vote on proportional representation for European Parliament elections (the proposal was defeated). The Liberals did not receive any ministerial posts, so the pact fell short of a formal government coalition, though an inter-party Consultative Committee was formed to institutionalise cross-party co-ordination. There was opposition to the pact in both parties, and disappointment for the Liberals regarding the timing of the general election and policy decisions.

Loi Defferre

The 'Defferre Law' (named for the Interior Minister in Mitterrand's first government) which in 1982 created a legislative basis for a series of other laws extending decentralisation in France. This decentralisation programme involved transferring powers from the prefects of the Departments to presidents of elected regional assemblies and various formerly centrally controlled field services were also put under the authority of the regional councils. A new corps of local civil servants was established, equating their status with the central civil service. Prefects were replaced by Commissioners, and changes were made in the planning process to the advantage of regional and local government. Other measures, such as local electoral reform and restriction of multiple office-holding, were designed to promote local political participation and foster greater democratic accountability.

Lombardy League [See: Northern Leagues]

Lomé Convention

Based on the requirement in the Preamble to the Rome Treaty obligating member states of the EEC to maintain and foster links with their former colonial possessions, the EEC in 1963 concluded the Youandé Convention with 18 such former colonies, providing privileged arrangements for exports from those states to countries of the EEC. The entry of the UK to the EEC meant that a new arrangement, covering the many former British colonial possessions and former dominions, had to be developed. This was the Lomé Convention of 1975, providing for free trade between 44 such countries and the EEC. The number of states covered by the Convention (which has been renewed at intervals since 1975) is now over 77. These countries also benefit from subsidies, loans on specially favourable terms and development aid from the EU. The Lomé arrangements have led to disputes with GATT concerning their compatibility with global free trade arrangements; the 'banana disputes' by which bananas from Lomé states are given privileged access compared to Latin American bananas, is an example. Lomé V (also known as Cotonou) of June 2000 features political conditionality and aims to create a free trade area by 2020.

Luxembourg compromise

An agreement among member states of the EEC in 1966 which allowed national veto power for any member state which declared that its vital national interests would be adversely affected by a proposed decision. It resulted from the rejection by France in 1965 of proposals for reform of financing of the Common Agricultural Policy and for extension of majority voting in the Council of Ministers. France refused to attend meetings of the Council of Ministers until some compromise on these issues had been reached. The main effect of this compromise was to prevent large-scale reform of the Community for many years, and, by emphasising the inter-governmental aspects of the EEC, delayed extension of supranational policies.

[See also: empty chair crisis]

Maastricht Treaty

The Maastricht Treaty (formally known as the Treaty on European Union (TEU)), which came into force in 1993, established the European Union (EU). It provides for an EU based on three 'pillars': the European Communities (the EEC, ECSC and EURATOM); a Common Foreign and Security Policy (CFSP); and co-operation in the fields of justice and home affairs (JHA). While foreign and security policies remain under the authority of national institutions, the Maastricht Treaty requires systematic co-operation among EU member states on matters of concern in this area, including immigration and asylum policy; police co-operation to combat drug trafficking and other serious crime; and judicial co-operation. The Treaty provisions on CFSP and JHA are open-ended, allowing for future moves towards integration in these areas. All member states except the UK agreed to co-operate over social and economic policy under the Social Chapter. The Treaty consolidated the Single European Act (SEA) by setting a strategy and timetable for implementing Economic and Monetary Union (EMU). It also created the Cohesion Fund: a regional fund to channel financial support for the improvement of transport infrastructures and for environmental upgrading in the poorer member states.

[See also: Economic and Monetary Union; Economic and Social Cohesion; Single European Act]

mafia

Originally linked specifically with eighteenth-century Sicily, the term: mafia is now used to refer generically to organised crime in the southern Italian Mezzogiorno. The mafia is no longer believed to be a single organisation with an integrated structure, but rather a network of criminal groups with local organisations, bound by strong personal connections and family ties. The network extends to Italian communities in other countries, such as the USA. The groups within the mafia network sometimes clash violently, but usually respect each other's status within the overall hierarchy and sphere of influence. Mafia members operate the principle of *omertà* (the 'anti-law' of silence) and *vendetta* (revenge), making it difficult for the authorities to penetrate the organisation. The network has infiltrated and entrenched corrupt relationships with the police, local government and the courts throughout the Mezzogiorno, through which it offers patronage. In spite of violent reprisals against informers, a series of 'maxi-trials' involving large numbers of mafia began in 1986 on the basis of inside evidence. The network is so significant in Italian politics that at the national level there is a High Commissioner responsible for the fight against the mafia. The extent of the mafia's involvement with Italy's political and administrative elites was one of the main reasons for the collapse of the traditional political parties in the Tangentopoli scandal of 1992–93.

[See also: Mezzogiorno; Tangentopoli]

Mani pulite ('clean hands' operation)

In 1992 it was found that the Milan branch of the Italian Socialist Party (PSI), a traditional party of the left, had broken the party finance laws. This discovery launched a thorough investigation into party and government affairs known as the mani pulite, or 'clean hands' operation. Mani pulite was the initial investigation which snowballed in 1993 as 'Tangentopoli' (bribe city), becoming a national investigation of corruption amongst Italian political elites.

[See also: Tangentopoli]

maquis

A name given to sections of the French resistance in the Second World War, usually those located in rural areas especially of southern France. The word derives from the scrubby undergrowth found especially in the mountainous areas where they had their bases.

[See also: Resistance groups]

Marshall Plan

A plan proposed by US Secretary of State General George Marshall in June 1947 to revive the war-devastated economies of Europe by offering financial and other forms of economic aid to those countries. It was initiated because the USA feared that the physical destruction and economic dislocation of European economies might both lead to increased support for communist parties in Europe and hamper the recovery of world trade, to the disadvantage of US commerce. European states were to propose their own plans for utilising US aid (the European Recovery Programme). The USSR, though invited to participate, rejected the conditions required, including publication of economic data, and anyway could not view such external aid as congruent with its tightly controlled centralised economic policies. This rejection led to the self-exclusion of other East European states from the scheme. An organisation, the OEEC, was created to administer and co-ordinate Marshall Aid (as US assistance under the scheme came to be known), and sixteen countries benefited from the food, raw materials, investment goods and financial aid supplied by the USA from 1948 onwards. Marshall later received the Nobel Peace Prize for his role in the scheme.

May Events (1968)

The May Events were a series of strikes and demonstrations culminating in riots which took place in France in May 1968, producing a situation so volatile as to threaten the French Fifth Republic. The events began with student protests in Paris over the outmoded system of higher education and the lack of facilities for study. Radical student leaders saw the protests as the basis for a full-scale social and political revolution and the demonstrations escalated into riots. When the police took violent counter-measures, the rioting spread from Paris to the provinces of France. The unions called a one-day strike to express solidarity with the students, but lost control of the action which developed into a general strike. The protests collapsed when President de Gaulle enlisted the support of the army, but a conciliatory approach was then adopted by Prime Minister Pompidou, who promised education and economic reforms. The May Events inspired similar student actions in other countries, particularly Germany, and were later judged to have damaged the authority of de Gaulle.

[See also: de Gaulle*, Pompidou*]

Médiateur [See: Ombudsman]

Mezzogiorno

The term: Mezzogiorno is applied to the southern regions of Italy: Abruzzi; Basilicata; Calabria; Campania; Molise; Puglia; Sardinia and Sicily. The Mezzogiorno has remained significantly less developed than the rest of Italy in socio-economic terms and as such represents a major problem for the national government. Several factors help to account for the north–south divide. The hotter, drier climate and the mountains in much of the Mezzogiorno have restricted the development of agriculture, road and rail communications, and services to support larger settlements. Moreover, the area is prone to earthquakes. The regime history of the Mezzogiorno was more repressive than that of other areas of Italy, which experienced a wider range of government styles in the past. The mafia, the notorious network of organised crime, has its stronghold in the Mezzogiorno to this day, where it has infiltrated local government structures and represents an important (and illegal) source of patronage for the area. In political terms, the south is more reactionary and pro-monarchist than the north; also, national political leaders are more likely to be recruited from the northern regions. The term: Mezzogiorno was also applied in unified Germany in the early 1990s, when some economists drew speculative parallels between Italy and the new Germany concerning the prospects for future economic development. They feared that, as for the Italian Mezzogiorno, the new eastern Länder (formerly the German Democratic Republic, GDR) of unified Germany might become permanently dependent on subsidies from the wealthier western Länder, those of the former Federal Republic of Germany (FRG).

[See also: mafia; reunification of Germany]

Modell Deutschland (the German model)

The 'German model' is the term used to indicate the system of political economy in Germany with its emphasis on social consensus and political regulation of the market economy. The success of this system, especially in the twenty years from 1960 to 1980 when the West German economy became dominant in Europe, led other countries to consider adopting elements of its structures. Co-determination, legal regulation of trade unions and industrial relations (but with guarantees for the status and role of the trade unions), the short-lived 'concerted action' system of tripartite discussion about economic parameters and, more recently, the 'Alliance for Jobs' (*Bündnis für Arbeit*) which has renewed that system of tripartite discussions have been significant elements of the 'German model'. The term is very similar in its meaning to the 'Rhineland model'.

[See also: co-determination; Rhineland model]

Mogadishu Affair

In 1977 the Red Army Faction (RAF) hi-jacked a West German plane, forcing it to land at Mogadishu airport in Somalia. The hostages were rescued by a daring raid on the plane by a special unit of the West German border guards. The failure of the hi-jacking (which had been intended to secure their release) led Baader and Meinhof to kill themselves in their cells in Stammheim prison.

[See also: Baader-Meinhof group; Red Army Faction]

Morgenthau Plan

A plan (formally: the 'Programme to Prevent the Initiation of a Third World War by Germany') proposed by Henry Morgenthau, US Secretary of the Treasury, which was adopted by the UK and USA at the 1944 Quebec conference as a basis for the treatment of Germany once the Second World War came to an end. Starting from the premise that Germany had been to blame for the war, and that the country had been dangerous because of its industrial strength as well as because of its aggressive leadership, the Plan proposed severe reduction of Germany's industrial capacity, turning the country into an agricultural region. The Plan was abandoned in 1945 because of the severity of these proposals, and assessment of the effect which the Plan's restriction of manufacturing and therefore on Germany's export trade would have on the ability of the Germans to feed themselves.

NATO twin-track decision

A policy pursued by NATO, based on a decision by the NATO Council in 1979. It involved simultaneously (a) making attempts to foster détente by negotiation with the USSR and (b) ensuring by means of the stationing of medium-range nuclear missiles in Western Europe that the USSR would be deterred from nuclear attack on Western European states. Despite protests in many West European states, those missiles were put in place.

[See also: détente]

nazism

The ideology of the Nazi Party and movement founded by Hitler after the First World War, and applied as state policy during the Third Reich (1933–45).

There is dispute concerning which features are distinctive to nazism, and which belong to more general categories such as fascism or totalitarianism. However, it is generally agreed that three core elements were at the heart of Nazi ideology. First was the belief in the racial superiority of the Aryan (and especially the German) people, and consequently the racial inferiority of Slavs, Jews and other races – as set out in Hitler's book: *Mein Kampf* (My Struggle). Second was the absolute authority of the leader (the Führer) and, through him, of the Nazi Party and its organisations. Third, the benefit of what the Nazis understood by 'community' and the harm done, as the Nazis perceived it, by political parties and other 'divisive' organisations to that sense of unifying community. From these ideas derive other elements, such as the threat to civilisation posed by communism, the need to 'correct' the penalties and humiliations imposed on Germany by the Treaty of Versailles, and the right of Germany to expand territorially: first to take in other areas regarded as rightfully 'German' (such as Austria, parts of Poland and Czechoslovakia, and Alsace-Lorraine), then to expand into Eastern Europe to acquire 'living space' (*Lebensraum*) for the German people.

The methods used to attain these goals involved the imposition of a totalitarian state apparatus, which involved genocide, terror, the forced inclusion of all social associations and institutions within the Nazi movement (from churches to trade unions) and the militarisation of German society.

Though nazism in this sense terminated with the destruction of Hitler's regime at the end of the Second World War, some extreme right-wing groups – within but also outside Germany – adopt some of the ideological elements of nazism and may cherish the symbols and memories of the Hitler period. These groups are sometimes called 'neo-Nazi' groups. However, not all European extreme right-wing groups possess this link to nazism.

[See also: anti-fascism; anti-Semitism; denazification; fascism; Holocaust; Nuremberg tribunal; Hitler*]

neocorporatism

Neocorporatism is a system of functional representation, that is, representation according to socio-economic interest or sector. Under neocorporatism, organisations which each represent a distinct socio-economic interest have institutionalised representation within government and key decision-making bodies. In Western European democracies, neocorporatist structures supplement the channels of representation effected by plural elections and competing political parties. It is clearest in the close and formalised collaboration between government and major socio-economic interests such as employers' federations and trade unions which takes place in countries such as Austria and the Scandinavian countries.

new politics

'New politics' or 'new paradigm politics' refers to a major shift in social attitudes and values which distinguishes Europeans growing up after the Second World War from previous generations. Writers in the 'new social movement' school generally agree that, in the post-war period, the increased economic development and prosperity of advanced Western industrialised societies have transformed the basic value priorities of succeeding generations of people. The 'old politics' of the years immediately following the Second World War encompassed values such as sustained economic growth; law and order; rigorous national security; and traditional, family-based lifestyles. These were the values embodied by and represented by the established political parties of Western Europe. The characteristic values of 'new politics' are environmental quality; social equality; alternative lifestyles; minority rights; and participation in political decision-making. These new issue demands initially manifested themselves in the new social movements of the 1960s to the 1980s.

[See also: new social movements]

new social movements

Social movements can be described as a conscious attempt to bring about a change in the established power structures and dominant norms and values in society and to have these new values reflected in national politics: a political challenge which attracts some mass support. The 'new social movements' were active across Western Europe from the late 1960s to the early 1980s. The ideologies and issues which prompted their protest action included feminism, nuclear disarmament and peace, and environmentalism (the 'green' movement). The new social movements challenged their states at various levels. They shared a common ideological outlook which was critical of the customary liberal democratic order and processes. They also challenged the values and policy consensus of the 1950s and 1960s. They demanded a radical new interpretation of democracy. They tried to promote individual participation in political decision-making in place of 'ritual' political activity, which was often in practice limited to voting. This effectively challenged the principle of representative democracy, which rests on established channels of representation through parties and parliaments. At the height of their activity, the new social movements sometimes posed a threat to public order through their unconventional protest tactics. The green movement became established as a new partisan family of political parties in Western Europe. The other movements did not translate to comprehensive party organisations in the same way.

[See also: Green movement; new politics; women's movement]

Northern Leagues

A number of political organisations formed in the north of Italy from 1979, to press for greater autonomy and a reduction in the economic burden imposed on the more prosperous northern areas of Italy in order to subsidise the poorer southern regions. Allegations of corruption in the central government and in southern regions such as Sicily, the perceived preference in public service appointments apparently given to southerners and the heavy tax burden on small businesses were other complaints of the supporters of these Leagues. The most successful of the Leagues was the Lombard League, led by Bossi, which in 1990 won a substantial share of the vote in regional elections. Following the creation in 1991 of an umbrella organisation (the Northern League), further electoral successes, in local and national elections, followed. For a time, the Northern League participated in Berlusconi's right-wing coalition government. The Northern League now wants a federal basis for the Italian state, in which the northern, central and southern areas would be responsible autonomously for many areas of domestic policy. Some of the more extreme supporters of the League want an independent northern state: Padania.

[See also: Berlusconi*; Bossi*]

Nuremberg tribunal

An international court created in 1945 to put leading German war criminals on trial. It was set up as a result of discussion among the Allies from 1943, as one of the methods by which denazification would be promoted. Judges were appointed by the British, French, American and Soviet Union governments. The tribunal sat from November 1945 until it delivered its verdicts in October 1946. Leading Nazi politicians, military leaders and others who occupied leading positions in the Nazi state were accused of various crimes, including 'crimes against humanity', and twelve were sentenced to death (including Goering, who committed suicide before he could be executed, Himmler and General Jodl), seven to periods of imprisonment (including Doenitz and Hess, who died in prison whilst serving a life sentence) and three were found not guilty and released. Other trials of lesser-known war criminals and organisations involved in Hitler's military and racial policies subsequently took place.

The Nuremberg tribunal in particular was criticised for lacking a firm basis in international law and for the clear political basis of some of the verdicts, especially by the Soviet Union judge. However, it did attempt to elevate standards of law above political expediency and emphasise that even war was subject to certain international standards of behaviour. It also served as a symbol of the Allies' determination to eradicate nazism from German society. The tribunal also set a precedent, which has been followed, for example, in the attempts to bring before an international court war criminals who were involved in the Yugoslavian conflicts.

[See also: denazification; nazism]

Oder–Neisse line

The post-war settlement concerning Germany reached at the Potsdam conference included a supposedly provisional agreement on the borders of Poland. As compensation for the territory formerly belonging to Poland which the Soviet Union had retained at the end of the Second World War, part of the former German state, east of the rivers Oder and Neisse, was placed under Polish administration pending a peace treaty with Germany which would officially terminate the Second World War and define Germany's future boundaries. With the intensification of

the Cold War and the division of Germany, it seemed that a peace treaty would never be negotiated, and Poland came to claim the Oder–Neisse boundary as permanent. The German Democratic Republic signed a treaty with Poland in 1950 which officially recognised this boundary between the two states. The German Federal Republic, however, claimed that the boundary could not be accepted by the Federal Republic nor be recognised in international law until such a peace treaty was signed, though in the Ostpolitik treaties it renounced any intention to use force to change existing boundaries. This attitude, though based on constitutional requirements included in the Basic Law, was regarded especially by states in the communist bloc as ravanchist, since it seemed to imply that a reunited Germany might claim back what had become de facto Polish territory. In fact, the Two plus Four talks and the agreements resulting from these made clear that a reunified German state would abandon all claims not only to territory east of the Oder–Neisse line, but anywhere in Europe.

[See also: Ostpolitik; Potsdam conference; 'Two plus Four' talks]

oil crisis

The first, and best-known, oil crisis occurred in 1973–74. The Arab oil-producing states used their control over a large proportion of the world's oil production to cut off supplies to states which had been in the forefront of support for Israel in the Arab–Israeli war which had commenced in October 1973, and by reduction of output increased the world price of oil very considerably. This had a shock effect on the economies of most developed states, many of which experienced a period of negative economic growth. Unemployment increased, and remained high for several years and inflation also increased, in some countries (including the United Kingdom) to very high levels at times. Developing states and those in the communist bloc also suffered economically.

A second oil crisis, similarly produced by Arab states limiting oil production, took place in 1979 following the overthrow of the Shah of Iran. While the price of oil had quadrupled in 1973–74, it more than doubled again in 1979–80, though this price increase was relatively short lived, since Iran and Iraq, at war with each other, were forced to export more than their quota to produce revenue to pay for the war.

The oil price increases, based upon agreed production quotas, were made possible by the authority of the Organisation of Petroleum Exporting Countries (OPEC), founded by five states in 1960, but which by 1973 had twelve member states. The price increases encouraged states to reduce their reliance on oil as a fuel, to promote energy conservation and to intensify the search for economic alternative fuels. The fact that states such as Norway and the United Kingdom were able to produce oil outside the quotas set by OPEC buffered the effect which such quotas would otherwise have had on national economies, and by the 1990s oil production by OPEC states accounted for less than half of total production outside the communist bloc.

There was talk of a third oil crisis in 2000, when oil producers, who had experienced a decline in the price of oil (and thus their revenues) throughout the 1990s, attempted with some success to engineer an increase in the price of oil by limiting production. However, though the world market price of oil did increase, this was nothing like as large an increase as had occurred in the two previous crises. Demonstrations and protests in Western states by farmers, lorry drivers and others dependent upon oil for their commercial activities were directed, with good reason, more at governments because of levels of taxation on oil fuels than at increases in producer prices. There was justification for this, since such producer price increases constituted only a small proportion of the total price of petrol and diesel.

Ombudsman

A Swedish word, the title of an independent official responsible for receiving and investigating grievances submitted by citizens relating to maladministration by government officials. The office was originally founded in 1809. It has been adopted as a means of protecting the citizen against maladministration in other countries such as Denmark, Spain, Italy (at the regional level) and Austria. Such officials are generally appointed by, and report to, Parliament. The United Kingdom has several such officials; as well as the Parliamentary Commissioner for Administration, others exist for health service and local government matters, for example. Germany has an Inspector General of the Armed Forces (*Wehrbeauftragter*) to investigate complaints by members of the military. In France, where the office was created in 1973, the mediator (*médiateur*) is an official who reports to the president. The *médiateur* seeks an equitable solution to conflicts between citizens and the bureaucracy, on matters such as entitlements to pensions and subsidies.

Ostpolitik

Literally: 'policy concerning the East'. The term refers to the innovative policy approach adopted by the coalition government of the Social Democrats (SPD) and the liberal Free Democrats (FDP) in the Federal Republic of

Germany following the 1969 Bundestag election. To some extent, Ostpolitik built upon developments which had already occurred in the period of the 'grand coalition' (1966–69), in which Brandt, the Chancellor of the SPD–FDP government from 1969, had served as Foreign Minister.

The Ostpolitik set out to replace confrontation with the communist bloc states of Central and Eastern Europe (a policy stance typified by the 'Hallstein Doctrine') with a policy focused upon diplomatic acceptance of the status quo in relation to state boundaries (especially the Oder–Neisse boundary between the German Democratic Republic (GDR) and Poland) and de facto, though not de jure, recognition of the GDR as a separate state. It also included efforts to encourage trade, cultural exchanges and other contacts with those states in an atmosphere of peace. Ostpolitik included within it 'Deutschlandpolitik': policy towards the German Democratic Republic, where progress depended very obviously upon the consent of the leadership of the Soviet Union.

In its own terms, 'Ostpolitik' could be regarded as successful. In particular, four treaties were concluded which permitted improved relations between the Federal Republic of Germany and communist bloc states: the treaties with the USSR and Poland (both in 1970), an Agreement concerning the status of Berlin to which France, the United Kingdom, the USA and USSR – the four former occupying powers – were signatories (1971), and in 1972 a treaty-like Basic Agreement between the two German states (which was not called a 'treaty' because the Federal Republic always refused to regard the GDR as a foreign state). Because the coalition only had a small majority in 1969, and because a number of FDP and SPD Members of the Bundestag refused to support 'Ostpolitik' and in some cases transferred to the opposition, this policy had cost the

coalition its majority by 1972. Chancellor Brandt survived a constructive vote of no confidence in April 1972, but this did not resolve the problem of not being able to put through legislation. So a premature Bundestag election was held in November 1972, which resulted in a safe majority for the Brandt coalition. Brandt himself was awarded the Nobel Peace Prize in 1971 for his diplomatic initiatives in relation to Ostpolitik.

[See also: Basic Treaty; constructive vote of no confidence; the German question; Hallstein Doctrine; Oder–Neisse line; Brandt*]

paedophile scandal (Belgium)

The Belgian paedophile scandal challenged the judicial establishment in Belgium and the ruling Dehaene government. In August 1996 a senior magistrate uncovered a paedophile ring based in Belgium which practised the kidnapping and murder of young girls. His dismissal from the case in October 1996 led to accusations of police incompetence and official corruption. The revelations prompted strikes and public demonstrations, notably the 'White March' of October 1996, in which some 300,000 people took part to call for reforms to the police and judicial system. In April 1997, a parliamentary commission recommended the establishment of an integrated national police force, but in February 1998 the government opted instead to recommend voluntary agreements for co-operation between the country's police services. In April 1998 claims of police incompetence were underlined by the temporary escape from custody of the man accused of heading the paedophile network. The Commander of the national police, the Minister of the Interior and the Minister of Justice all resigned in the aftermath of this incident.

pantouflage

A French term referring to the practice in the French political system of civil servants resigning to take up more profitable employment in the private sector.

peaceful revolution (East Germany)

The peaceful revolution of 1989 took place in the former German Democratic Republic (GDR) and proved to be the first step in the process of German unification. It took the form of large-scale, peaceful weekly demonstrations in urban centres throughout the GDR. The demonstrations gathered strength from late September 1989. Initially the demonstrators demanded the reform of the socialist state under the leading Communist Party, the Socialist Unity Party (SED), at least in line with the liberalisation achieved in Central and Eastern European countries. However, when the party leadership failed to respond to popular demands and even resisted calls for reform from Mikhail Gorbachev, General Secretary of the Soviet Communist Party, the demonstrators became disillusioned and some demanded reunification with the Federal Republic of Germany.

[See also: reunification of Germany]

perestroika

Perestroika (reconstruction) was one of the innovative principles adopted by Mikhail Gorbachev after his appointment as General Secretary of the Communist Party of the Soviet Union in 1985. Together with glasnost (openness), the term: perestroika entered into common currency also in Western Europe, symbolising the new approach to government and international relations promoted by Gorbachev. The two concepts galvanised a reform process throughout Central and Eastern Europe and eventually helped to overthrow communist rule in these countries and in the Soviet Union itself. Gorbachev applied the perestroika principle to carry out institutional restructuring in the Soviet Union, but did not at first attempt a thorough economic reform. Economic policy remained heavily centralised and led by the 1986–90 Four Year Plan, and, in place of the anticipated upturn, the Soviet Union's economic problems worsened dramatically. The Communist Party factionalised around Gorbachev's programme, and he was soon under attack from all sides. Economic reform was finally introduced in January 1989, but by this time farmers had begun to establish their own means of distributing their produce for profit. The institutional reform process continued – a partly competitive election for the Parliament, the Congress of People's Deputies, was held in 1989 – but opposition to Gorbachev mounted. By 1990 Gorbachev had acknowledged that reform of the existing system was not enough. He now advocated a comprehensive transformation, including the introduction of fully competitive elections and a free market economy. In August 1991 there was an attempted coup by right-wing elements and on Christmas day 1991 Gorbachev resigned. The following day, the Soviet Parliament dissolved the Soviet Union.

[See also: glasnost]

Petersberg Agreements (Germany)

A set of agreements between the Western Allied occupation authorities and the Adenauer government signed on 22 November 1949 in the hotel on the Petersberg (near Bonn) to revise some of the terms and conditions constraining the sovereignty of the new Federal Republic of Germany. The Federal Republic was permitted to have consular representation in other countries. Its foreign policy remained a responsibility of the occupation

53 EVENTS, GROUPS AND DEVELOPMENTS

EVENTS, GROUPS AND DEVELOPMENTS

authorities, though the Federal Republic could become a member of certain international organisations (including the Council of Europe). The Agreements affected other matters such as limitation of dismantling of industrial production and restrictions on the merchant navy. The Agreements clarified several ambiguities in the occupation statute and the occasion was used by Adenauer as a symbolic gesture to assert the independent status of the Federal Republic.

pillarisation

A translation of a Dutch term (*verzuiling*), which refers to the social and political structures in the Netherlands by which the major groupings in society (especially Catholics, Protestants, socialists and liberals) control a proportion of political and social institutions, and individuals utilise the institutions related to their social grouping, such as schools, newspapers, broadcasting stations, churches and trade unions. These proportions reflect the weight of social groups within society. Modernisation of the economy and society (and the consequent erosion of deep-seated class conflicts) and the decline in affiliation to religious groups and religious-based or ideologically-based political parties have meant that pillarisation is no longer as relevant in present-day Dutch society.

political asylum [See: asylum]

Politikverdrossenheit

Literally: alienation from politics. The term became fashionable in the early 1990s in Germany to refer to a set of developments, ranging from much-reduced electoral turnout to declines in party membership and activism, from distrust of politicians and the political process to criticism of particular policies. A series of scandals since the 1970s, the apparent inability of politicians to deal effectively with perceived problems such as immigration, unemployment and criminality, the tensions created by reunification in 1990 and the long period in office of the ruling Christian Democrat–Free Democrat coalition are among the factors blamed for this phenomenon. It is also related to the unusual degree of penetration by political parties into the economic and social spheres within German society.

poll tax

A form of local taxation to provide finance for local government authorities, introduced by the Thatcher government in Scotland in 1988 and in the rest of Britain in 1990. Officially termed the 'community charge', it replaced an out-moded system of taxes (the rates) based on historic valuations of homes, shops and other premises. This system of rates was inequitable, since it took no direct account of either aggregate household income or the number of earners in a household. It was not even based on up-to-date assessments of property values. The community charge was based upon the number of income-earners in a household, so was fairer in that respect, but took no account of levels of income. It was also intended to link payment of local taxes to levels of spending by local councils, and thus act as an electoral restraint on high-spending councils, where previously those who benefited from costly levels of services often escaped any payment towards them through the rating system. Protests against the inequity of the new system were immediate and became violent, coupled with a campaign of non-payment of the charge. It was asserted that the new system would benefit the wealthier sections of local communities. The poll tax damaged the image and popularity of both the Prime Minister,

Mrs Thatcher, and her party, and was a factor in her replacement as Prime Minister by John Major. Major abandoned the poll tax, and instead introduced a different system of local taxation: the council tax, based on property values, with concession for single-person households.

popular front

The term: popular front referred to alliances of communists, socialists and liberal democrats which overcame their differences to fight fascism in Europe between 1935 and 1939. Popular front movements were brought about by a directive of the world communist movement, the Communist International, which reversed a previous policy of non-co-operation with other partisan groups to permit collaboration with other pro-democratic parties. Popular front governments formed in Spain and France in 1936. In Spain, the narrow victory of Azaña's Popular Front government in the context of a deeply divided society precipitated the outbreak of the Spanish civil war. In France, the government, led by Léon Blum, tried to introduce social and economic reforms including the introduction of a 40-hour working week, paid holidays and collective bargaining. However, it faced difficulties in paying for the reforms in conjunction with a sharp rise in military expenditure. The Communist Party of France had refused to join the Popular Front government, but upheld its majority in Parliament. However, the Communists withdrew their support over Blum's policy of non-intervention in the Spanish civil war.

[See also: Spanish civil war]

populism

Populist parties do not operate according to the pluralist principle in democratic politics. They do not seek to represent the interests of a particular sector of society against those of other sectors, but instead try to unite a whole society behind them. In the late 1950s and early 1960s, the French Gaullist Party adopted a populist approach, appealing to the nation to support the personal leadership of General de Gaulle. De Gaulle saw himself as above politics, and did not align himself with any of the traditional 'tendencies' (political divisions) in French party competition. The contemporary Gaullist Party has modernised its approach. It no longer campaigns on a populist platform, instead competing with other sectoral parties for the vote of a centre-right electorate. A more extreme populist approach is found, for example, in European political parties of the extreme right.

[See also: de Gaulle*]

postmaterialism

Postmaterialism is a concept associated with the 'new politics' which developed from the students' movements of the late 1960s. Postmaterialism is linked to the values of the new politics: environmental quality; social equality; alternative lifestyles; minority rights and participation in political decision-making. It is typically found in the first generation to be born after the Second World War in Western Europe and especially amongst the middle classes: people who are well-educated and who have grown up without the direct constraints of war, hunger or poverty. In particular, it criticises the 'old politics' values which prioritise material satisfaction, even to the point of material excess, above other life values such as spirituality and leisure. Postmaterialism has been expressed in electoral politics through environmentalist and ecologist movements (the latter is the more radical expression) and through the Green parties which developed in Western Europe from the late 1970s.

Greens argue that constant economic growth is neither essential nor desirable: because of this they believe that they are fundamentally different from Western Europe's traditional parties.

[See also: citizen initiative groups; Green movement; new politics]

Potsdam conference

The conference involving the USSR, USA and United Kingdom heads of government held in Potsdam (near Berlin) in July 1945, immediately after the end of the Second World War. It confirmed or asserted the principles upon which Germany should be governed by the occupation regime, including denazification, demilitarisation, removal of all cartels, democratisation and decentralisation of administration. Germany was to be treated as a single economic unit, with its industry to be so controlled that its people enjoyed a living standard below that of other European states. An agreement on reparations – in money and in plant and machinery – was reached. Parts of eastern Prussia were placed under Polish and USSR administration pending a peace conference to decide on Germany's future borders (which gave rise to the Oder–Neisse border issue concerning Poland's borders). As with the Yalta conference, differing interpretations of often rather ambiguously worded decisions led to the division of Germany and intensification of the Cold War.

Because the United Kingdom held a general election at about this time, Churchill took Attlee with him to the conference, and, when the election results showed that Attlee was to replace Churchill as Prime Minister, Churchill withdrew from the conference.

[See also: Cold War; denazification; German question; Oder–Neisse line; Petersberg Agreements; Yalta conference]

Poujadism

Poujadism, named after its founder Pierre Poujade, was a reactionary political movement which gained electoral support in France in the mid-1950s. Poujadism was anti-state (particularly anti-taxation), anti-socialist, anti-intellectual and anti-European. Its members were drawn largely from shopkeepers and the petit-bourgeoisie. The movement's political arm was the Union for the Protection of Businesses and Craftsmen (UDCA). Initially a small sectoral group, the party soon took on a wider protest role, attacking aspects of modernisation including foreign influences in France, republicanism, bureaucracy, Paris and urbanisation. In 1955 Poujade formed a new political party, the Union and Fraternity of the French (UFF) and conducted major rallies throughout France. In the 1956 elections, the UFF won 52 seats in the parliament, the National Assembly, but declined from 1958 under the French Fifth Republic with its modernising ethos.

[See also: Poujade*]

privatisation

The transfer of ownership of economic enterprises, such as water supply or telephone services, from the state or other public authorities to private ownership. One of the first instances was the denationalisation of the iron and steel industry by the Conservative government in 1953 (though it was renationalised by the Wilson Labour government in 1967) but the policy in Britain is especially associated with the Thatcher government from 1979 onwards, when the public utilities and other state-owned commercial assets were transferred to private ownership. This policy was imitated by several West European countries for at least some of their state-owned assets (especially telecommunications, power supply and aviation) and, though in a different context, by states of the former Soviet bloc following the collapse of communist rule.

Profumo Affair

John Profumo was a minister in Macmillan's cabinet. He resigned in disgrace from his government post and as an MP in 1963 after admitting that he had earlier lied to the House of Commons concerning a relationship with Christine Keeler. Ms Keeler was associated with, among others, a diplomat from the Soviet Union, which raised fears concerning breaches of security by Mr Profumo. The scandal was a factor in weakening support for the Conservative government, which narrowly lost the 1964 general election.

proportional representation

In the context of parliamentary and other public elections, any electoral system designed to reflect the proportion of votes cast for a particular political party in the proportion of seats obtained by that party. Proportional representation systems vary in the details of their operation. Some are based on fixed party lists of candidates, so that the elector votes for a party directly. Others allow electors to influence the order of the list, and thus which candidates are elected. The German system (imitated by New Zealand, Scotland and Wales, for example) uses an 'additional member system' to combine local constituency representation with overall proportionality. Many political scientists claim the Single Transferable Vote (STV) system to be one of proportional representation. Under STV, though, the vote of any single elector cannot be easily identified as being a vote for a particular party since that vote may be significant in electing the second or third or later preference candidate. It is therefore difficult to see how anyone

can calculate the percentages of votes which each party has received, and thus compare that with the percentages of seats for each party.

[See also: Additional Member System; Single Transferable Vote]

quango

The word is a short form of 'quasi non-governmental organisation'. A quango differs from other non-governmental organisations because it is usually founded by a government, and is wholly or largely financed from government sources, though such an organisation operates independently (within regulatory parameters). This form of organisation can be found in the USA as well as in Western European states. Quangos include: public sector broadcasting authorities such as the British Broadcasting Corporation (BBC), the political party foundations such as the Konrad Adenauer Foundation (KAS) in Germany, organisations concerned with public funding of scientific research and university education, agencies with a quasi-judicial function such as labour relations tribunals, and institutions concerned with racial or gender discrimination. Some political scientists prefer to emphasise the role of the state in creating and maintaining these institutions, rather than their independent operation, so instead use the term: 'quagos' (quasi governmental organisations).

radicals' decree

A joint decision in 1972 by the governments of the Länder and the federal government concerning the application of standards of political loyalty to those wishing to enter the public service in the German Federal Republic. These standards included the readiness 'at all times' to defend actively the democratic and constitutional principles embodied in

57 EVENTS, GROUPS AND DEVELOPMENTS

the Basic Law (the constitution of the Federal Republic), and avoidance of any appearance of toleration or support of extremist groups or movements which might be regarded as critical of the constitutional order. Though the utilisation of this decree in fact resulted in a very small minority of applicants for employment in the public service being rejected, it was nevertheless criticised strongly particularly by left-wing opponents as amounting to an anti-democratic 'ban on pursuit of a profession' (*Berufsverbot*), the more so as in the Federal Republic of Germany various types of career, such as teachers, university professors, some postmen and even railway employees, were classified as 'civil servants'. The fact that many more applicants were rejected because of association with extreme left-wing, rather than right-wing, groups, also gave rise to criticism.

Realos and Fundis

Opposed factions within the German Green Party. The terms are shortened versions of the German words for 'realists' and 'fundamentalists'. The 'Realos' pursue a pragmatic political strategy, and are willing to compromise in order to secure desired political changes. They have participated as junior coalition partners in Land and national governments as a means of securing such changes. 'Fundis' have taken a more radical and uncompromising stance, regarding many issues, especially those relating to the environment, as matters of principle and as non-negotiable, even though that stance may well prevent any progress being made by governments towards goals desired by the Greens generally and the 'Fundis' in particular. Some, indeed, will not co-operate with 'old paradigm' parties at all. Such factional conflicts have also extended to matters of Green Party organisation, such as

rotation in office and quotas among office-holders. The 'Realos' have been dominant in the national and regional parties since the unexpectedly poor results secured by the Greens in the Bundestag election of 1990. Since then, the Greens have modified their organisational rules to become more like orthodox political parties, and have participated in several Land coalition governments. Many 'Fundis' have left the party, though several are still very active in the environmental movement.

The terms: 'realos' and 'fundis' have been applied to factions in Green parties in other countries.

[See also: Kelly*]

Rechtsstaat

A German term to refer to a state based on the rule of law, anchored in the constitution, as contrasted to a state based on ideology, dictatorship or some other principle. The Rechtsstaat incorporates values of liberal constitutionalism, including: the separation of powers, the equality of all persons under the law, the supremacy of the constitution over other legislation or regulations, and the guarantee of personal liberties (such as freedom of speech) especially vis-à-vis the organs of the state. The Basic Law, the constitution of the German Federal Republic, includes all these attributes. Article 3 refers to equality before the law, and Article 28 refers to the state and its component Länder being based on the principles of a republican, democratic and social state based on the rule of law.

[See also: constitutionalism]

Red Army Faction (Germany)

The West German Red Army Faction was originally founded by members of the Baader-Meinhof group in 1971. The 'second generation' RAF, the successors of the original Baader-Meinhof group, became active from the mid-1970s. In their terrorist activity, the second generation was more ruthless even than their forerunners, and have been described as the most serious threat to the internal security of the FRG to date. In the spring of 1977, the second generation RAF embarked on their 'Offensive '77', apparently with the main aim of releasing their RAF comrades from prison. The 'Offensive '77', which ran until the end of 1978, was directed at first against 'representatives of the system'. It involved taking prominent personalities as hostages, some of whom were killed. Among the victims of the Offensive were Chief Public Prosecutor Siegfried Buback; Jürgen Ponto, head of the Dresden Bank and uncle of one of the RAF members, Susanne Albrecht; and Hanns-Martin Schleyer, president of the West German employers' federation and president of the Federal Association of German Industry. There were plans also to kidnap the FDP leader Genscher and NATO commander Haig. In an attempt to increase pressure on the West German government, Palestinian associates of the RAF took a Lufthansa plane hostage at Mogadishu. The hostages, a group of tourists, were freed by the West German commando unit GSG-9. The Offensive prompted the introduction of increased security and anti-terrorist legislation in what was later referred to as the 'German autumn'. In 1982, the second generation RAF published their tract the 'May paper', which depicted various forms of military and political uprisings as evidence of a world-wide anti-imperialist front with revolutionary potential. A late victim of the RAF was Rohwedder, head of the privatisation agency for East Germany, killed in 1991. In January 1992, the 'Kinkel initiative' headed by the Federal Minister of Justice Klaus Kinkel, paved the way for a 'reconciliation' between the state and the RAF. On 20 April 1998, the RAF issued an eight-page statement

announcing its formal dissolution. The statement may speak for only a faction within the group: jailed hard-liners such as Brigitte Mohnhaupt, Christian Klar and Adelheid Schulz have always argued against dissolution. Further, in 1995 a new extremist organisation, apparently a further successor organisation to the RAF, became active under the name of the Anti-Imperialist Cells (AIZ).

[See also: Baader-Meinhof group; Mogadishu Affair; Schleyer Affair]

Red Brigades (Italy)

During the 1970s, Italy suffered terrorist attacks by extremist groups of both the right and the left. The most notorious of the left-wing groups were the Red Brigades (Brigate Rosse – BR) founded by Renato Curcio in Milan in 1970. The Red Brigades at first kidnapped their victims without physically harming them. However, after Curcio was jailed in 1976, the group's tactics became more violent. From 1977 to 1978, they adopted a 'strategy of annihilation', targeting 'servants of the state' including policemen, magistrates and journalists. On 16 March 1978, the BR kidnapped the former Prime Minister Moro. When the government refused to accede to their demands, the group 'tried' him and killed him. The incident lost the BR their public support and launched an anti-terrorist campaign. Sixty-three members of the BR were tried in 1982–83 and 32 received life sentences for the murder of Moro. These included Mario Moretti, who was believed to have directed the kidnapping, and Prospero Gallinari, one of the group thought to have carried out the murder. By the end of the 1970s the activity of the BR had declined, but isolated attacks continued into the 1980s. In December 1981 a senior NATO officer, US Brigadier-General Dozier, was kidnapped, but was later freed by police unharmed. In 1985 a new BR faction emerged, the Union of Fighting

Communists (UCC), which carried out a number of murders. The UCC was believed to have links with other European left-wing extremist groups, notably Action Directe in France and the Red Army Faction in Germany. A further splinter group, the Fighting Communist Party (PCC), claimed responsibility for the murder in 1988 of one of Prime Minister de Mita's chief advisers, Ruffili.

[See also: Action Directe; Red Army Faction; Moro*]

resistance groups

The resistance was the popular term for the organised opposition to Germany's Nazi regime, both within Germany itself and in those European countries occupied by Germany during the Second World War. The resistance movements engaged in guerrilla warfare and sabotage against Nazi Germany and collaboration governments. They also prepared plans for reform in Europe for when the war was over. From January 1942, the Free French began to organise resistance groups and in May 1943 the maquis liberated Corsica. By 1945 resistance groups were active throughout Europe, but were often divided on ideological grounds. After the war, political parties whose members had been active in the resistance initially gained an electoral bonus with the voters and in some countries communist parties were viewed for the first time as responsible and electable on account of their resistance record. The participation of resistance leaders in the foundation of new political systems in post-war Europe initially helped to promote the ideal of a united Europe.

[See also: maquis; nazism]

reunification of Germany

The process whereby the two former German states, divided from each other in 1949 by the creation of the Federal Republic of Germany and the German Democratic Republic (GDR) as a result of the Cold War, merged on 3 October 1990 to become a single state. The process was made possible by the events of the second half of 1989, when citizen protests in the GDR relating to fraudulent local council election results in May and the migration of large numbers of GDR citizens through the border between Hungary and Austria during the summer led to further protests and demonstrations, and to the formation of new political groups, such as New Forum. The celebrations of the fortieth anniversary of the founding of the GDR in October were an occasion for further demonstrations, and soon afterwards the GDR communist leader, Honecker, was compelled to resign his offices. Krenz, the new party leader, was widely distrusted and was unable to introduce political reform swiftly enough to satisfy protesters and dissidents. Efforts to introduce a more liberal set of arrangements for travel outside the GDR led to the opening of the Berlin Wall on 9 November. By the end of 1989 the communist regime had been displaced by a provisional government, ruling in conjunction with a 'Round Table' on which dissident groups and established political parties and other organisations were represented. Democratic elections to the People's Chamber (*Volkskammer*), originally scheduled for May 1990, were brought forward to March because of the economic and political situation in the GDR. That election gave victory to the right-wing electoral alliance led by the Christian Democrats, whose leader, de Maizière, formed a coalition government which aimed at introducing currency union with the Federal Republic without delay. This was achieved on 1 July 1990, but by then it was obvious that a political union would soon have to follow. Following negotiations, it was agreed to merge the GDR with the Federal Republic, using the route offered by Article 23 of the Basic Law of the Federal Republic, which permitted 'other parts' of Germany to join the Federal Republic. This meant that the Basic Law was retained as the constitutional foundation of the enlarged Federal Republic, rather than using the mode envisaged in Article 146 of the Basic Law, by which a totally new constitution for reunified Germany would have had to have been designed and presented to the public for ratification by referendum. The former GDR was divided into the five 'new' Länder, plus East Berlin, which merged with West Berlin to form one Land.

Some authorities prefer to use the term: 'unification' to indicate the merger of the two German states, on the grounds that there never was a 'Germany' which only consisted of the territories of the Federal Republic and GDR, therefore they could not be re-unified. However, the existence of an earlier 'unification of Germany' (in 1871) means that there could be ambiguity if the term were used also to describe the events of 1990.

[See also: Berlin Wall; Bonn Republic–Berlin Republic transition; Cold War; German question; Round Table; Stalin Note; Honecker*; Krenz*; de Maizière*]

Rhineland model

Alternatively known as 'Rhineland capitalism', this term is applied to the system of political economy developed in the Federal Republic of Germany, at least until German reunification, and, some would assert, even to the present day. It is distinguished from the Anglo-Saxon model of political economy by its emphasis on corporate structures which encourage consensus among the principal economic actors (the government, the trade unions, owners of business enterprises, the banks, etc.). Unlike economic systems in other parts of the world which also emphasise corporatist consensus, this model requires the existence of a market

economy and a democratic political system, combined with a complex and comprehensive system of social welfare provision, as provided by Erhard's social market system. Globalisation, privatisation of formerly state-owned enterprises and greater emphasis on shareholder interests are all tendencies which recently have eroded the distinctive structure of the Rhineland model.

[See also: social market economy]

Round Table

Several 'round tables' have occurred in recent history, providing relatively informal modes of discussion involving representatives of conflicting groups. The most famous is that created in December 1989 in East Berlin, which played a role in the transition of the GDR from a communist dictatorship to a multi-party democracy. It arose from an appeal on 21 November 1989 by the new citizen movement group: 'Democracy Now' to all parties to join in a series of discussions about the desperate political and economic situation of the GDR and possible paths of development in the future. It was to serve as a democratically based forum at a time when the institutions of party and state in the GDR had lost all legitimacy, and a democratically elected parliament had not yet been created. Several parties, including the Socialist Unity Party and its former associated 'bloc parties', accepted the formal invitation issued by the Protestant and Catholic churches on 30 November 1989, and a first meeting was held on 7 December 1989. There was a balance of representatives from, on the one hand, the SED, its affiliated communist organisations and the former bloc parties, and newly formed citizen movement organisations on the other. Two clergy served as impartial chairs of the meetings of the Round Table.

Several key issues were discussed,

such as the future of the State Security Service, the draft of a new, democratic, constitution for the GDR and the economic situation. The Round Table was instrumental in bringing forward the planned May date for new elections to the Volkskammer (the GDR Parliament) to 18 March, because of the increasing crisis situation of the GDR.

However, once the Volkskammer election had been held and it was clear that German reunification was inevitable in the near future, the Round Table was dissolved, having no longer a useful role.

[See also: reunification of Germany; Stasi]

Saarland question

The Saarland is a territory in south-west Germany bordering France and Luxembourg. Because of its strategic location and its large coal reserves and steel production capacity, it has been of great significance in conflicts involving Germany and France. After the First World War it was ceded to France for a period of fifteen years under a League of Nations mandate, with rights to extract minerals in that period. The plebiscite at the end of that term, which took place in the period of Hitler's dictatorship, led to a majority of over 90 per cent voting to rejoin Germany. At the end of the Second World War, France was again given control of the Saarland. As it became clear that the Federal Republic of Germany was becoming much more prosperous than France or the Saarland, opinion among Saarland residents was strongly in favour of inclusion in the Federal Republic. Attempts by France to repress opposition to French rule and to place the Saarland under some form of international control came to nothing. In 1957, following a plebiscite, the Saarland became a Land of the Federal Republic.

[See also: Young Turks' revolt]

Schengen Agreement

An agreement entered into by the Benelux countries (which already enjoyed open borders with each other), Germany and France to remove border controls on persons and goods moving from one of those states to another. It was originally agreed at a meeting in 1985 of delegates from the signatory states in Schengen, a Luxembourg town on the Moselle across the river from Germany. It was not implemented until 1994, and even then some limitations on its application still existed. The limited number of states which signed the Schengen Agreement did so because it was clear that the introduction of open borders between all member states of the EU under the terms of the Single European Act would not occur in the foreseeable future. A Declaration accompanying that Act provided for retention of border controls where required to combat immigration from countries outside the EU, terrorism, crime, drug trafficking and smuggling of works of art. The United Kingdom, in particular, stood firm against opening its borders to intra-EU traffic. Later all other states of the EU (together with Iceland and Norway as associate signatories) with the exception of the United Kingdom and Ireland, joined the Schengen arrangements. A complex system of co-operation on matters such as cross-border pursuit of criminals, extradition and the treatment of asylum-seekers has developed under the umbrella of this Agreement. The terms of the Schengen Agreement were incorporated into the Treaty of Amsterdam (1997), allowing states to adopt or not adopt the conditions of the Schengen Agreement.

[See also: Benelux]

Schleyer Affair

Dr Hanns-Martin Schleyer was a victim of the 'Offensive '77' conducted by the extreme left-wing terrorists, the West German Red Army Faction (RAF). President of the West German employers' federation and president of the Federal Association of German Industry, Schleyer was targeted by the group as a 'representative of the system' and was taken hostage by the group in an attempt to pressurise the West German government into releasing imprisoned RAF members. When Schleyer was kidnapped, his four companions were killed. In an attempt to increase pressure on the government, Palestinian associates of the RAF took a Lufthansa plane hostage at Mogadishu. The hostages, a group of tourists, were freed by the West German commando unit GSG 9. Hours later, the RAF took revenge by murdering Schleyer.

[See also: Baader-Meinhof group; Mogadishu Affair; Red Army Faction]

Secret Army Organisation (OAS)

The *Organisation de l'Armée Secrète* (OAS) was an extreme pro-French nationalist organisation of French Algerian settlers led by General Jouhad and General Salan. The group was founded in 1961 and conducted reciprocal terror campaigns with the rival Algerian nationalist National Liberation Front (FLN). The OAS wanted to retain the French colonial control of Algeria and did not accept the French government's decision to award Algeria self-determination with the prospect of independence. Once it became clear that they had lost their cause, the OAS reacted with an unsuccessful revolt in Algiers and with a spate of terrorist bomb attacks in Algeria and metropolitan France. The French public turned against the movement and several large anti-OAS demonstrations took place. Some 1,200 OAS members were arrested and Jouhad and Salan were sentenced to life imprisonment. The movement made two attempts to murder General de Gaulle, who had

devised the settlement, but failed. When the independence referendum was confirmed by 75 per cent of the vote, Muslim nationalists took revenge on the OAS. On 5 July 1962 over 100 Europeans were killed in Oran. Soon afterwards, some 500 Europeans suspected of being OAS sympathisers were kidnapped: some were tortured and released, others disappeared.

[See also: Algerian conflict; de Gaulle*]

Single European Act (SEA)

The central aim of the Single European Act (SEA), which came into force in 1987, was to improve the economic efficiency of the EC by creating a single European market (SEM) between member states by 1992. In 1957, the Treaties of Rome had removed tariff barriers among the member states. In practice, though, non-tariff barriers continued to restrict trade, reducing the competitiveness of the EC in world trade. The SEA provided for tighter control of EC economic policy and related areas. It formally expanded the EC's policy competences to include environmental policy, research and technological development and regional policy (termed 'economic and social cohesion'). It established new legislative procedures to improve the efficiency and control of decision-making in specific policy areas (the 'co-operation' and 'assent' procedures) which gave the European Parliament slightly more influence in EC decision-making.

[See also: Economic and Social Cohesion; Treaties of Rome]

Single Transferable Vote (STV)

An electoral system utilising preferential voting, in which voters indicate their preferences by placing numbers: 1, 2, 3, … etc., by the names of candidates. Unlike the otherwise similar Alternative Vote System, STV must be used in

63 EVENTS, GROUPS AND DEVELOPMENTS

multi-member constituencies, usually of up to about 5 seats. Larger numbers are possible, but involve increased complication of the counting procedure and increased length of the ballot paper. Ireland uses constituencies electing 3–5 members each. Candidates are elected if they receive a quota of votes. This quota is the lowest number of votes which will elect the required number of candidates, but no more. As a formula: the Quota = the number of valid votes cast, divided by the number of seats to be filled plus one, and one is added to that sum; so $Q = V/(S+1) + 1$. Votes in excess of the quota for a candidate are redistributed according to indicated next preferences, and, where candidates are eliminated because they have fewest votes, the next preferences of votes they have received are also redistributed until sufficient candidates are elected.

Though not an electoral system designed to produce a close correspondence between a party's share of the vote and its share of seats, the STV system does give results which are much closer to proportionality than first-past-the-post systems such as that used in House of Commons elections in Britain. The principal advantage of the system is that it provides the voter with great freedom of choice as to the criteria the voter uses to select candidates, and greatly reduces wasted votes. A voter may choose to vote for all the candidates of one party first (but even then can exercise choice among them), for candidates irrespective of party who support or oppose some particular policy issue, for candidates on the basis of personal qualities such as gender, occupation, age or place of residence, or whatever other criteria the voter wishes to employ. As well as Ireland, Malta uses STV for its legislative elections, and Northern Ireland uses it for the election of its representatives to the European Parliament.

[See also: Alternative Vote System]

social capital

A term applied to the network of voluntary associations in a political system, with reference to the political resources which such a network contributes to a democracy. The hypothesis underlying the use of the term is that groups such as sports clubs, trade unions, churches, professional organisations, charitable groups and leisure-based groups such as dramatic societies and choirs, contribute to democracy in various ways. On occasion, they may act as pressure groups to promote policies advantageous to the group or its clients (such as working mothers or pensioners). Moreover, even if a group never becomes engaged in political activity directly, its members learn skills of participation, activist involvement (such as office-holding) and leadership. Therefore a society where membership of such groups is low or declining may have a less robust democratic base than one where membership of such groups is high and rising. Some studies of non-participation in elections have found a link between propensity of an individual to vote in an election and membership of that individual in such voluntary organisations.

social market economy

The label applied to the system of political economy developed in the Federal Republic of Germany by Erhard (Minister of Economics in Adenauer's government). The system sought to combine production and sales based upon the principle of the free market, qualified by protection against cartels and monopolies and by regulatory legislation concerning health and safety in the workplace, with provision of social welfare, based upon the insurance principle, to provide employees with adequate pensions, unemployment and sickness benefits and other payments. This system depended upon the co-operation of the trade unions and business organisations. Such co-operation was made easier by the introduction after the Second World War of a system of industrial trade unions, in which employees, of whatever trade or skill, in, say, the chemical industry were all members of the Chemical Workers' Union – in contrast to the United Kingdom, where each factory could contain employees in a dozen or more different trade unions. Legislation promoting co-determination in industry, at first in the coal and steel sectors, then from 1976 in medium- and large-sized firms in all sectors of industry, also played a role in developing the social market economy. The system of workers' councils, whose representatives were elected by employees, and the short-lived system of tripartite discussions on economic and industrial policy known as 'Concerted Action' (*konzertierte Aktion*) or the new version called 'Alliance for Jobs' (*Bündnis für Arbeit*) introduced in 1998 by the Schröder government to focus especially on reduction of unemployment are other examples of policy initiatives designed to promote the social market economy.

The term has been used in other countries to describe either actual or desired economic systems, but the German version is the most developed example of such a system.

[See also: Erhard*]

South Tyrol question

South Tyrol is an area in north Italy consisting of a mainly German-speaking population. Previously part of the Austro-Hungarian empire, it was given to Italy as part of the peace settlement after the First World War. Mussolini took measures to suppress the German language and culture of the region, and agreed with Hitler to resettle German speakers in Germany (though only a small number were transferred). After the Second World War, a degree of protection for the German-speaking population was provided in the 1948 Italian constitution. However, actions by the Italian government to repress the German-speaking inhabitants by merging the area into a larger area so that Italian-speakers would be in a majority led to increased support for the South Tyrol People's Party, to mass demonstrations and even violence and terrorist activity. An agreement was negotiated which was embodied in a treaty in 1971, guaranteeing proportional provision of resources to both the Italian-speaking and German-speaking communities in the area, and in 1992 the region (in Italian: Alto Adige-Trentino) was given special status within the system of regional government in Italy.

Spanish civil war

Spain's democratic Second Republic was founded in 1931 by centre-left political forces, but the regime was not fully acceptable to the country's reactionary elements. In July 1936 a military uprising against the leftist 'Popular Front' government led by Manuel Azaña led to a bitter civil war between the Republicans and the opposition Nationalists which lasted until 1939. The Republicans were supported by organised labour, regional nationalists and secular forces in society. The Nationalists based their support on the Catholic church (except in the Basque country), the business community and landowners, the peasantry, most of the military and traditional monarchists. The Nationalists won the civil war, aided in their military campaign by the country's armed forces and by subsidies from Nazi Germany and fascist Italy, more substantial than those provided to the Republicans by Stalin. The Nationalists were able to ban and disperse political parties, movements and trade unions which did not support their stance. The civil war cost between 75,000 and 200,000 lives and caused major economic problems. The victorious Nationalists established a repressive authoritarian state under General Franco, which continued to persecute those forces which had supported the Republican cause. It was not until Spain's transition to democracy from the mid-1970s that Spanish society began to recover from this war.

[See also: fascism; nazism; Franco*]

Spanish coup attempt (1981)

Spain's current constitutional monarchy was established in 1978, but many powerful interests remained suspicious of the new democratic regime. On 23 February 1981, reactionaries in the army were alarmed by moves towards regional autonomy and mounting terrorist action, so attempted a coup against the democratic state. A paramilitary Civil Guard unit led by Lieutenant-Colonel Tejero Molina broke into the Cortes, the parliament building, and took the elected MPs hostage. There was no agreement amongst the army officers involved as to the desired outcome: some, like Tejero, wanted a Chilean-style coup, while others wanted a 'soft' coup leading to the formation of a national government. King Juan Carlos acted quickly to restore the status quo. He contacted those military leaders not involved in the coup to assure them that he did not support it. He told the coup leaders that he was not prepared to abdicate or to leave the country and would rather be shot than accept the take-over. He then made a television address to the nation to declare that the Crown would not tolerate the coup. The coup collapsed and the captured MPs were released.

[See also: Juan Carlos*]

Spiegel Affair

In October 1962 the Hamburg news weekly, *Der Spiegel*, published a report of recent NATO military manoeuvres which criticised the performance of the German military in those exercises. A fortnight later the federal state prosecutor ordered the arrest of Augstein (the publisher), Ahlers (chief editor), and several other staff on charges of treason and bribery, since it was suspected that members of the military had sold secret information to the magazine. Police occupied the editorial offices of the magazine in Hamburg and Bonn and copies of the magazine were seized. This high-handed and seemingly anti-democratic action was severely criticised by the mass media and the public, as well as by politicians from the liberal Free Democrats (coalition partner to the governing Christian Democrats) and the opposition Social Democrats. The way in which action was taken, at night and without warning, as well as the dubious procedures concerning the arrest of Ahlers, who was on holiday in Spain, were compared to methods used in the Hitler regime against opponents. It was revealed that the Minister of Defence, Strauss, had been largely responsible for initiating the action against the magazine, and that, in a debate in the Bundestag, he had made misleading statements about his responsibility for what had occurred. Adenauer's own position was affected by opposition criticism and the threat of the FDP to resign from his government. To avoid having to dismiss Strauss, Adenauer reshuffled his cabinet, excluding some FDP ministers and some other Christian Democrat ministers from the previous cabinet, as well as Strauss. The affair was a factor in Adenauer's decision to resign as Chancellor in 1963, finally fulfilling his promise made at the time of the formation of the coalition in 1961.

Neither charges of treason against Augstein and Ahlers, nor a constitutional court complaint by *Der Spiegel* concerning the government's breach of the constitutional guarantee of press freedom, were successful. The FDP insisted that Strauss be excluded from Erhard's cabinets in 1963 and 1965, though he returned as a minister in the grand coalition. However, the FDP managed also to prevent Strauss gaining the Foreign Ministry in 1982 and 1983, which meant, since Strauss would take no lesser post, that after 1969 he never again became a federal minister.

[See also: Adenauer*; Strauss*]

spin doctor

A term applied in recent years to those public relations advisers in politics whose function is to put the best possible interpretation (or 'spin') on events relevant to the government or party which they serve, and to try to ensure that stories favourable to their party or government appear prominently and at the best times in the press or the broadcasting media. In Britain Peter Mandelson and Alistair Campbell have been among the most prominent 'spin doctors' for the Labour Party, and were held to have contributed considerably to the Labour Party victory in the 1997 general election. The US president and other US politicians have employed the services of 'spin doctors', and the campaigns of German and French politicians in recent years have also laid emphasis on the work of 'spin doctors'.

Stability and Growth Pact [See: Economic and Monetary Union]

Stalin Note

Following initiatives in 1950 and 1951 from the Prime Minister of the German Democratic Republic, Grotewohl, offering all-German negotiations leading to the reunification of Germany, Stalin made an offer (the 'Stalin Note') on 10 March 1952 to the Western Allies. This proposed that a German state should be created within the borders of Germany as they were at the end of the Second World War. This new German state would be neutral, but would be allowed to possess its own defence force. A peace treaty would be signed by the Allies and Germany, following which free elections would be held. As this Note was communicated during negotiations for Germany's membership in a European Defence Community, it was regarded in the West as a delaying tactic, so its offer was not pursued. Some historians consider the offer to have been genuine, and its rejection therefore a missed opportunity for early reunification. Others, however, consider it to have been only a tactical manoeuvre, which Stalin would not have permitted to have led to German reunification. Certainly a large majority of West Germans supported rejection of Stalin's proposals in opinion polls at the time.

[See also: Cold War; European Defence Community; the German question; reunification of Germany]

Stammheim trials [See: Baader-Meinhof group]

Stasi

A German term, an abbreviation of 'Staatssicherheitsdienst' (state security service), referring to the secret police employed by the Ministry for State Security in the GDR and beyond its borders for purposes of spying on its own citizens and foreign visitors, for gathering intelligence and other activities required by the government of a totalitarian system. It was regarded as an essential mechanism by which the GDR communist party (the SED) could retain power. When the SED lost its monopoly of political power in late

1989, the public sought to occupy the offices of the Stasi, and – though many files and other forms of data were destroyed – a large number of files were rescued and passed into the custody of the reunified Federal Republic, which created a special agency (called the 'Gauck agency' after its first Director, Joachim Gauck, an East German associated with the citizen movement in 1989) to manage the archive of files and regulate access by individuals to those files.

Stormont

The name of the location of the legislature of Northern Ireland, and thus, by extension, applied to the legislature itself. This legislature was created by the Northern Ireland Act 1920, and, following the first elections in 1921, consisted of two chambers: a Senate and a House of Commons. Following a revival of civil unrest in Northern Ireland in the 1960s, the British Parliament passed a law in 1972 suspending the powers of the Northern Ireland legislature. Attempts were made from time to time to reach a settlement among the conflicting factions within Northern Ireland, which would have resulted in an agreed basis for an elected legislature; indeed, elections for a constitutional convention were held in 1975 and for an Assembly in 1982, but with no lasting effect. It was not until the Good Friday Agreement in 1999 produced a more settled agreement, validated by a referendum, that elections could be held for an Assembly and a devolved form of government could be established based on that Assembly, though even then the new Assembly at Stormont faced an uncertain future because of a failure by the IRA to comply with requirements to abandon their arsenals of weapons.

[See also: Good Friday Agreement; IRA]

streitbare Demokratie

A German term (translatable as 'combative', 'militant' or 'aggressive' democracy) which refers to constitutional, legislative and administrative provisions in the political system of the Federal Republic of Germany by which the democratic political order is able to defend itself against its potential enemies. This is in contrast to the Weimar Republic which, lacking those devices, through its own democratic tolerance allowed the enemies of democracy to threaten, pervert, destabilise and eventually overthrow the constitutional democracy of that Republic. Instruments of 'streitbare Demokratie' include: the provision in the constitution which allows the Federal Constitutional Court to prohibit the existence of political parties which are themselves internally undemocratic or which seek to overthrow the democratic regime; a constitutional provision to permit the minister of the interior to ban organisations (other than political parties) which pursue criminal or unconstitutional ends; an explicit listing of civic rights in the forefront of the constitution and an effective constitutional court which can protect those rights, but which can suspend or deny some of them by due process to those who engage in activity opposed to the constitutional order. Federal and Länder Offices for the Protection of the Constitution investigate and produce information concerning groups considered to be extreme and potentially dangerous to democracy. There is an emphasis on the obligation of state employees to defend the constitutional order at all times (which led to the formal codification of this obligation in the so-called 'radicals decree', requiring that applicants for posts in state employment with a record of association with anti-constitutional groups or parties should be refused appointment). Critics of some of these measures claim that their application sometimes necessitates undemocratic actions, so in themselves they may pose a danger to democracy.

[See also: radicals' decree]

Structural Funds [See: Economic and Social Cohesion]

subsidiarity

Subsidiarity is a concept applicable to federal political systems or to those which operate in a similar way, such as the multi-tiered political system of the European Union (EU). It is a constitutional principle which holds that policy decisions should be taken by the lowest tier of government possible within the territorial hierarchy. If a policy matter cannot be dealt with effectively by the lowest tier in the territorial hierarchy, say, local government, then it should be passed to the next tier up, say, regional government, until it arrives at an appropriate level of government. The subsidiarity principle can enhance the accountability of decision-making and can also help to avoid problems of government overload at higher levels of government. The concept has been widely used in discussions about the development of the EU, but was at first rather ambiguous. In a speech in Bruges in September 1988, the UK Prime Minister Margaret Thatcher used the concept to promote decision-making at the level of the member state national governments rather than by the supranational institutions of the EU. Other proponents have used the concept to promote an enhanced role for local and regional government. The Edinburgh European Council (December 1992) provided a working definition and laid down guidelines for interpreting Article 5 (formerly Article 3b) on subsidiarity in the EU. The Amsterdam Treaty (1997) produced a further protocol on how the principle of subsidiarity should be applied within the EU.

[See also: Amsterdam Treaty; Thatcher*]

Suez crisis

The Suez canal linking the Mediterranean Sea to the Red Sea and thus to the Indian Ocean was jointly owned by British and French shareholders. In July 1956, one month after the withdrawal of British troops stationed in the Canal Zone under the terms of a Treaty between Britain and Egypt, the canal was threatened by nationalisation by the Egyptian government of President Nasser. This threat was in retaliation for withdrawal of development funding by the USA and Britain for Egypt's Aswan Dam project. The Suez canal was of vital commercial and military importance to the Western powers.

In response to this threat, Britain and France colluded with Israel in order to produce a legitimate excuse for invasion of the 'Canal Zone', which would lead to their assumption of the direct operation of the Suez canal. France and Britain had been victims of Nasser's anti-Western and anti-colonial policies (such as aid for Algerian nationalist groups). Israel, suffering from a naval blockade by Egypt, invaded Egyptian territory at the end of October 1956, the British and French took military action a few days later (as they claimed: to protect the canal's viability) and Egypt retaliated by sinking ships to block the canal. The British and French were forced to withdraw their invasion forces by US diplomatic and financial threats. The canal was nationalised. Israel was compelled to withdraw from Egyptian territory. The crisis contributed to the collapse eighteen months later of the Fourth Republic in France. In Britain, Prime Minister Eden, who had seen Nasser as a new version of Hitler, resigned following deep divisions over his policies and actions in connection with the crisis, and was replaced in January 1957 by Macmillan. The crisis acted as a deterrent to British military involvement overseas for many years.

[See also: Eden*; Macmillan*]

Tangentopoli

The term: Tangentopoli ('bribe city') refers to a major corruption scandal which was uncovered in Milan in early 1992 and which challenged some of the highest office-holders in Italian politics, eventually resulting in the collapse of the traditional party system and in calls for a major constitutional review. By the end of the 1980s, political corruption in Italy, based on party clientelism, had become systemic and routine. On 17 February 1992 Mario Chiesa, the Socialist head of an old people's home in Milan, was arrested for taking a 7 million lire bribe from the owner of a cleaning company. Chiesa was a 'business politician': a type familiar in the Italian politics of the 1980s as high-living, corrupt fixers involved in politics only for personal advantage. Chiesa's confession implicated many others who were then obliged to confess corrupt dealings of their own. This uncovered a vast network of illicit dealings between the political parties and economic interests in Milan. The crisis soon spread far beyond Milan. By the end of 1993 251 members of Parliament were under judicial investigation, including four former prime ministers, five former party leaders, and seven members of the governing Amato cabinet. Amongst those implicated were the Christian Democrat (DC) President Cossiga who resigned early in 1992; Craxi, the leader of the Socialist Party (PSI) who resigned in February 1993; and Andreotti (DC), one of the country's most influential politicians of the 1970s and 1980s. Tangentopoli thoroughly discredited

Italy's five traditional parties, which were either seriously weakened or were forced to reinvent themselves as 'new' parties, having undergone damaging splits. The parties and party system remain in a state of flux.

[See also: clientelism; Mani pulite; Andreotti*; Cossiga*; Craxi*]

terrorism

Terrorism involves the deliberate and systematic use of physical or psychological violence to intimidate others. In Europe, it has been used by various groups in an attempt to resolve political conflicts in their favour. Although typically only very small numbers of people have engaged in terrorism, it has been a recurrent problem for the countries of Western Europe and has at times caused the widespread disruption of social and working life. Terrorists in Europe have been motivated by three general causes: extreme ideologies of the left and right; centre–periphery or regional conflicts; and single issue conflicts. Terrorist actions have included arson, bombings, kidnappings, hijackings and killings.

[See also: Baader-Meinhof group; ETA; Irish Republican Army; Red Army Faction; Red Brigades; Secret Army Organisation]

Treaties of Rome

In 1957, two separate treaties, together known as the Treaties of Rome, established the European Communities (the European Economic Community (EEC) and the European Atomic Energy Community (EURATOM)), taking effect in January 1958. The Treaties of Rome established a customs union amongst the six founder states (Belgium, France, Italy, Luxembourg, the Netherlands and West Germany). This entailed a phased programme to remove all tariffs and quotas from trade between the member states while setting a Common External

Tariff (CET) on imports from outside the EEC. Common policies, notably in agriculture and transport, were introduced to promote trade within the EEC. A common social policy was designed to offset hardship suffered in the transition to a more open market. The Rome Treaties established a set of governing institutions: a supranational Commission; a Parliamentary Assembly; a Court of Justice; and a Council of Ministers made up of government representatives of the member states.

[See also: Common Agricultural Policy; European Coal and Steel Community]

Treaty of European Union (TEU) [See: Maastricht Treaty]

Treaty of Nice

The Treaty of Nice was concluded at the European Union summit of 7–11 December 2000 and was signed on 26 February 2001. A target deadline for member state ratification of the Treaty has been set for December 2002. The Treaty proposes extensive reform of EU institutions to cater in particular for enlargement to the east. The 'big five' member states (Germany, UK, France, Italy and Spain) have agreed to reduce their allocation of EU commissioners from two to one. Otherwise, though, the proposed institutional reforms on qualified majority voting (QMV) and the post-enlargement composition of the European Parliament would generally strengthen the power of the large member states. Policy areas to be added to those in the QMV category include trade policy in services; some immigration and asylum matters; and the appointment of the Commission president.

Treuhandanstalt

A German term meaning: trustee agency. This was an institution created by the GDR government on 1 March 1990 to acquire and administer economic enterprises (with the exception of certain utilities such as the railways and postal service) which had previously been owned by the state, with the task of preparing the GDR economy for monetary union with the FRG, preparations which involved privatising the almost entirely state-owned economy. So the Treuhandanstalt had to investigate the financial situation of economic enterprises, undertaking restructuring where advisable, and, following a law passed by the GDR Parliament on 17 June 1990, disposing of them to private ownership. It became clear that many of these enterprises were unviable in an open and competitive economy, so about one-third of them had to be closed down, causing unemployment and economic and social dislocation. Following reunification, the processes of restructuring, sale and closure accelerated, but a variety of problems confronted the agency, including accusations of favouring certain bidders in sales of businesses and the high costs of restructuring. A process that had been hoped would produce a surplus for public funds ended by costing the German taxpayer several billion Deutschmarks. The second Director of the Treuhandanstalt, Rohwedder, was assassinated in 1991 by terrorists in protest against the economic hardships resulting from closures in eastern Germany. The Treuhandanstalt terminated its operations in 1994.

[See also: Rohwedder*]

Trizonia [See: Bizonia]

two-ballot electoral system

A system of election in which voters may cast two ballots, separated in time, in order to elect representatives. Such a system is used for elections to the

National Assembly and to elect the president in the French Fifth Republic. For National Assembly elections, single-member constituencies are used. If a candidate wins more than 50 per cent of votes in the first round of balloting, he or she is elected. In constituencies where no candidate secures that absolute majority, a second round is held two weeks later. Only those candidates who secured on the first round votes equal to at least 12.5 per cent of *the registered electorate* (not just of those who turned out to vote) are eligible to participate in the second round. In fact, for reasons of political strategy, usually only two candidates present themselves: one from the right-wing and one from the left-wing party blocs. In the second round, the candidate with the most votes is elected, irrespective of whether an absolute majority is secured or only a relative majority. The system to elect the president is similar. The differences are that only the two candidates with the highest first-round votes contest the second round, and the interval between the two rounds is one week.

'Two plus Four' talks

In preparation for the reunification of Germany, a series of international conferences took place in 1990 involving representatives of the two German states and of the four former occupying powers (the USA, France, the United Kingdom and the USSR). No peace treaty had been concluded after the Second World War, so the previous occupying powers had retained responsibilities for Berlin and, though in a very restricted and formal manner, for the rest of Germany. The consent of these four former occupying powers was essential before reunification under conditions of complete sovereignty could come about. Four meetings took place between February and September 1990, two in Germany and one each

in Paris and Moscow. The Paris meeting also involved representatives of Poland, since that meeting discussed the issue of the borders of reunified Germany, including the Oder–Neisse border with Poland. The Moscow meeting in September 1990 produced a Treaty between the four powers and the two German states which amounted to a post-Second World War peace treaty, including as it did acceptance of the right of Germany to be a member of the North Atlantic Treaty Organisation.

[See also: Cold War; German question; Oder–Neisse line; reunification of Germany]

Vergangenheitsbewältigung (coming to terms with the past)

A German term used to describe the problems and processes connected with Germany's ability to deal with its especially turbulent recent history. It was originally applied to dealing with the Nazi period: how and why Hitler came to power; the totalitarian policies of the Third Reich; the aggressive foreign policies of the Hitler regime; and especially the genocidal policies against the Jewish peoples of Europe. It could be applied to other countries, such as post-war France in relation to the Vichy regime and with Algeria. More recently, it has also been applied to the problems raised by the collapse of the Communist regime in the GDR and reunification, concerning the policies and activities of the state and the ruling Communist party in the GDR, such as the 'shoot to kill' orders relating to those seeking to flee across the border, or the crimes of the secret police (the Stasi). Methods employed to foster the process of 'coming to terms with the past' include the denazification procedures introduced by the occupation powers after the Second World War (including the Nuremberg tribunal), re-education policies, historical programmes on radio and television, publication of memoirs by those involved in the Third Reich or the GDR regime, the Bundestag Commission on the activities of the Communist regime in the GDR, and speeches of the federal president (whose functions include such moral interpretations of the country's history).

[See also: denazification; Nuremberg tribunal; Stasi]

Vichy regime

When France capitulated following its invasion by Germany in 1940, the armistice agreement allowed for a rump state to be governed by the French, rather than be occupied as was the remainder of France. This government of this state, in southern France, was known as the Vichy regime (the town of Vichy being the seat of government). The government was led by President Pétain, a First World War hero, who presided over a government that collaborated with the German authorities on matters such as the deportation to Germany of Jews and recruitment of French workers for forced labour. Following the landing of Allied troops in Normandy in June 1944, the Vichy regime territory was occupied by the Germans and its leaders sent to Germany. After the war Pétain was sentenced to death by a French court for treason, but his sentence was commuted to life imprisonment. He died in 1951. Pétain's Prime Minister, Laval, was executed after the war for treason.

[See also: Vergangenheitsbewältigung]

Voeren dispute (Belgium)

The Voeren dispute became a symbol of the tension between linguistic communities in Belgium. In 1962 the administrative authority for Voeren/Fourons, a largely French-speaking group of villages in north-eastern Belgium, passed from French-speaking Liège to Flemish-speaking Limburg, launching repeated clashes between the two linguistic groups. José Happart, a militant French speaker, was elected mayor of Voeren in 1986, but his nomination was rejected by the Flemish Chamber of the Council of State because he refused to take a competency test in Flemish, which was by now the official language of the villages. Happart's repeated re-election obliged Belgian Prime Minister Wilfried Martens to resign in October 1987 and call an early general election. In December 1988 Happart agreed not to stand as mayor of Voeren again in exchange for a place on the French-speaking Socialist Party electoral list in the June 1989 European elections.

Volkspartei

A German term (literally: 'people's party') referring to parties which seek to attract voting support and membership from many or all of the different groups in society, instead of being confined to a particular set of supporters (e.g. trade unions, farmers or Catholics), utilising policy programmes and electoral manifestos which are sufficiently diffuse to appeal to a broad spectrum of the electorate, rather than emphasising ideologically derived political aims. Such parties must, almost by definition, possess sufficiently large electoral support to be able to lead a government, alone or as principal partner in a coalition. The Christian Democrats and Social Democrats in Germany and Austria are obvious examples of the Volkspartei type. The decision of the SPD to adopt its Bad Godesberg Programme in 1959 is a clear example of a party seeking to become a Volkspartei after being very much a working-class party in earlier years.

[See also: Godesberg Programme]

Waldheim Affair

Dr Kurt Waldheim was President of Austria from 1986 to 1991. During his presidential campaign, he was accused of having been implicated in atrocities committed by the Nazis in the Balkans in 1942–45. When he took office, the allegations surrounding his wartime activities led him to be barred from entering the United States. During his incumbency, relations between Austria and many other states, particularly Israel, became strained. In 1988 an international commission of historians concluded that Waldheim must have been aware of the atrocities at the time they were taking place. He refused to stand down as President, but did not seek re-election when his term of office came to an end.
[See also: nazism; Waldheim*]

'Wende'

A German term meaning 'change of direction'. It has been utilised in two different political contexts. (a) The term was applied to the strategy of Helmut Kohl and his coalition when he became Chancellor in 1982. The change of direction he promised was especially to do with restrictions on public expenditure (especially social welfare payments and subsidies) and, in consequence, of the rising levels of public debt. (b) It is also applied to the situation in the GDR in 1989–90, and to German reunification. Here it refers to the downfall of the communist regime in the GDR, its replacement by a multi-party democracy, and then to its incorporation in the Federal Republic of Germany. Germans refer to events or developments in eastern Germany as occurring 'before' or 'after' the 'Wende'.

West Lothian question

The Scottish MP Tam Dalyell is credited with raising the West Lothian question in debates on Scottish devolution in the 1970s. The West Lothian question refers to a constitutional anomaly which exists where only part of the United Kingdom possesses regionally devolved powers. In such a case, pointed out Dalyell, MPs in the House of Commons would be prevented from debating or voting upon laws affecting education in West Lothian (and other parts of Scotland), but would still be able to vote on laws affecting education in West Bromwich (and other parts of England). So a Scottish MP could vote on educational matters for England, but neither that MP nor any English MP could vote on educational matters for Scotland, since that would be one of the policy areas devolved to a Scottish parliament.

This potential has become a reality since the opening of the Scottish Parliament in 1999. There is no equivalent parliament for England as such, though some have suggested that there should be such a parliament, or else that the House of Commons when dealing with matters parallel to those devolved to the Scottish parliament (such as education) should sit without Scottish MPs being allowed to vote. This, though, could mean that a government possessing a parliamentary majority dependent upon Scottish MPs would be outvoted by the opposition on such English policies. Others maintain that the anomaly really does not have much effect on policy, and that few members of the public are aware of its existence.

winter of discontent

A phrase from Shakespeare's *Richard III*, applied to the winter of 1978–79 in Britain, when trade union action eventually made the Labour government so deeply unpopular that it suffered a heavy defeat in the May 1979 general election. It was caused especially by the combined effects of high levels of inflation and a restrictive incomes policy by the Wilson and Callaghan governments, which had reduced the standard of living of many employees. First strikes in the private sector produced pay increases of 17–20 per cent. Then a series of strikes by public sector employees, especially manual workers employed in local government, caused great inconvenience and hardship to the general public, closing schools and hospitals, leaving refuse to pile up in the streets, and even, in the most publicised case, preventing burials of the dead. The Labour government was hampered by its close financial connection to the trade unions and by a lack of legislation to prevent strikes. This was especially the case in key public services, where the closed shop existed (meaning that all employees had to be members of the trade union, and were subject to sanctions by that trade union if, for example, they refused to strike) and there were sometimes questionable practices concerning strike ballots. When the Conservative government won the election, it introduced legislation to restrict the powers of trade union leaders. The Labour Party started to question its reliance on the trade unions, leading eventually to reforms within the party initiated by Kinnock, John Smith and Blair.

[See also: Blair*; Callaghan*; Kinnock*; Smith J.*]

women's movement

The feminist movement that emerged in Western Europe in the 1960s to 1970s was divided into two branches: the women's rights movement and the women's liberation movement. The women's rights movement had its historical roots in the suffrage movement at the turn of the twentieth century, which secured women's right of access to education and to professional qualifications. In the 1960s and 1970s, this branch of the feminist movement was particularly successful in France and Britain. The women's rights activists were concerned with promoting gender equality; that is, the same rights as men to work and participate in society. They tried to secure political reforms largely by traditional methods, often working through political parties and trade unions. In contrast, the women's liberation movement adopted the idea of gender difference. Their aim was to develop a feminist counter-culture. For them, influencing the political establishment took second place to changing women's attitudes. The women's liberation movement was organised at the grassroots level and their campaigns were conducted through mass protests. The women's movements have succeeded in creating an ongoing public debate on women's role in society, even if their values have been accorded rather limited recognition within national politics. One substantive area of success has been in their demand for easier access to legal abortion. Mainstream political parties have adopted a broadly supportive, if unspecific, stance on women's issues, and European governments have introduced a range of state bodies to promote gender equality. However, some feminists feel that parties are only paying lip service to women's issues, are using feminist ideas for their own purposes, or have failed to reflect their ideas accurately.

xenophobia

Literally: fear of strangers. Xenophobia has been regarded as a cause of race hatred and as an element in the politics of the extreme right-wing, manifesting itself as hatred of foreigners (especially immigrants) and their culture. It is therefore found especially in societies where either a sudden influx of immigrants occurs, immigrants whose cultural separateness makes them difficult to integrate into the host society, or in societies where contact with foreigners has been very restricted, such as the GDR before the fall of the

75 EVENTS, GROUPS AND DEVELOPMENTS

Berlin Wall. After reunification, some of the worst acts of violence in Germany against foreigners occurred in the area of the former GDR.

[See also: anti-Semitism; immigration]

Yalta conference

One of a series of wartime conferences among leaders of the Allies in the Second World War. The conference at Yalta (in the Crimea) was held in February 1945, at a time when it was obvious that Germany would soon be defeated. It therefore focused on the post-war treatment of Germany. Decisions reached included the division of Germany into three zones of occupation (it was later agreed that France should also have a zone of occupation – in territory originally allocated to British and American occupation), confirmation of a policy of unconditional surrender of Germany and its total disarmament, acceptance of the Atlantic Charter and the founding of the United Nations Organisation, and the declaration of war on Japan by the USSR. Differing interpretation of the decisions reached at Yalta (as well as those reached at the Potsdam conference) contributed to the Cold War and the division of Germany.

[See also: Cold War; the German question; Potsdam conference]

Youandé Convention [See: Lomé Convention]

Young Turks' revolt

In 1955–56 discussions took place within the parties in the Federal Republic of Germany concerning revision of the Electoral Law, ahead of the scheduled 1957 Bundestag election. Because Chancellor Adenauer had had a number of conflicts with his coalition partner, the Free Democratic Party (FDP), over issues such as the Saarland question, he permitted some in his party to float the idea of a revised form of proportional representation in which only half the Bundestag (rather than all its membership, as was then the case) would be elected on the basis of proportional representation with the remainder being elected in constituencies on the basis of 'first past the post' but not taken into account when seats were distributed proportionally among parties: the Grabenwahlsystem (meaning two systems of election separated by a 'ditch'). This would have greatly diminished the number of FDP candidates elected to the Bundestag and would very likely have eliminated their role as a coalition partner. The FDP sought to dissuade the Christian Democrats from proceeding with this idea. In the largest Land: North Rhine-Westphalia (NRW), the FDP withdrew from their coalition with the Christian Democrats and instead joined a coalition government led by the Social Democrats. This had the effect of switching votes to the opposition from the Christian Democrats in the upper chamber (the Bundesrat, where the Länder governments had veto powers over certain types of legislation), making it more difficult for Adenauer to govern. Because many of those involved in this coup in the NRW FDP, such as Weyer, Döring and Scheel, were relatively young, it became known as the Young Turks' revolt. The principal consequences were that the Grabenwahlsystem idea was dropped, but a break-up of the coalition in Bonn followed. This forced Adenauer to govern with the aid of a number of renegade FDP Members of the Bundestag. In the Bundestag election in 1957, which took place under very much a similar electoral system to that used in 1953, Adenauer obtained an absolute majority for his party, and did not need the FDP as a coalition partner.

[See also: Grabenwahlsystem; Saarland question]

Section 2
Biographies

Biographies

Related entries are listed at the end of an entry by '[See also: ...]'. An asterisk indicates a cross-reference to Section 1, 'Events, groups and developments'. For example, the entry for **Auriol, Vincent** has at the end '[See also: de Gaulle; Vichy regime*]'. The entry for de Gaulle is in this section; that for Vichy regime is in Section 1.

Adams, (Gerry) Gerard

Leader of the Northern Ireland party Sinn Féin (Ourselves). Born in the Falls Road area of Belfast in 1948, Adams was a founder member of the Northern Ireland Civil Rights Association and a member of the Belfast Housing Action Committee. He joined the Republican movement in 1964. In March 1972 Adams was interned in Long Kesh under suspicion of terrorism but was released in July 1972 to take part in secret talks between the UK Secretary of State for Northern Ireland and the Irish Republican Army (IRA). He was rearrested in 1973 and tried to escape from the Maze Prison. After his release in 1977, he was charged in 1978 with membership of the Provisional IRA but released after seven months through lack of evidence. Vice-President of Sinn Féin 1978–83, he became President of the party in 1983. He was elected MP for Belfast West 1983–92 and again from 1997. In 1988 and 1993 he met with John Hume, leader of the nationalist Social Democratic and Labour Party (SDLP), to discuss proposals for the future of Northern Ireland. He has been the key representative of the nationalist Catholic community in negotiations with the UK government. He has been member for Belfast West of the Northern Ireland Assembly from 1998.

[See also: Hume; Irish Republican Army*]

Adenauer, Konrad

Chancellor of the Federal Republic of Germany 1949–63; leader of the Christian Democratic Union (CDU) 1950–66. Adenauer was born in Cologne in 1876. He studied law and economics, then practised law in Cologne. He joined the Catholic Centre Party in 1906, and was elected to the Cologne city council in 1908, becoming Lord Mayor in 1917, an office he filled until 1933. In the Weimar Republic he was elected to the Prussian legislature. He was dismissed from his offices by the Nazis, and was twice imprisoned by them. Appointed Lord Mayor of Cologne in 1945 by the US occupation authorities, when the British took over the administration of the region, they dismissed Adenauer for non-co-operation. He was active in founding the CDU in the British zone of occupation, and became Chairman of the Parliamentary Council (1948–49) which met in Bonn to draft the Basic Law (the provisional constitution for the Federal Republic). He was elected by the Bundestag as the first federal Chancellor in September 1949, and led his party to victory in the federal elections in 1953, 1957 and 1961. Following coalition negotiations which required of Adenauer that he resign the chancellorship before the 1965 elections, and a series of governmental crises (including the Spiegel Affair) which damaged his authority, he left the chancellorship in 1963. He was elected as federal Chairman of the CDU in 1950, when the CDU created an organisation for the Federal Republic (having previously existed as zonal and Land parties). Adenauer was tempted to seek the office of federal president in 1959, but withdrew when he was assured that he could not extend the very limited powers of that office. His chancellorship was marked by a search for the security of the Federal Republic through close alliances with other West European countries and with the USA, leading to the Federal Republic becoming an enthusiastic partner in the institutions of European integration and NATO. The Friendship Treaty between the Federal Republic and France in 1963 was another indication of this diplomatic policy. Adenauer was accused of being insufficiently enthusiastic about promoting German reunification, and it was under his leadership that the Hallstein Doctrine was promulgated. The Federal Republic became extremely prosperous during Adenauer's chancellorship. As Chancellor, Adenauer frequently experienced difficulties with his coalition partners, especially the FDP. His authoritarian style similarly led to problems within his own party. Nevertheless, his undoubted success in developing the new Federal Republic as a secure and prosperous democratic state during the period of the Cold War, and his active utilisation of the office of federal chancellor to promote his policies, led commentators to apply the term 'chancellor democracy' to the period of his leadership. Adenauer died in 1967.

[See also: Basic Law*; chancellor democracy*; economic miracle*; German question*; Hallstein Doctrine*; Spiegel Affair*; Stalin Note*; Young Turks' revolt*]

Andreotti, Giulio

Andreotti was Prime Minister of Italy 1972–73; 1976–79; and 1989–92. Born in Rome in 1919, Andreotti graduated in law from the University of Rome and served as President of the Federation of Catholic Universities 1942–45. A member of the Christian Democrats (DC), he was elected to the Italian Constituent Assembly in 1945 and served in the Chamber of Deputies from 1946, becoming a life senator in 1992. In a ministerial career spanning four decades, Andreotti had responsibility for many policy areas including the interior, finance, the treasury, defence, industry and commerce, the budget and economic planning and foreign affairs. He was Chairman of the DC parliamentary party group 1948–72. In February 1972 he became Prime Minister for the first time at the head of a single party interim government. He then formed a coalition government of the centre, but resigned in June 1973. From 1976, Andreotti led a DC government with the support of the Communist Party until the Communists withdrew their backing in 1979. In July 1989 he formed a five-party coalition which fell after the elections of 1992. In 1993 he became embroiled in the Tangentopoli scandal: in 1993 his immunity was lifted and in March 1995 he was charged with links to the Mafia (acquitted in 1999), with complicity in murder in November 1995, and with financial corruption.

[See also: Tangentopoli*]

Arias Navarro, Carlos

General Franco's feared head of security and Prime Minister of Spain 1973–76. Arias Navarro was born in 1908 in Madrid and received a doctorate in law from the Central University of Madrid. He worked at the Ministry of Justice as a civil servant before becoming a public prosecutor in Malaga in 1933. He supported the rebellion led by General Franco during the Spanish civil war and was arrested by the republican government in 1936. He was freed by pro-Franco Falangist forces and joined Franco's army. When Franco won the civil war, Arias Navarro was appointed to a series of provincial governorships before becoming Director General of security in 1957, renowned for his harsh dealings with enemies of the regime. He was appointed Minister of the Interior in Carrero Blanco's government of 1973. When Carrero Blanco was assassinated by terrorists in December 1973, Arias Navarro succeeded him as Prime Minister. He was faced with the difficult task of promoting a gradual political liberalisation to ensure a peaceful transfer of executive power from the failing Franco to King Juan Carlos. He was reappointed by King Juan Carlos after Franco's death in 1975 but the King was critical of his slow progress in democratising Spain. Arias Navarro resigned in 1976 and retired from politics. He died on 27 November 1989.

[See also: Carrero Blanco; Franco; Juan Carlos, King; Spanish civil war*]

Ashdown, Paddy

Former leader of the British Liberal Democratic Party. Ashdown was born in New Delhi in 1941. After a career as an officer in the Royal Marines (1959–72), work for the Foreign Office and a period in private industry, he entered the House of Commons in 1983. He became leader of the Liberal Democrats in 1988, but resigned in 1999. He led the party to an astonishing electoral success in 1997, when – thanks to a successful electoral campaign focused on 'target' seats and a clear identity as an anti-Conservative party – it acquired nearly fifty MPs, more than at any time since the 1920s (though it had a slightly lower vote-share in 1997 than in 1992). Ashdown had hopes that Blair would invite him to take a cabinet post, as a symbol of cross-party co-operation, but the large size of Labour's majority dissuaded Blair from doing this. Ashdown did obtain the creation of a cabinet committee to deal with constitutional issues, upon which the

Liberals had representation, and the appointment of a Commission to examine the case for some kind of electoral reform, though it soon became clear that electoral reform would not be brought forward as Labour policy in the foreseeable future.

[See also: Blair]

Attlee, Clement

Prime Minister of the United Kingdom 1945–51; leader of the Labour Party 1935–55. Attlee was born in London in 1883, and studied at Oxford University. He became a lawyer, then a lecturer in social sciences. He served in the First World War, and was then briefly mayor of Stepney, in London. He became an MP in 1922, and served as a junior minister in the Labour governments led by Ramsay MacDonald in 1924 and 1929–31. As leader of the Labour Party during the Second World War, he was brought into Churchill's coalition cabinet. After the general election of 1945 had taken place (but before votes had been counted, a delay because of the large numbers of votes from the armed forces serving overseas), Attlee accompanied Churchill to the Potsdam conference, in case it turned out that Labour would form a government after the election results were known. Attlee's Labour government introduced an ambitious programme of radical policies, particularly implementation of welfare state provisions (including the National Health Service) outlined in the Beveridge Report, and nationalisation of public utilities such as the coal mines, railways and gas and electricity supply, as well as policies to cope with post-war reconstruction in a context of severe austerity and adjustments of Britain's international status during a period when parts of the British Empire were seeking self-rule. Attlee died in 1967.

[See also: Beveridge Report*; Potsdam conference*]

Auriol, Vincent

President of the French Fourth Republic 1947–53. Auriol was born in the Haute-Garonne in 1884. After studying law, he practised as a lawyer, entering the Parliament of the Third Republic as a Socialist deputy in 1914. He served as Finance Minister and Justice Minister in 1936–38. After internment as an opponent of Marshal Pétain and the Vichy regime, he fled to Britain in 1942 and became associated with de Gaulle's Free French group in London. After representing France at the United Nations, then serving briefly as president of the National Assembly, he was elected as first President of the new Fourth Republic in 1947. He died in 1966.

[See also: de Gaulle; Vichy regime*]

Aznar López, José María

Prime Minister of Spain since 1996. Born in 1953 in Madrid, Aznar studied law at the University Complutense of Madrid before working as a tax inspector. He joined the Alianza Popular (AP) in 1978 (the forerunner of the Partido Popular (PP)) and was elected to the Spanish Parliament in 1982. In 1987 he was elected President of the autonomous community of Castilla-León, a position he held until 1989. He has been president of the PP since 1990. He re-entered Parliament in 1989. He became Prime Minister of Spain in 1996 following the general election that year, and again following his party's successes in the general election in March 2000. He played a major role in modernising his party, enabling it to discard its Francoist legacy and bringing it electoral success. His leadership of the government has been largely responsible for Spain's economic growth in recent years. He survived a car-bomb attack by ETA terrorists in 1995.

[See also: ETA*]

Bahr, Egon

Bahr was born in 1922 in Treffurt (Thuringia). He became a journalist, and joined the West German Social Democratic Party in 1957. Bahr was given a leading foreign policy advisory role during the grand coalition, serving under Foreign Minister Brandt. When Brandt became Chancellor in 1969, Bahr became a senior negotiator of the agreements later embodied in the 'Ostpolitik' treaties with the USSR, Poland and the German Democratic Republic. Having been elected to the Bundestag in 1972, he was appointed as Minister without Portfolio 1972–74, and Minister for Overseas Development 1974–76. He served as federal business manager (the equivalent of party general secretary) of the SPD 1976–81.

[See also: Ostpolitik*]

Bahro, Rudolf

East German dissident and one of the founders of the German Green Party. Bahro was born in Bad Flinsberg in 1935, and studied philosophy at the Humboldt University in Berlin. He was a member of the SED (the East German communist party). Employed first in journalism, then as an economist in a factory, Bahro became increasingly critical of the regime of the German Democratic Republic. This criticism, based on the conclusion that the ruling party in the GDR had distorted true communism, was laid out in his book: *The Alternative*, which was published in West Germany in 1977. The decision to publish led to his arrest and Bahro was sentenced to eight years' imprisonment in 1978 on grounds of anti-socialist and subversive activity, but under an amnesty was then allowed to emigrate to the Federal Republic of Germany in 1979. There Bahro associated himself with the nascent Green movement, helping to found the Green Party in 1980, and aligning himself with the fundamentalist wing of that party. His Marxist and environmentalist beliefs led him to resign from the party in 1985 in protest at the party's failure to persist with 'pure' ecological policy positions.

[See also: Realos and Fundis*]

Balladur, Edouard

Prime Minister of France 1993–95. Balladur was born in 1929 at Smyrna in Turkey. He studied law at Aix-en-Provence and at the Paris Institute of Political Studies and graduated from the National College of Administration in 1957. In 1963 he joined the staff of Prime Minister Pompidou to advise on social and industrial relations. He was part of Pompidou's May 1968 crisis team, taking part in the Grenelle negotiations with the unions. When Pompidou became President, Balladur worked for him, becoming the Elyseé Secretary-General in 1972. After Pompidou's death in 1974, Balladur moved to the private sector. From 1980, Chirac often consulted him informally on political and economic issues. Balladur was elected a Deputy of the National Assembly on the Rassemblement pour la République (RPR) list in 1986. A supporter of 'cohabitation', he joined Prime Minister Chirac's cabinet as Minister of the Economy and Finance, taking responsibility for the government's free-market programme. Re-elected in 1988, Balladur worked to transform the alliance between the RPR and the Union pour la Démocratie Française (UDF) into a moderate conservative grouping putting forward a single presidential candidate. He was Prime Minister of France 1993–95.

[See also: Chirac; Pompidou]

Barre, Raymond

Prime Minister of France 1976–81. Barre was born on the island of Réunion in 1924. After studying political science and law at the University of Paris, he entered the civil service, became a professor at Paris University, and joined the EEC Commission as Vice-President responsible for financial and economic affairs (1967–73). In 1976 he served briefly as Minister for Foreign Trade in Chirac's government, before succeeding Chirac in August 1976 as Prime Minister, serving as his own Minister for Economics and Finance until 1978. His 'Barre Plan' sought to deal with the economic and currency problems facing France. He became Prime Minister for a second term following the general election of 1978, but resigned in 1981 following Mitterrand's election as President. He stood unsuccessfully as presidential candidate in 1988.

[See also: Chirac]

Barzel, Rainer

Leader of the West German Christian Democrats 1971–73. Born in 1924 in East Prussia, Barzel qualified as a lawyer. He was elected as a Christian Democratic candidate in the Bundestag election of 1957. He served briefly as Adenauer's Minister for All-German Affairs (1962–63). On the death of von Brentano in 1964, Barzel became leader of the Christian Democrat parliamentary party, retaining that post until he resigned in 1973. Barzel was elected as party leader in 1971, was the unsuccessful nominee for chancellor in the first ever 'constructive vote of no confidence' in 1972 and was selected as chancellor-candidate for the Christian Democrats for the 1972 Bundestag election. After resigning as party leader and leader of the parliamentary party in 1973, he returned as Minister for Inner-German Relations in Kohl's cabinet in 1982, and became Chairman of the Bundestag in 1983 (equivalent to the Speaker in the House of Commons), a post he retained until he resigned in 1984 because of his involvement in the scandal surrounding the Flick Affair.

[See also: Adenauer; constructive vote of no confidence*; Flick Affair*]

Bastian, Gerd [See: Kelly, Petra]

Baudouin, King of Belgium

King of Belgium 1951–93. Baudouin was born in 1930 in Stuyvenberg, near Brussels. Reflecting the divisions in Belgian society, his education was conducted half in French, half in Flemish. The reigning King Leopold's clumsy attempts at intervening in politics during the inter-war period caused resentment against the royal family in Belgium, and, after the Second World War, they went into exile in Switzerland. Leopold was only allowed to return to the throne in 1950 on condition that his son Baudouin take on most of his powers, becoming Prince Royal of Belgium and head of state. Leopold abdicated on 16 July 1951 in Baudouin's favour. Unlike his father, Baudouin was widely respected, particularly for his scrupulously neutral dealings with the Flemish and Walloon (French-speaking) communities and for his part in securing the country's long transition to a federal state. His reign restored faith in the monarchy in Belgium. The extent of his popularity was revealed when he caused a potential constitutional crisis in April 1989. The Belgian Parliament had passed legislation to legalise abortion, but Baudouin, childless and a staunch Catholic, could not in good conscience sign the bill. The crisis was resolved through the co-operation of the government: the Council of Ministers ruled that Baudouin was unfit to govern, giving them the right to enact the abortion measure on their own authority. The following day, Parliament was convened and Baudouin's royal powers were returned to him in full. Baudouin died on 31 July 1993 and was succeeded by his brother, Prince Albert.

Bérégovoy, Pierre

Prime Minister of France 1992–93. Bérégovoy was born in Deville-les-Rouen in 1925. He left school at 16, becoming a manual worker who eventually became Director of the national gas utility in 1978. A member of the French resistance, after the Second World War he joined the Socialist Party (SFIO), but broke with the party over his opposition to the Algerian War. A prominent member of various left-wing groups, Bérégovoy played a leading role in the Parti Socialiste (PS) as it consolidated 1969–71. One of Mitterrand's closest supporters, Bérégovoy managed the PS co-operation with the Communist Party (PCF). He failed, though, to revive the 1972 electoral pact (the Joint Programme for Government between the PS, PCF and left radicals) for the 1978 elections. Bérégovoy was campaign manager for Mitterrand in the Socialist presidential election victory of 1981, and again in 1988. Under Mitterrand, he was appointed Secretary-General of the President's Office, the first in the Fifth Republic not to have been a senior civil servant. As Minister of Social Affairs and National Solidarity (1982–84), he improved the social security system and as Minister of Finance (1984–86), he modernised the financial markets and implemented the Socialists' policy of economic austerity. After the 1988 campaign, he returned as Minister of Finance under the Rocard government, becoming Prime Minister in 1992. When the PS suffered a major defeat in the parliamentary election of 1993, Bérégovoy was replaced by Edouard Balladur. Bérégovoy was implicated in a minor financial scandal concerning the personal use of campaign funds. Blaming himself for the Socialist Party's parliamentary defeat, he committed suicide on 1 May 1993.

[See also: Balladur; Mitterrand; Rocard; Resistance groups*]

Berlinguer, Enrico

Former leader of the Italian Communist Party (PCI). Berlinguer was born in Sardinia in 1922. He led the PCI at the height of its 'eurocommunist' phase. Since the Second World War, the PCI had been marginalised in Italian politics through the successful tactics of its rival, the Christian Democratic DC. The PCI had retreated into a stance of fundamental opposition and alignment with the Soviet Union. After the Soviet invasion of Hungary in 1956, though, the party adopted an independent, eurocommunist position which aimed to achieve socialism within the existing form of regime. Berlinguer in 1973 adopted the strategy of 'historic compromise', aiming to establish the PCI as a mainstream party. The strategy culminated in the agreement in 1976 to tolerate DC Prime Minister Andreotti's coalition government, but was abandoned in 1980 after anticipated electoral gains had failed to materialise. Berlinguer died in 1984.

[See also: Andreotti; eurocommunism*; historic compromise*]

Berlusconi, Silvio

Berlusconi, controversial politician and businessman, leader of the Italian party Forza Italia (FI). He became Prime Minister of Italy in 1994 and again in June 2001. Born in Milan in 1936, Berlusconi studied at the University of Milan before embarking on a successful business career. Starting with a building and property development business at the age of 26, his business empire came to span commercial TV, the printed media, publishing, advertising, insurance and financial services, retailing and football (through AC Milan

football club). In 1993 he formed the populist, right-wing political movement FI and began a full-time political career in 1994, leading his party to win the general elections of that year in alliance with the separatist Northern League and far-right National Alliance. As Prime Minister of this coalition government (called the 'Freedom Pole') in 1994 he broke with standard conventions of liberal democracy. The coalition terminated through inter-party disagreements at the end of 1994, and Berlusconi became leader of the opposition. In 1996 he was charged with fraud, bribery of tax officials and illegal party financing and in 1998 was sentenced to over five years' imprisonment for these offences. On 9 May 2000 various convictions on charges of bribery were overturned on appeal. He became Prime Minister again following the general election in May 2001, when his party formed a coalition with the Northern Alliance and Northern League.

[See also: Northern Leagues*]

Bevan, Aneurin

Minister of Health 1945–51 and Minister of Labour 1951; deputy leader of the Labour Party (1959–60). Bevan, son of a Welsh coalminer, was born in Tredegar in 1897, and worked as a coalminer from the age of 13. He became an active trade unionist, leading the Welsh miners during the 1926 general strike. He was first elected to Parliament in 1929 as an Independent Labour Party candidate. He joined the Labour Party in 1931. He was frequently in trouble with the party leadership because of his outspoken left-wing views, and was expelled briefly from the party in 1939 and resigned as Minister of Labour in 1951, along with Harold Wilson, over Chancellor of the Exchequer Gaitskell's imposition of charges within the National Health Service (of which Bevan had been the principal founder in 1948).

In opposition, Bevan was the standard-bearer of the left wing in the party, and his followers acquired the name of 'Bevanites', seeking to reduce defence expenditure and expand social services, though Bevan himself renounced unilateral disarmament in a speech at the party conference of 1957. He sought the party leadership in 1955, but was defeated by Gaitskell. He died in 1960.

[See also: Gaitskell; Wilson]

Bevin, Ernest

Trade union leader and Labour Party minister during and after the Second World War. Bevin was born in Somerset in 1881, and became a trade union official, then creator and General-Secretary (1921–40) of the Transport and General Workers' Union (a federation of numerous smaller separate trade unions). Bevin was a leading organiser of the general strike in 1926. In 1940 Churchill invited him to join the all-party war cabinet, as minister responsible for employment and national service. Attlee selected him as his Foreign Secretary in the Labour government of 1945–51, during which period he coped capably with the many challenges of post-war diplomacy and the Cold War. He was regarded as a stalwart of the moderate centre of the Labour Party, attracting the scorn of left-wingers as a result. Bevin died in 1951.

[See also: Attlee; Churchill]

Bildt, Carl

Prime Minister of Sweden, 1991–94 and international statesman. Bildt was born in 1949 in Halmstad. He studied at the University of Stockholm and was Chairman of the Confederation of Liberal and Conservative Students 1973–74 and of the European Democratic Students 1974–76. He worked as an adviser on policy co-ordination for the Swedish Ministry of Economic Affairs 1976–78 and with the cabinet office 1979–81. He joined the executive committee of the conservative Moderate Party (MP) in 1981 and was the party's Chairman from 1986 to 1999. He successfully led the moderate coalition in the elections of 1991 and replaced Social Democrat Carlsson as Prime Minister. Sweden was renowned for the highly developed welfare state which had been promoted under Social Democratic rule, but Bildt stood for rolling back the state, reducing taxation and government interference in private enterprise. He also pressed for Sweden to join the European Union (EU). He became EU peace envoy to the former Yugoslavia in 1995 and acted as High Representative of the International Community in Bosnia and Herzegovina 1995–97. He was Vice-Chairman of the International Democrat Union 1989–92 and Chairman 1992–99. In 1999 he was appointed Special Envoy of the Secretary-General of the United Nations to the Balkans.

Blair, Tony

British Prime Minister since 1997 and leader of the British Labour Party. Blair was born in Edinburgh in 1953, studied at Oxford University and qualified as a lawyer. He entered Parliament in 1983, and was appointed to a shadow cabinet position responsible for employment policy by Neil Kinnock in 1988; he later became opposition spokesman for home affairs. On the death of John Smith, he became a candidate for the party leadership in 1994, and was elected by a large margin. In the period between his election as leader and the general election in 1997, Blair made radical changes to the organisation of the party, making it a more centralised and efficiently managed organisation, and improving dramatically its public relations performance. He also did all he could to rid the party – which he referred to as 'new Labour' – of those aspects of its policy likely to arouse distrust among uncommitted voters; this involved the abandonment of Clause Four of the party's constitution, which committed the party to nationalisation of 'the means of production and exchange'. Labour's overwhelming victory (in terms of seats, though not in terms of vote-share) in the 1997 election made Blair's position as leader totally secure, despite continuing criticism from a minority of socialists within the party. In government, he has introduced a number of major constitutional changes, ranging from the introduction of elected assemblies for Scotland and Wales and a directly elected mayor for London to removal in stages of the hereditary peers from the House of Lords. His government's economic policies, implemented by Gordon Brown as Chancellor of the Exchequer, have been conservative and have produced large public sector surpluses. He has made statements expressing commitment to European integration and favours eventual British membership of the European currency project, provided economic conditions permit this. Blair has been criticised for seeking to exercise control over the party at the expense of democratic choice by members, in matters such as selection of the candidate for mayor of London and leadership of the Labour Party group in the Welsh Assembly. He has also diluted several conventional practices connected with cabinet government, such as using cabinet meetings less than his predecessors, and he attends the House of Commons very infrequently. He led his party to another sweeping general election victory in 2001. He played a significant international role in the diplomatic and military developments following the 11 September 2001 attack by terrorists on New York.

[See also: Kinnock; Smith; Clause Four*]

Bohley, Bärbel

Campaigner active in the citizen movement during the fall of the GDR regime. Bohley was born in Berlin in 1945. She became an artist in the GDR. Her activities as a peace campaigner brought her into conflict with the authorities, leading on two occasions to her arrest and then to her expulsion from the GDR. Pressure from her associates in West Germany led to revocation of that expulsion. During the period of crisis for the communist regime in Autumn 1989, Bohley was among those instrumental in founding New Forum, the best known of the new groups which tried to provide a structure for discussion within the burgeoning citizen movement. The pace of events in the GDR in 1989–90 tended to force the citizen movement to the margins of the political process, and Bohley became an opponent of the rush to reunification, arguing for a 'third way' which would produce a democratic but socialist form of state within the GDR.

[See also: reunification of Germany*]

Böll, Heinrich

German author and political campaigner. Böll was born in Cologne in 1917. After the Second World War he became renowned for his novels and short stories, dealing with life in the Nazi period, the war and the post-war years. He was awarded the Nobel Prize for Literature in 1972. Böll's fame enabled him to publicise his views on political matters such as the radicals' decree and what he regarded as the revival of militarism in the Federal Republic of Germany. His commitment to the protection of the persecuted was demonstrated by his welcome to Solzhenitsyn when that author left the Soviet Union in 1974. Böll died in 1985.

[See also: nazism*; radicals' decree*]

87 BIOGRAPHIES

Bossi, Umberto

Leader of the Italian party, the Lombardy League, then of the Northern League. Born in 1941 in Varese, Bossi studied at Pavia University. He co-founded the Lombardy Autonomy League in 1982 and has led the party (which changed its name to Lombardy League) since 1984. He was elected as a Senator in 1987 and has been leader of the Federation of Northern League Movements from 1989. In 1991 he played a leading part in creating the Northern League from five regional parties, and became its leader. He served as minister responsible for reform and devolution in Berlusconi's coalition government in 1994, one of five Northern League ministers in that government. Personal and political disagreements between Bossi and Berlusconi led to the break-up of that coalition at the end of 1994. In 1995 he called for the secession of the northern area of Italy to form a new state called: 'Padania'. He rejoined Berlusconi in the new coalition formed in 2001. In 1995 he was sentenced to five months' imprisonment for libel and eight months' for illegal party financing.

[See also: Northern Leagues*]

Brandt, Willy

Chancellor of the FRG 1969–74 and leader of the SPD 1964–87. Brandt (born as Herbert Frahm) was born in Lübeck in 1913. He joined the SPD in 1930, and then the Socialist Workers' Party – which had broken away from the SDP – in 1931. When Hitler came to power in 1933 Brandt fled to Norway, assuming the name 'Willy Brandt' which he was to retain after the war, and spent the war in that country and Sweden, studying history and law and working as a journalist, reporting for a time on the Spanish civil war. Having rejoined the SPD in 1947, Brandt was elected to the Bundestag in 1949 and remained a Member until 1957, then again from 1969 to 1992. He was elected to the Berlin city legislature in 1950 and became lord mayor of West Berlin in 1957, a post he held until 1966, including the period of the erection of the Berlin Wall. He was chancellor-candidate of the SPD in the federal elections of 1961 and 1965. After a period as Deputy Chancellor and Foreign Minister in the grand coalition (1966–69), Brandt was again chancellor-candidate of his party in 1969, and because after that election the FDP preferred to ally with the SPD rather than the CDU, Brandt was elected as Chancellor. He pursued a very active policy of improvement of relations with the Soviet Union, the GDR and other East European states, in contrast to the policies of the Adenauer government. Having survived the first ever constructive vote of no confidence in the Bundestag in 1972, Brandt led his party to victory in the Bundestag election later that year. He resigned as Chancellor in 1974 following the Guillaume Affair, but remained as party leader. He had been awarded the Nobel Peace Prize in 1971 for his Ostpolitik achievements, and went on to take an active role in several international organisations, including the Socialist International. He served for a period as a Member of the European Parliament, and was Chairman of the Independent Commission on International Development Issues (the Brandt Commission) which produced reports on the North–South divide and other 'third world' issues. Brandt died on 9 November 1992.

[See also: Adenauer; Hitler; Berlin Wall*; Guillaume Affair*; Hallstein Doctrine*; Ostpolitik*; Spanish civil war*]

Brundtland, Gro Harlem

Norwegian Prime Minister February–October 1981; 1986–89; 1990–96 and leading international politician. Born in Oslo in 1939,

Brundtland studied medicine at the Universities of Oslo and Harvard. She acted as a consultant to the Norwegian Ministry of Health and Social Affairs 1965–67, was medical officer for Oslo city health department 1968–69 and Deputy Director of Oslo's school health service in 1969. Minister of the Environment 1974–79, she was deputy leader of the Labour Party 1975–81 and leader of the parliamentary party group 1981–92. In 1981, she became Norway's first woman Prime Minister. During her first two periods in office, she introduced several controversial economic reforms to reduce Norway's budget deficit. She became active internationally as a leading spokeswoman on the environment, the equality of women, and international co-operation. Her report as Chair of the UN World Commission on the Environment and Development (1987) established the concept of sustainable growth. She was a leading figure in the 1995 UN womens' conference in China, and was appointed Director-General of the WHO in 1998. A pro-European, she was unable to mobilise the majority of Norwegians to agree to entry of the EU, but remains a popular leader.

Callaghan, James

British Prime Minister 1976–79. Callaghan was born in Portsmouth in 1912. He became a civil servant, and was elected to the House of Commons in 1945. He failed in his attempt to be elected as Labour Party leader in 1963, following the death of Gaitskell. He was appointed as Chancellor of the Exchequer, Home Secretary and Foreign Secretary by Wilson in the period 1964–76 (one of the few politicians ever to hold all three of these leading ministerial positions). Following Wilson's resignation in 1976, Callaghan was elected as party leader and thus became Wilson's successor as Prime

Minister. The Labour government lost its small majority due to defeats in by-elections, and Callaghan had to negotiate with, first, the Liberals, then the Scottish and Welsh Nationalists and Northern Irish MPs, to retain a majority over the Conservative opposition. He was Prime Minister during the 'winter of discontent' when strikes plagued the British economy. That, and his misjudgement concerning the timing of the general election, are generally held to have contributed to the heavy defeat of his party in the 1979 general election. He continued as party leader and thus as leader of the opposition only until 1980, when he was replaced by Kinnock. He became a member of the House of Lords in 1980.

[See also: Gaitskell; Kinnock; Wilson; Lib–Lab pact*; winter of discontent*]

Carrero Blanco, Luis

Prime Minister of Spain June–December 1973. Carrero Blanco was born in Santona in 1903. He graduated from the Spanish naval academy, becoming an ensign in 1922, a lieutenant in 1926 and later a submarine commander. He joined the staff of the naval academy in 1934 and in 1966 was promoted to admiral. He joined the Nationalist navy during the Spanish civil war and in 1939 became Franco's chief of naval operations. He was appointed Under-Secretary to the presidency of the government in 1941 and became Vice-President of the Parliament, the Cortes, in 1942. In 1951 he joined Franco's cabinet and was a trusted adviser throughout the 1950s and 1960s, serving as Deputy Prime Minister from 1968, and was viewed as the likely successor to Franco. He favoured changes in the regime which would restore the monarchy, though he did not favour political reform of a democratic type. In 1973, when a new constitution was introduced in Spain, Franco kept the presidency, but handed his powers as head of government to Carrero Blanco. On 20 December 1973 Carrero Blanco was killed in a car-bomb attack, believed to have been carried out by ETA, the Basque separatist organisation. His death made political reform in Spain more likely.

[See also: Franco; ETA*]

Carrillo, Santiago

Leader of the Spanish Communist Party (CP), 1960–82 and of the United Communists (UC) since 1985. Born in 1915 in Gijón, Carrillo became leader of the United Socialist Youth in 1936. Having close links to the Italian Communist Party, Carillo tried to introduce their ideas of eurocommunism to his party, with some success. A member of the Congress of Deputies from 1977, he was expelled from the Communist Party in 1985, becoming President of the United Communists in the same year, a party which became absorbed in the PSOE. He left politics in 1993, and has since published his memoirs and several other books.

[See also: eurocommunism*]

Carstens, Karl

CDU politician and President of the Federal Republic of Germany 1979–84. Carstens was born in Bremen in 1914. He studied law and political science in Germany, France and the USA. After service in the army in the Second World War he practised law and served the Bremen government. He followed this with a period as a professor combined with diplomatic service. He was appointed as State Secretary, first in the Defence Ministry in 1967, then in the Chancellor's Office from 1968 to 1969. He was elected to the Bundestag in 1972, and became parliamentary leader of the Christian Democrats in 1973 until his election as President of the Bundestag in 1976. He then served a

single term as federal President, during which he became noted for his plan to walk – in stages and accompanied by local citizens – the length of the Federal Republic from the Danish border to the Lake of Constance. He died in 1992.

Chaban-Delmas, Jacques

A leading Gaullist figure in post-war French politics and Prime Minister of France 1969–72. Born Jacques Delmas in 1915 in Paris, he studied law and politics and worked as a journalist for the Radical Socialist economic daily *L'Information* before fighting in the Italian campaign. From 1941 to 1943 he worked in the Ministry of Industrial Production and joined the resistance, afterwards adopting 'Chaban', his resistance pseudonym, as part of his surname. He became the national military delegate of de Gaulle's provisional government and was closely involved in the liberation of Paris. After a brief association with the Radical Party, in 1947 he joined the Gaullist Rassemblement du Peuple Français (RPF). He served as Minister of Public Works, Transport and Tourism; Minister of State and Defence Minister. Following the upheavals of 1968, in 1969 Pompidou appointed Chaban-Delmas as Prime Minister to try to stabilise the situation. Chaban-Delmas formed a government which included two members of the social democratic opposition. He promised his government would create a 'new society' in France, setting out to reduce the inequalities and rigidity of French society through progressive social measures including more effective collective bargaining and the liberalisation of government, particularly in public sector broadcasting. However, Chaban-Delmas' initiative failed to integrate the more hard-line Gaullists and the parties of the left. Pompidou increasingly came to see Chaban-Delmas as irresponsible and in danger of alienating conservative support for the party. Relations between President and Prime Minister deteriorated and in 1972 Pompidou was furious when Chaban-Delmas called (and won) a parliamentary vote of confidence on his own initiative. Six weeks later, the President dismissed him. Chaban-Delmas at first appeared to be consolidating his position as a future leader of the Gaullist party, but in the presidential election of 1974 he lost heavily to his rival, Giscard d'Estaing, and withdrew to his provincial stronghold of Bordeaux, allowing Chirac to take over leadership of the Gaullists. He continued to figure large in parliamentary politics (he was three times President of the National Assembly), but did not regain a party leadership role.

[See also: Chirac; de Gaulle; Giscard d'Estaing; Pompidou; resistance groups*]

Chirac, Jacques

Prime Minister of France 1974–76; 1986–88 and President of France 1995–. Chirac was born in 1932 in Paris and studied at the Paris Institute of Political Studies. After active service in Algeria, he graduated from the National College of Administration in 1959. During the early part of his political career, Chirac was appointed to Prime Minister Pompidou's staff and forged close links with him. His ministerial career spanned employment (1967–68); finance (1968–71); relations with Parliament (at which he was not judged a success, having little interest in Parliament) (1971–72); agriculture (1972–73; 1973–74) and the interior (1974). He was instrumental in Giscard d'Estaing's nomination as Gaullist presidential candidate in 1974 and was rewarded by Giscard with the post of Prime Minister. Giscard and Chirac soon clashed personally and over policy and in 1976, following Giscard's refusal to dissolve the Parliament and hold fresh elections,

Chirac resigned. Chirac then became party leader of the new Gaullist Rassemblement pour la Republique (RPR), a post which he held until 1994. He was elected mayor of Paris (1977–95), an important power base. After his resignation as Prime Minister, Chirac worked to undermine Giscard. In the presidential elections of 1981, he split the right by standing against Giscard, consolidating his reputation for being divisive and ambitious. During Mitterrand's first presidency, Chirac was effectively leader of the opposition in France. When the right won a narrow majority in the parliamentary elections of 1986, Mitterrand called on Chirac to form a 'cohabitation' government to work in tandem with his Socialist presidency. France's poor economic performance during Chirac's premiership (1986–88) hampered him in the presidential race of 1988, again won by Mitterrand. Chirac finally succeeded in his ambition to become President in 1995. He resumed a Gaullist foreign policy in launching nuclear testing at Mururoa and through adopting a Eurosceptic stance. His economic policy had two central but conflicting aims: to fight unemployment and to reduce the budget deficit. Chirac's popularity plummetted during his first year as President, but he was able to shift much of the blame for his policies onto his Prime Minister, Juppé. He made a political blunder by calling an early general election, which the Socialists won, forcing Chirac to govern in cohabitation with Prime Minister Jospin.

[See also: Giscard d'Estaing; Mitterrand; Pompidou; Algerian conflict*]

Churchill, Winston

British Prime Minister 1940–45 and 1951–55. Churchill was born at Blenheim Palace in 1874. He took up a military career after training at Sandhurst military college. He was elected to Parliament as a Conservative in 1900, but switched to the Liberal Party in 1906, and held various ministerial posts, including Home Secretary and First Lord of the Admiralty, a post he resigned following the failed Dardanelles military landings in 1915. Churchill served in the army in France until, in 1917, Lloyd George appointed him Minister for Munitions. Changing back to the Conservatives in 1924, Churchill was Chancellor of the Exchequer 1924–29. His critical attitude towards the Baldwin and Chamberlain governments' appeasement policies towards European dictators aroused hostility towards him among the more orthodox members of his party, but when the Second World War commenced, he accepted office as First Lord of the Admiralty again. The downfall of Chamberlain in 1940 left the way open for Churchill to become Prime Minister and lead an all-party national government. After the war, this government broke up, and in the general election of 1945 Churchill, despite the accolades given him for his leadership in the war, was heavily defeated by the Labour Party. He returned as Prime Minister in 1951, but was by then ageing and unwell. He was persuaded to retire in 1955. He remained an MP until 1964. He was awarded the Nobel Prize for Literature in 1953, and was made a Knight of the Garter in that same year. On his death in 1965 he was given a state funeral.

Ciampi, Carlo

Italian Prime Minister 1993–94. Born in Livorno in 1920, Ciampi studied at the University of Pisa, and, after serving with the Italian army 1941–44, joined the Bank of Italy in 1946 and pursued a career as a research economist. He was Governor of the Bank of Italy 1979–93, after which he was asked to form a 'government of technocrats' in order to restore confidence in the collapsing parliamentary institutions while

constitutional reform was pursued. After his term as Prime Minister he served as Minister of the Treasury and the Budget in the d'Alema government (1996–98). From 1998 until 1999 he was Chairman of the IMF Interim Committee and has been a member of numerous economic institutions. In 1999 he was elected President of Italy.

[See also: Tangentopoli*]

Constantine II of Greece

Deposed King of Greece. Born in 1940 near Athens, Constantine studied law at Athens University and received military training 1956–58. He won a gold medal in the Rome 1960 Olympic Games for yachting. When his father King Paul I died in March 1964, he succeeded to the throne. Constantine had a tense relationship with the left-wing Prime Minister Georgios Papandreou and dismissed him in 1965. This launched a period of civil disorder and a vacuum in government culminating in a military coup on 21 April 1967. Constantine had little choice but to accept the military dictatorship which was imposed after the coup. He called for a return to a democratic civil regime, but, when an attempt in 1967 to topple the military government failed, he was forced to leave Greece for Rome, then London. Constantine was formally deposed on 1 June 1973. The abolition of the Greek monarchy was confirmed by popular referendum in December 1974. In 1994 Constantine was deprived of his Greek citizenship and the property he owned in Greece was nationalised.

[See also: Papandreou; Colonels' coup (Greece)*]

Cosgrave, Liam

Leader of the Irish Fine Gael (FG) party 1965–77; Prime Minister of Ireland 1973–77. Cosgrave was born in 1920 in Templeogue, County Dublin. His father was William T. Cosgrave, President of the Executive Council of the Irish Free State 1922–32. Liam Cosgrave studied in Dublin and Kings Inns and was called to the Bar in 1943, becoming a Senior Counsel in 1958. In 1943 he was elected to Parliament as a representative of the FG. He acted as Parliamentary Secretary to the Prime Minister and to the Minister for Industry and Commerce 1948–51. In 1956, as Minister for External Affairs, he led the first Irish delegation to the United Nations General Assembly. In 1965 he was elected leader of the FG and in 1973 became Prime Minister at the head of an FG–Labour coalition. He was respected as a moderate leader who tried to ease tensions between the Republic of Ireland and Northern Ireland, although his attempt to promote compromise through the Sunningdale Agreement of December 1973 met with little success. In 1977 the National Coalition government was defeated by the Fianna Fail (FF) and Cosgrave stepped down both as Prime Minister and as leader of the FG. He retired from politics in 1981.

Cossiga, Francesco

Prime Minister of Italy 1979–80; President of Italy 1985–92. Cossiga was born in 1928 in Sassari, Sardinia, and received a law degree from Sassari University in 1948. He joined the Christian Democrats (DC) in 1945, becoming a provincial secretary 1956–58 and a member of the party's national council 1956–85. In 1958 he was elected to the Chamber of Deputies. He was Under-Secretary of State for Defence 1966–70 and Minister for Public Administration 1974–76. As Minister of the Interior 1976–78 in the cabinet of Aldo Moro he had to deal with an upsurge in urban violence and political terrorism. In April 1977, his offices were bombed by radicals. In March 1978 Cossiga took charge of the investigation into the kidnapping of Aldo Moro. He refused to negotiate with the terrorists

and when Moro was murdered in May 1978, Cossiga resigned. In 1979 he agreed to form a coalition government and immediately introduced legislation to curb terrorism. He resigned as Prime Minister in March 1980 in the face of a vote of no confidence, but immediately formed another coalition government of Christian Democrats and Socialists. He resigned again in October 1980 when his economic plan to support the value of the lira was defeated in Parliament. He was President of the Italian Senate 1983–85 before being elected President of the Republic 1985–92. He was implicated in the corruption crisis which engulfed the Italian political elite in the early 1990s and resigned early in 1992.

[See also: Moro; Tangentopoli*; terrorism*]

Coty, René

As President of the Fourth French Republic 1954–59, Coty guided the peaceful transition between the Fourth and the Fifth Republics. Coty was born in Le Havre in 1882 and studied law at the University of Caen. He was elected to the National Assembly in 1923, sitting with the left Republican party group. From 1935 to 1940 he was a member of the Senate, and was amongst those who supported the transfer of powers to Pétain. After the Second World War he led the Independent party group in the National Assembly and was Minister for Reconstruction and Town Planning 1947–48. In the presidential election of 1953, it took seven days of negotiations and thirteen ballots before Coty, an outsider who entered the field only on the eleventh ballot, emerged as President. Aware of his shaky mandate, he worked to restore the dignity and unity of the parliamentary institutions, exercising his powers with restraint and adopting a conciliatory stance towards the Communist Party. In 1958, when France faced a crisis over Algerian independence and the threat of military intervention, Coty helped to secure the transition to the Fifth Republic. He threatened to resign, potentially leaving the way open for a Popular Front government, unless de Gaulle was allowed to introduce the new republic. Once the Fifth Republic was inaugurated, Coty stepped down as President in favour of de Gaulle. Coty died on 22 November 1962.

[See also: de Gaulle; Algerian conflict*; Vichy regime*]

Craxi, 'Bettino' (Benedetto)

Prime Minister of Italy 1983–87 and leader of the Italian Socialist Party. Born in 1934 in Milan, Craxi joined the Italian Socialist Youth Movement in the early 1950s and became active in the Socialist Party. He was elected to the Chamber of Deputies in 1968. He became Deputy Secretary of his party in 1970, and General Secretary in 1976 and succeeded in integrating the various factions of the party. In 1983 he became the first Socialist Italian Prime Minister. His government's austerity programme was met with a series of strikes. In October 1985, the Italian liner the Achille Lauro was hijacked by Palestinian terrorists. Craxi's government negotiated with the terrorists through the Palestinian Liberation Organisation and released the suspected organiser of the hijacking. These events caused a government crisis, but Craxi was able to stay in power until 1987. After his resignation he remained sufficiently powerful to force the resignation of several subsequent governments. He resigned as leader of the Socialist Party in February 1993 following allegations of political corruption. He fled to Tunisia and in 1994 he was sentenced in his absence to eight and a half years' imprisonment for having accepted 7 billion lire from the corrupt Milanese Banco Ambrosiano for the Socialist Party. He died in January 2000.

[See also: Tangentopoli*]

Cresson, Edith

First woman Prime Minister of France 1991–92. Born in Boulogne-sur-Seine in 1934, Cresson graduated from a prestigious Paris business school and took a doctorate in demography before beginning a career in economic investment and marketing. She was national secretary of the Socialist Party (PS) 1974–79 and was also responsible for its youth section. She was elected to the European Parliament in 1979 and to the National Assembly in 1981. She was a member of all three Mauroy cabinets: Minister for Agriculture 1981–83; Foreign Trade and Tourism 1983–84; and Industrial Restructuring and Foreign Trade 1984–86. From 1988 to 1990 she was Minister for European Affairs, famously attacking Mrs Thatcher by declaring that the EC was 'more than a glorified grocer's shop'. As Prime Minister 1991–92 she often caused offence with her rash comments and failed to promote the popularity of the PS. When the party lost support in the March 1992 parliamentary elections, she stood down. From 1994 to 1999 she was EU Commissioner for Science, Research and Development. She was deeply implicated in the scandal which brought down the commission team in 1995.

[See also: Mauroy]

Debré, Michel

Prime Minister of France 1959–62 and designer of the constitution of the Fifth French Republic. Debré was born in Paris in 1912. After studying law, he served as an officer in the Second World War, became a prisoner of war but escaped in 1940 and fled to England. Here he worked closely with de Gaulle's Free French resistance movement. He became a Senator in the Fourth Republic, and, when de Gaulle accepted the call to introduce a new constitution in 1958, Debré played a leading role in drafting that constitution.

After serving as Prime Minister, he later became Foreign Minister and Defence Minister. In 1981 he was a candidate for the presidency, but received only about 1 per cent of the vote on the first round of balloting.

[See also: de Gaulle; resistance groups*]

Delors, Jacques

French christian democrat/socialist and President of the EC/EU Commission 1985–95. Delors was born in 1925 in Paris, where he studied law and banking before joining the Bank of France in 1944. He acted as consultant in social and economic affairs in the preparation of the Fifth Plan (1962–69), a position he gained partly through his ties with the Catholic union, the CFTC. He associated briefly with the Mouvement Républicain Populaire and with socialist splinter groups before leading the Catholic Citoyen 60 club. After the social upheaval of May 1968, his vision of a less authoritarian, consensus-led mode of conducting industrial relations became more popular. In 1969, Prime Minister Chaban-Delmas, keen to promote a 'new society' in France, appointed Delors as his adviser on social affairs. In 1974, Delors joined the Socialist Party (PS) and became a supporter of Mitterrand. When Mitterrand became President in 1981, Delors was appointed Minister of Finance. He kept France in the European Monetary System (EMS), and, in the Spring of 1982, implemented an austerity programme aimed at curbing consumption to reduce the trade deficit. A second, more stringent phase adopted in March 1983 curtailed collective bargaining, particularly in the public sector. Although the government proved unpopular, Delors' performance was approved by the financial community. First elected MEP in 1979, Delors became President of the EC Commission in 1985. As President, he

engineered major changes including a restructuring of the EC's finances and agricultural policy and significant constitutional and institutional reform. Encouraged by a proactive Franco-German leadership (Mitterrand and Kohl), he moved the EC towards further integration. His efforts were consolidated in the Single European Act (SEA) and the Treaty on European Union (TEU or Maastricht Treaty). In addition to various EU posts, he has acted as special adviser on economic and social affairs to the OECD since 1999.

[See also: Chaban-Delmas; Kohl; Mitterrand; Maastricht Treaty*; Single European Act*]

Dewar, Donald

First Minister (Prime Minister) of the Scottish Executive 1999–2000. Dewar was born in Glasgow in 1937. He studied history and law at Glasgow University. Dewar was first elected as a Labour Party MP to the House of Commons in 1966, but was defeated in the 1970 general election. He returned as an MP in 1978, and became the Opposition spokesman on Scottish affairs in 1983, a post he held until 1992. He became a strong supporter of the idea of a devolved Parliament for Scotland, campaigning in favour of devolution in the unsuccessful 1979 referendum, supporting the Scottish Constitutional Convention created in 1988 which investigated ways and means of bringing about a Scottish Parliament, and managing the campaign in 1997 which produced an overwhelming majority in a referendum favouring a Scottish Parliament. When that Parliament was elected in 1999, Dewar, as leader of the largest parliamentary party group, became the First Minister and formed a coalition government with the Liberal Democrats. In 2000 he had treatment for a heart condition, and died in October 2000.

Dini, Lamberto

Leading Italian economist and 'technocratic' Prime Minister of Italy 1995–96. Dini was born in 1931 in Florence and studied at the Universities of Florence, Minnesota and Michigan. He became an economist with the IMF in Washington and took various consultancy posts before joining the Bank of Italy, first, in 1979, as Assistant General Manager, then as General Manager. He was a member of the Monetary Committee of the EU. He was Minister of the Treasury 1994–95, Prime Minister 1995–96 and Minister of Foreign Affairs 1996–2000. In spite of a bitterly divided Parliament in the wake of Berlusconi's failed government of 1994, Dini was able to find majorities to pass a new budget in March 1995 and a significant pension reform to introduce a new system of benefits by 2008. However, he was not able to pass anti-cartel laws directed against Berlusconi's control of the media: the measure was rejected by referendum by 57 per cent of the vote. He resigned as Prime Minister under growing pressure from the established parties, but formed a new party: the centrist Italian Renewal Party, shortly before the 1996 general election, and became a prominent member of Prodi's 'Olive Tree' coalition government in 1996.

[See also: Berlusconi; Prodi; Tangentopoli*]

Duncan Smith, Iain

Leader of the Conservative Party since 2001. Duncan Smith was born in Edinburgh in 1954 and educated at Sandhurst, following which he became an army officer, then a business executive. He was first elected to the House of Commons in 1992. He established a reputation within the party for his outspoken opposition to further developments in European integration, and especially British entry into the single European currency scheme. He was appointed by Hague in 1997 as opposition spokesman for social security policy. In the leadership election in 2001, he rather surprisingly obtained more votes from Conservative MPs than Portillo, and competed successfully against Clarke in the membership ballot among the top two contenders.

[See also: Hague]

Dutschke, Rudi

Leading figure in the German student movement, especially in the late 1960s. Dutschke was born in Schönefeld near Luckenwalde (south of Berlin) in 1940. As a conscientious objector in the GDR he was excluded from higher education, so moved to West Berlin to study sociology. As a leading member of the left-wing Socialist German Student Association (SDS), he organised demonstrations in the late 1960s, including a protest demonstration against the visit of the Shah of Iran in 1967, against the grand coalition and its policies and against what the SDS perceived to be undemocratic dominance in universities and other institutions by elites. In April 1968 Dutschke was shot by an assassin, and for a time his life was in danger. He made a recovery, eventually finding employment at Aarhus University (Denmark). He supported the founding of the Green Party in Germany. Dutschke died in 1979 from the effects of his gunshot injuries.

[See also: extra-parliamentary opposition*]

Eanes, General António

An army officer, General Eanes was President of Portugal 1976–86. Eanes was born in 1935 in Alcains. He studied psychology and law before military training in 1953. He was commissioned to Portuguese India 1958–60; Mozambique 1962–64, 1966–67;

Portuguese Guinea 1969–73; and Angola 1973–74. He became a General in 1978. After the April Revolution he was named to the first 'Ad hoc' Committee for mass media in June 1974 and subsequently to other media posts, but resigned after accusations of 'probable implication' in the abortive counter-coup of March 1975. He was later cleared of this charge. He was a member of the Military Committee of the Council of the Revolution and was responsible for the Constitutional Law approved in December 1975. In addition to the presidency, Eanes was Commander-in-Chief of the Armed Force 1976–80, 1980–81. After his presidency, he led the Portuguese Democratic Renewal Party 1986–87.

Eden, Anthony

British Prime Minister and Conservative Party leader 1955–57. Eden was born in 1897 in Durham. After studying at Oxford, he was awarded the Military Cross during his service in the First World War. He was first elected to the House of Commons in 1923. After holding junior ministerial posts, he was appointed Foreign Secretary in 1935. Disagreements with Prime Minister Chamberlain, especially concerning the need actively to resist aggression by Italy in Abyssinia, caused Eden to resign from the cabinet in 1938. Eden became Dominions Secretary in Chamberlain's government when the Second World War commenced in 1939. Churchill appointed him in 1940 as Secretary of State for War, then as Foreign Secretary, which involved Eden closely in the war-time conferences with the USA and USSR. When Churchill returned as Prime Minister in 1951, Eden became Foreign Secretary for the third time, and was the recognised successor-in-waiting to the aged and ailing Churchill. He became Prime Minister when Churchill resigned in 1955, but in 1956 became embroiled in the Suez crisis, which led to his humiliation as Prime Minister and to divisions within his party. He resigned as Prime Minister on grounds of ill-health in January 1957. He became Earl of Avon in 1961. He died in 1977.

[See also: Churchill; Suez crisis*]

Eichmann, Karl Adolf

Nazi war criminal responsible for administration of the Holocaust. Eichmann was born in Solingen in 1906. He joined the Nazi Party in 1932 and was recruited to the SS (state security service). As a high-level bureaucrat with experience in managing anti-Jewish policies in Vienna, he attended the Wannsee conference which planned the so-called 'final solution' and was in charge of administration of this policy of eliminating Jews in Europe by murder in concentration camps. Escaping from American custody after the war, he fled to Argentina, but a group of so-called 'Nazi hunters' located his residence there in 1960 and he was kidnapped by Israeli security agents, transported to Israel and put on trial. Found guilty of crimes against the Jewish people, he was sentenced to death and executed in 1962.

[See also: anti-Semitism*; final solution*; Holocaust*; nazism*]

Engholm, Björn

Prime Minister of Schleswig-Holstein, 1988–93 and leader of the West German Social Democratic Party 1991–93. Engholm was born in Lübeck in 1939. He had been a Member of the Bundestag, and, briefly, a minister in Helmut Schmidt's coalition government. Engholm was a popular politician, who seemed set to become chancellor-candidate for the SPD for the 1994 Bundestag election. However, his admission that he had given false evidence to an inquiry into the Barschel Affair led to his resignation from party and public office in 1993. He was

replaced as SPD leader by Rudolf
Scharping.

[See also: Scharping; Schmidt;
Barschel Affair*]

Eppelmann, Rainer

Dissident and leading eastern German
politician during German reunification
(1989–90). Eppelmann was born in
Berlin in 1943. After his trade
apprenticeship he was jailed as a
conscientious objector. He studied
theology and became a leading pacifist
and critic of the German Democratic
Republic (GDR). As a pastor, he housed
meetings for opponents of the regime
in his East Berlin church. He was
co-founder of the political movement:
Democratic Renewal (Demokratische
Aufbruch) and represented it at the
Round Table talks on constitutional and
political reform which took place in late
1989 and early 1990 under the Modrow
government. From February 1990 he
was Minister without Portfolio in the
Modrow cabinet. When the leader of
Democratic Renewal, Wolfgang Schnur,
resigned over alleged links with the
GDR state security police (Stasi), he
was replaced by Eppelmann.
Eppelmann was Minister for
Disarmament and Defence in the de
Maizière cabinet in 1990 following the
parliamentary elections. He became a
member of the CDU when Democratic
Renewal was merged with the CDU
shortly before reunification, and took a
leading role in the CDU employees'
organisation. He chaired committees of
inquiry into past events in the GDR. He
has been a Member of the Bundestag
since 1990.

[See also: de Maizière; Modrow;
reunification of Germany*; Round
Table*; Stasi*]

Erhard, Ludwig

Chancellor of the Federal Republic of
Germany 1963–66. Erhard was born in

1897 in Fürth (Bavaria). Prior to and
during the Second World War he
directed an economics research
institute. In 1944 he produced a scheme
for the economic recovery of post-war
Germany based on the notion of a
social market economy, a combination
of the free market and welfare state
provisions, which guided West German
economic policy after the war. After the
war he was appointed as Professor of
Economics at Munich University, served
as Bavarian Minister for Industry in
1945–46 and became Economic Director
in the Bizone Economic Council
Executive in 1948. In this post he
implemented the currency reform of
1948, designed to produce a stable
currency and eliminate the black
market in the western zones of
occupation. He was elected to the
Bundestag in 1949, and became Minister
of Economics in Adenauer's
government, serving in that post until he
succeeded Adenauer as Federal
Chancellor in 1963. His skills as an
economist and administrator, though
earning him the title of 'Father of the
Economic Miracle', did not benefit him
in election campaigns, and the failure of
the CDU–CSU to do as well as expected
in the 1965 Bundestag election left
Erhard in a vulnerable position. When
the Free Democrats forced a coalition
crisis in 1966 over taxation policy,
Erhard was forced to resign as
Chancellor, and was replaced by
Kiesinger. Erhard succeeded Adenauer
briefly as leader of the Christian
Democratic Union (1966–67). Erhard
died in 1977.

[See also: Adenauer; Kiesinger;
economic miracle*; social market
economy*]

Erlander, Tage

Prime Minister of Sweden 1946–69.
Erlander was born in Ransäter in 1901.
He entered the Swedish Parliament
(Riksdag) in 1933 as a Social Democrat,

and rapidly rose to become a member of the cabinet in 1944. In 1946 he was elected as party leader and became Prime Minister. His main achievement was the development of Sweden's welfare state system. He emphasised consensus in his relations with other parties, which enabled many of his policies to be adopted without much political controversy. He defended the policy of neutrality for Sweden, but combined this with internationalism expressed through generous foreign aid and Swedish membership in the European Free Trade Association.

Fabius, Laurent

Prime Minister of France 1984–86, the youngest to hold this office since Decazes in 1815. Fabius was born in Paris in 1946 and studied there at the Institute of Political Studies and at the National College of Administration. In 1973 he joined the Council of State, France's highest administrative tribunal, becoming Master of Petitions in 1981. In 1974 he joined the Socialist Party (PS) and rose rapidly from economic adviser to Mitterrand in 1975 to First Secretary of the party, and, in 1976, Director of Mitterrand's advisory staff. Together with Jospin, Fabius worked to secure Mitterrand's power base within the party. In 1978, Fabius became PS parliamentary spokesman on budgetary matters, and, in 1981, Minister for the Budget. His reflationary budget of 1982 aimed to implement the series of social and economic reforms proposed by the Socialist–Communist coalition. In March 1983, Fabius was promoted to the flagship 'superministry' of Research, Industry and Telecommunications, intended to mastermind France's 'third industrial revolution'. When Mauroy resigned as Prime Minister in 1984, Mitterrand replaced him with Fabius, who introduced the surprisingly successful austerity programme. Popular with the public, Fabius clashed with

rivals in the party, and also with Mitterrand. He was criticised for his pragmatism and viewed as not being a true socialist: he was dubbed the 'Giscard of the left'. Lacking an independent political power base, Fabius lost public profile when the right regained the government in 1986. He failed to gain the leadership of the PS during the election year of 1988 and his selection as President of the National Assembly in that year was understood as a consolation prize. He was briefly First Secretary of the PS (1992–93) and led the PS party group in the National Assembly 1995–97.

[See also: Giscard d'Estaing; Jospin; Mauroy; Mitterrand]

Fini, Gianfranco

Leader of the right-wing National Alliance party in Italy, and Deputy Prime Minister in Berlusconi's government. Fini was born in Bologna in 1952, and studied education and psychology at university. He played a leading role in Italy's neo-fascist youth group (the Fronte della Gioventú) and was elected to Parliament for the neo-fascist Italian Social Movement (MSI) in 1983. He became leader of that party in 1987, but, because of problems affecting that party, decided to form a new party in 1994: the National Alliance (AN), which took a more moderate and orthodox political stance than had the MSI. That same year the AN joined in Berlusconi's coalition government, and it also became a partner in Berlusconi's 2001 coalition government.

[See also: Berlusconi]

Finnbogadóttir, Vigdís

President of Iceland 1980–96. Finnbogadóttir was born in 1930 in Reykjavik and studied at the Universities of Iceland, Grenoble and the Sorbonne before becoming a French teacher. She became involved in the Icelandic tourist industry, was Director of the Reykjavik Theatre Company 1972–80 and taught French drama at the University of Iceland. In politics, she was first a Member, then Chair, of the Advisory Committee on Cultural Affairs in the Nordic countries 1976–80 before becoming President of Iceland 1980–96.

Fischer, Joschka

Foreign Minister of Germany, and leading personality in the Green Party. Fischer was born in Gerabronn in 1948. He was one of the more notorious radicals of the '1968 movement'. He joined the Green Party in 1982, as it was first developing into a national political force. In 1985 he became Minister for the Environment in the Hesse Land government, in what was the first Land coalition government in which the Green Party had participated. He retained that office until 1987, and was again Minister for the Environment in the second SPD–Green Party coalition in Hesse, from 1991 to 1994. He had been a Member of the Bundestag 1983–85, and was again elected to the Bundestag in 1994. In the period 1987–94 he was a Member of the Hesse Land Parliament. Fischer was always seen to be a supporter of a more pragmatic policy for the Green Party: one of the 'Realos'. He was the most widely recognised personality in that party, certainly since the death of Petra Kelly. When the SPD formed a governing coalition after the 1998 Bundestag election, Fischer became Foreign Minister and Deputy Chancellor. His policies whilst in office have sometimes met with strong disapproval from elements within his own party, such as his support for German military participation in peacekeeping in areas of the former Yugoslavia. In 2001 allegations concerning his radical activities in the early 1970s cast a shadow over his position in the Schröder government.

[See also: Kelly; Realos and Fundis*]

Fitzgerald, Garret

Leading Irish and EU politician and economist, leader of the Fine Gael (FG) party 1977–87 and Prime Minister of Ireland 1981–82, 1982–87. Fitzgerald was born in 1926 in Dublin, where he graduated in law from University College. From 1947 to 1958 he worked as a manager for Aer Lingus before taking up posts in political economy at Dublin University 1958–73. He was a member of the Irish Senate (Seanad Éireann) 1965–69, then of the lower house (Dáil Éireann) for Dublin South-East 1969–92. He was Minister for Foreign Affairs 1973–77 before first becoming Prime Minister (Taoiseach) in 1981. During this period in office he set up an Inter-Governmental Council on Northern Ireland with the UK Prime Minister, Margaret Thatcher. His coalition government with the Labour Party fell when its budget was defeated in 1982, and fresh elections gave power to the opposition, the Fianna Fail (FF). Fitzgerald led the FG from 1977 to 1987. He again became Prime Minister in December 1982. On 15 November 1985 he signed the Anglo-Irish Agreement with Thatcher. This gave the Republic a consultative role in Northern Ireland for the first time, while recognising the right of the majority in Northern Ireland to decide the political allegiance of the province. With respect to domestic policy, Fitzgerald failed to reduce government spending or bring down the rate of unemployment and barely survived a no-confidence motion in October 1986. His government collapsed, again over the budget, in January 1987, and Fitzgerald promptly resigned from the leadership of FG. He has held numerous national and international positions relating to economics and in association with the EU. While Minister for Foreign Affairs, he was President of the Council of Ministers of the EEC January–June 1975. He was a leading figure in the

European People's Party of the European Parliament. He has been active as a political journalist, working for the BBC, the *Financial Times*, *The Economist* and the *Irish Times*.

[See also: Thatcher]

Foot, Michael

Leader of the British Labour Party 1980–83. Foot was born in Plymouth in 1913. Educated at Oxford University, he became a journalist noted for his left-wing views. He was first elected to the House of Commons in 1960 and became a minister in the 1974 Wilson government. He was leader of the House of Commons 1976–79. He was elected deputy leader of the Labour Party in 1976, and then leader in succession to Callaghan in 1980. His left-wing views were blamed for the heavy defeat of the Labour Party in the 1983 general election, after which Foot resigned as party leader. He has always been associated with pacifist causes, in particular the Campaign for Nuclear Disarmament.

[See also: Callaghan; Wilson; Campaign for Nuclear Disarmament*]

Fraga Iribarne, Manuel

Leader of the former Spanish party Alianza Popular (AP) (now Partido Popular (PP)) 1979–86, 1989–90 and a leading writer and diplomat. Fraga was born in 1922 in Villalba, Lugo and studied at the Universities of Santiago and Madrid before becoming a Professor at the Universities of Valencia (1945) and Madrid (1948). He was active in the diplomatic service from 1945. From 1951 to 1961 he held various public posts related to culture, education and political studies. He was Minister of Information and Tourism 1962–69 and also Secretary-General of the cabinet 1967–69. He was Ambassador to the UK 1973–75. After Franco's death, Fraga became Minister

for the Interior and Deputy Prime Minister 1975–76. In 1976 he formed the AP which he led for much of the 1980s. He was a Member of the European Parliament 1987–89 and was involved in regional politics in Galicia, becoming the President of the region in 1990 (and re-elected to that post in 1993, 1997 and 2000). During the Franco regime he was a supporter of partial liberalisation, both of the ruling party and of the regime. He removed aspects of censorship of the press by legislation in 1966, for instance. However, he was too closely linked to Franco's regime to be a key figure in the transition to democracy in Spain.

Franco, Francisco

Military leader of Spain from the civil war until his death in 1975. Franco was born in Galicia in 1892. He entered upon a military career, and became Chief of Staff in 1935. His overt opposition to the democratic regime in Spain at the time led to his posting as military commander in the Canary Islands, and Franco's decision in 1936 to lead a military uprising against the socialist government. This led to the Spanish civil war, which ended in a victory for the military forces in 1939. He then ruled Spain as a dictatorship in which he was head of state and Prime Minister, with the aid of his Falange party. Other parties were prohibited, democratic rights were abolished, regional identity was suppressed and a corporate form of economic regulation introduced. Franco was regarded by some as fascist and he benefited during the civil war from military aid sent by the Nazi government. Nevertheless, he refused to join in the Second World War, maintaining Spanish neutrality. Before his death, Franco arranged that the monarchy should be restored and that Juan Carlos should succeed him as head of state, in the hope that his style of regime would persist after his death.

[See also: Juan Carlos, King; Spanish civil war*]

Gaitskell, Hugh

Leader of the British Labour Party 1955–63. Gaitskell was born in London in 1906. He studied at Oxford University and then became a lecturer in economics. He was elected to the House of Commons in 1945 and held a number of ministerial positions in the Attlee governments, becoming Chancellor of the Exchequer in 1950. His decision to introduce charges for certain National Health Service provisions led to a bitter feud with Bevan (who resigned from the government on this issue) and the left wing of the party, and to criticism of Gaitskell's revisionism. In 1955 Gaitskell defeated Bevan in the election for the party leadership. He tried to modify Labour's commitment to nationalisation, and strongly opposed attempts to impose unilateral nuclear disarmament as party policy. He died in 1963.

[See also: Bevan]

de Gasperi, Alcide

Prime Minister of Italy 1945–53 during the reconstruction period after the Second World War. De Gasperi was born in 1881 in Pieve Tesino in Trentino. He studied at the University of Vienna before becoming editor of the newspaper *Nuovo Trentino*. He was elected to the Austrian Parliament in 1911 as a representative of the Italian Irredentist movement. After the union of his province with Italy, he was elected to the Italian Parliament in 1921. An opponent of Mussolini's dictatorship, he was arrested in 1926 and his newspaper was banned. He was jailed for 16 months. During the Second World War, de Gasperi was an active member of

the Italian resistance. When Mussolini fell, de Gasperi joined the Bonomi government of 1944, becoming Foreign Minister in December. He was elected leader of the newly founded Christian Democrats (DC) and in 1945 became Prime Minister, introducing a period of DC participation in government which was to last until the party's dissolution in 1994. As Prime Minister, de Gasperi committed the Italian Republic to NATO, promoted links with the USA, established a fairly liberal economic policy and remained staunchly anti-communist. He grew increasingly committed to the goal of European integration. During his period in office, Italy recovered its international standing and the economy improved. After losing a vote of confidence in June 1953, de Gasperi stepped down. He resigned as leader of the DC in June 1954 and died on 19 August 1954.

[See also: Mussolini; resistance groups*]

de Gaulle, Charles

Leader of the Free French resistance during the Second World War and President of France 1958–69. De Gaulle was born in Lille in 1890. He made a career in the army, and was a prisoner-of-war in the First World War. When France was defeated in 1940 by the German military, de Gaulle, at the time a General with a post in the Ministry of Defence, fled to London and set up a committee of the Free French to continue resistance to the Germans. Following the liberation of France in 1944–45, de Gaulle became head of the provisional government, until the Fourth Republic was established in 1946, following a referendum. He removed himself from an active role in national politics, but in 1958, as a result of the growing crisis in Algeria and the lack of support for the Fourth Republic, he was invited to become Prime Minister with the mandate to produce a new constitution. He became the first President of the new Fifth Republic, introduced direct election for the presidency and was re-elected in 1965 under this new system. He successfully managed the Algerian crisis, eventually ensuring that Algeria became independent. He played an active part in shaping the politics of European integration, though always with a view to protecting the interests of France. In particular, he negotiated the Franco-German treaty with Adenauer which was signed in 1963 and twice exercised a veto against the entry of the United Kingdom into the European Economic Community. He withdrew France from various aspects of NATO membership in 1966. The events surrounding the student and left-wing demonstrations in 1968 seemed to weaken his position, though he agreed to a range of reforms in an effort to meet popular demands. In 1969 de Gaulle's plans for regional reform were defeated in a referendum which was perceived as a test of confidence in his leadership, and he resigned. He died in 1970.

[See also: Adenauer; Algerian conflict*; empty chair crisis*; May Events*; resistance groups*]

Genscher, Hans-Dietrich

Foreign Minister of the German Federal Republic 1974–92 and leader of the Free Democratic Party (FDP) 1974–85. Genscher was born near Halle, in what later became the German Democratic Republic, in 1927. He studied law at the Universities of Halle and Leipzig, then migrated to the Federal Republic in 1952, the year in which he joined the FDP. He was appointed to the staff of the FDP parliamentary party in the Bundestag in 1956, becoming business manager of that parliamentary party in 1959, and business manager of the FDP in 1962. He was first elected to the Bundestag in 1965. He was elected as a deputy leader of his party in 1968. He served as Minister of the Interior in the Brandt government from 1969 to 1974. The resignation in 1974 of the incumbent Foreign Minister and party leader, Scheel, allowed Genscher to assume both those positions. Genscher played a leading role in bringing about the fall of the Schmidt government and its replacement by a Christian Democrat–FDP coalition in 1982 by use of the constructive vote of no confidence. As Foreign Minister under two Chancellors of different parties: Helmut Schmidt (Social Democrats) and Helmut Kohl (Christian Democrats), Genscher provided continuity of foreign policy and was able to promote his strategy of combining the pursuit of détente with measures to ensure the military and diplomatic security of the Federal Republic – a policy stance that became known as 'Genscherism'. He soon became the most prominent of all the FDP politicians, and his reputation and fame contributed much to the electoral survival of the FDP in 1983 and its electoral successes in 1987 and 1990. He played a leading role both in dealing with diplomatic incidents during the collapse of the communist regime in the GDR (such as emigration of GDR refugees in Western embassies in Eastern Europe in 1989) and in the diplomatic strategies which led to the reunification of Germany in 1990.

[See also: Brandt; Scheel; Schmidt; constructive vote of no confidence*; reunification of Germany*]

Giscard d'Estaing, Valéry

President of France 1974–81. Giscard was born in 1926 in Koblenz (Germany). He served in the Second World War and then received an elite civil service education, graduating from the newly created National College of Administration to take a post at the Bank of France. Minister of Finance

Edgar Fauré appointed Giscard to his staff in 1954, keeping him on when Fauré became Prime Minister in 1955. In 1956 Giscard inherited his grandfather's parliamentary seat of Puy-le-Dôme. In the 1958 crisis, Giscard backed de Gaulle and retained his seat at the first elections of the Fifth Republic. In 1962 he became Minister of Finance and Economic Affairs. From 1962 to 1974, Giscard led the development of liberalism in French politics. After the 1962 elections, his party group, the Independent Republicans, supported the Gaullist government as a coalition partner with the aim of promoting European integration and a less authoritarian style of government. In 1966 Giscard left the government and openly criticised de Gaulle, refusing to support him over the 1969 referendum on regional and senate reform. The failure of the referendum was to bring down de Gaulle's presidency. Giscard transferred his loyalty to Pompidou and was rewarded by the new President with the Finance Ministry (1969–74). When Pompidou died in 1974, Giscard won the presidential elections. Determined to be a new-style 'popular' president, the high expectations at the start of his term of office faded to disillusionment. Giscard took office as the oil crises of 1973 and 1979 were taking their toll in economic recession and inflation. Giscard had promised liberal social reforms, but failed to deliver as anticipated. On Europe, Giscard backed significant initiatives including the establishment of the European Council, the EMS and the Franco-German entente, but his administration was not noticeably less nationalist than that of his predecessors. From 1976 to 1981, the Gaullists became increasingly critical of the way in which Giscard himself kept tight control over policy. Jacques Chirac, Giscard's first Prime Minister, became his bitterest rival, and played a major part in Giscard's defeat in the

presidential election of 1981. Giscard's presidency ended in a welter of scandals, including the murder of a Giscardian Deputy of the National Assembly and the suspicious suicide of a government minister. The last straw was Giscard's refusal to account for his acceptance of a gift of diamonds from the African dictator Emperor Bokassa. Giscard returned to the National Assembly as a Deputy in 1984. He was President of a weakened UDF 1988–96. He became President of the European international movement 1989–97 and led the UDF–RPR list in the 1989 European elections. In 1997, he became President of the Council of European Municipalities and Regions.

[See also: Chirac; de Gaulle; Pompidou; oil crisis*]

Goldsmith, James

Founder and principal financier of the Referendum Party, which presented candidates at the 1997 British general election. Goldsmith was born in Paris in 1933. He became a businessman, amassing great wealth as a result of founding and developing companies. He became convinced that British entry into the single European currency system would be a national disaster, so he first campaigned vigorously for a promise by the Conservative government that they would promise a referendum on the issue on his terms, and, when that demand was rejected, financed candidacies of Referendum Party supporters in constituencies where he and his party regarded the Conservative candidate as unsound on the referendum issue. None of his candidates was elected, but some received several thousand votes in their constituencies, and could, in some cases, be regarded as having cost the Conservative candidate that seat. The Referendum Party was wound up after the election. Goldsmith died in 1997.

González Márquez, Felipe

Prime Minister of Spain 1982–96 and leader of the Spanish Socialist Party (PSOE) 1979–97. González was born in 1942 in Seville and studied law at the Catholic University of Louvain in Belgium. Working in Seville as a lawyer, in 1966 he introduced the first labour law centre specifically for workers. During Franco's regime, he was arrested several times for his association with the banned socialists. He had joined the Spanish Socialist Youth in 1962 and the PSOE in 1964 and rose rapidly in the party ranks, becoming a member of the Seville Provincial Committee 1965–69, the National Committee 1969–70, and the Executive Board in 1970. In 1972, he became leader of the largest faction within the party. He became first Secretary of the PSOE 1974–79, resigned for a brief period before being re-elected in September 1979 and then held the post of Secretary-General of the party until his resignation in 1997. In 1982, the Socialists won a landslide election and replaced Súarez's centre-right government. González was Prime Minister of Spain 1982–96, as well as leading the PSOE party group in Parliament. Initially very popular, his government was increasingly troubled by economic problems and by corruption scandals, including the FILESA scandal, when a judge ordered searches of party records which revealed illegal payments to the PSOE and later the trial of several officials of the party. These scandals, although not directly involving González in criminal charges, affected his reputation and probably prevented him being considered as successor to the discredited Jacques Santer as President of the EU Commission. González has now retired from politics.

[See also: Franco; Suárez González; Felipeism*]

Grass, Günther

German leftist intellectual, writer and artist: a vocal critic of the values of the Federal Republic of Germany and particularly of the reunification project. Grass was born in 1927 in Danzig (now Gdánsk, Poland) and went to art school. Best known as an author, Grass received numerous prizes for literature and the arts, notably the West German Group 47 Prize 1959; the literary prize of the Association of German Critics 1960; the Thomas Mann prize 1996 and the Nobel Prize for Literature 1999. His best known works are the fictional *Tin Drum* (1959); *From the Diary of a Snail* (1972); and the political commentary *Two States – One Nation?* (1990). He was President of the Berlin Academy of the Arts 1983–86 and a member of the American Academy of Arts and Sciences. A long-standing member of the Social Democratic Party (SPD), he resigned in 1992.

[See also: reunification of Germany*]

Grimond, Jo

Leader of the British Liberal Party 1956–67. Grimond was born in 1913. Trained as a lawyer, he fought in the Second World War, then entered Parliament in 1950 as MP for Orkney and Shetland. Elected as party leader in 1956, Grimond succeeded in increasing the very small number of Liberal MPs, and brought about a general, if limited, revival of the party. He acted briefly as provisional party leader in 1976 following the resignation of Jeremy Thorpe. He left Parliament in 1983. Grimond died in 1993.

[See also: Thorpe]

Gysi, Gregor

First leader of the Party of Democratic Socialism (PDS), after its emergence from the Socialist Unity Party (SED) at the end of 1989. Gysi was born in Berlin in 1948. He joined the SED in 1967. He was a lawyer by profession, and gained a reputation as a defender of dissidents. He became known as a reformer within the SED in the closing months of the communist regime. This led to his election as Chairman of the SED at its emergency congress in December 1989, leading a provisional committee given the task of adapting the party to the change of regime in the German Democratic Republic. He led the PDS in its electoral campaign for the elections to the People's Chamber in March 1990, and entered the Bundestag in 1990 as a delegate in October following reunification, and became an elected Member in December 1990. Gysi had to cope with accusations that the SED had misused funds and had improperly sought to avoid public accountability for its finances by sending large sums of money to foreign bank accounts. Despite suspicions of association with the Stasi, Gysi remained leader of the PDS until 1993, when he voluntarily gave up that office in order to concentrate on his activities as leader of the PDS parliamentary group in the Bundestag. Gysi was re-elected to the Bundestag in 1994 and 1998, retaining his Berlin constituency seat in each case.

[See also: reunification of Germany*; Stasi*]

Hague, William

Leader of the British Conservative Party and leader of the opposition in the House of Commons 1997–2001. Hague was born in 1961 in Rotherham and studied at Oxford University, where he was President of the Union 1981. After university he worked as a management consultant for McKinsey and Co. 1983–88 and acted as a political adviser to the Treasury. He made an early start to his political career when he addressed the annual Conservative Conference at the age of 15. He has been MP for Richmond, Yorkshire since

1989. Prior to becoming leader of the Conservative Party, he was Parliamentary Private Secretary to the Chancellor of the Exchequer 1990–93; Parliamentary Under-Secretary of State in the Department of Social Security 1993–94; Minister for Social Security and Disabled People 1994–95; and Secretary of State for Wales 1995–97. He has been Chair of the International Democratic Union since 1999. Following the defeat of his party in the general election of 2001, he announced his intention to resign as party leader. Following a lengthy and complex electoral process, he was replaced by Iain Duncan Smith in September 2001.

[See also: Duncan Smith]

Haider, Jörg

Leader of the far right Austrian Freedom Party. Haider was born in 1950 in Carinthia and studied at Vienna University. He joined the Liberal Youth Movement in 1964 and the Freedom Party in 1971. He worked in private industry 1976–77 and was a Member of Parliament 1979–83 and again from 1986. His controversial and charismatic leadership of the Freedom Party promoted the party to the third force in Austrian politics. There was an international outcry, particularly amongst EU countries, when Haider's party was asked to participate in a coalition government after the elections in February 2000, and EU states imposed various sanctions. He gave up the leadership of his party, but remains active in the regional politics of Carinthia.

Hallstein, Walter

German diplomat and first President of the European Commission 1958–67. Hallstein was born in Mainz in 1901. He studied law and became a Professor of Law at Rostock and Frankfurt Universities. He became a senior civil servant in Adenauer's government, first in the Federal Chancellery, then in the newly established Foreign Office. In this position he was the chief negotiator for the Federal Republic in the creation of the European Coal and Steel Community and the Messina negotiations which led to the Treaty of Rome. In 1955 he formulated the famous 'Hallstein Doctrine' concerning relations with states which recognised the GDR. He served as President of the EEC Commission, but French opposition prevented him from accepting the presidency of the EC Commission following fusion of the EEC, ECSC and EURATOM institutions. He served as a Member of the Bundestag for the CDU 1969–72. Hallstein died in 1982.

[See also: ECSC*; Hallstein Doctrine*]

Haughey, Charles

Former Prime Minister of the Irish Republic. Haughey was born in County Mayo in 1925. After studying law and accountancy, he went into the property business before entering politics. He became a member of the Irish legislature for Fianna Fail in 1957, and held a number of ministerial posts from 1961 onwards. He resigned as Minister of Finance in 1970 because of allegations of links to Irish Nationalist groups, but following his acquittal on charges arising from those allegations he was again appointed as Minister in 1977, and became Prime Minister and leader of his party in 1979. He remained Prime Minister until 1981, and was again Prime Minister briefly in 1982. In opposition, internal party conflicts led to a break-away from Fianna Fail by some of its parliamentary group, to form a new party: the Progressive Democrats. Haughey was again Prime Minister from 1987. In 1992 he resigned as Prime Minister because of his association with cases of illegal phone-tapping by his government. In retirement, further

accusations of financial impropriety were made against him concerning large political donations made by industrialists.

Havemann, Robert

German scientist and political dissident. Havemann was born in Munich in 1910. After studying chemistry at Munich and Berlin Universities, he was employed in a scientific research institute until forced from his post because of his membership of the Communist Party in 1933. He was active in resistance groups in the Hitler period, and on one occasion was caught, tried and sentenced to death, but reprieved because the research he was engaged in was of relevance to the German military. After the war, he became a Professor at the Humboldt University in East Berlin, a post he held until he was expelled from the SED in 1964 because of his dissident views. He was also an SED member of the Volkskammer (the GDR Parliament) 1950–63. He continued to publicise his dissident views, and was regarded as the leading theorist of a democratic form of socialism in the GDR. This led to his being placed under house arrest in 1976. He died in 1982.

[See also: Hitler; Resistance groups*]

Heath, Edward

Leader of the Conservative Party 1965–75 and British Prime Minister 1970–74. Heath was born in Broadstairs in 1916. He studied at Oxford University and served as an officer in the Second World War. He was first elected to the House of Commons in 1950, becoming his party's chief whip in 1955 and Minister of Labour in 1959. In 1960 he was appointed as Lord Privy Seal (a ministerial post without specific departmental responsibilities) and was principal negotiator – though unsuccessful – of British entry to the

EEC. He was Secretary of State for Industry in Home's government (1963–64). He became leader of the Conservatives in 1965 and, somewhat unexpectedly, led his party to victory in the 1970 general election. He called an early general election in February 1974 to try to defeat a series of strikes by coalminers. However, he failed to obtain a majority and the Labour Party formed the government. Heath also failed to win the general election in October 1974, and he was defeated in a leadership election by Margaret Thatcher in 1975. He never seemed to reconcile himself to this loss of party leadership, the more especially as Mrs Thatcher was electorally more successful than he had been and because she represented a very sceptical approach to further developments in European integration, developments which Heath seemed to welcome uncritically. Heath became 'Father of the House of Commons' in 1992, having served longer than any other sitting MP. He was re-elected in the 1997 general election, and as such presided over the controversial election of a Speaker in 2000, following the resignation of Mrs Boothroyd. When he left the House of Commons in 2001 Heath had served over half a century in the House of Commons.

[See also: Thatcher]

Herzog, Roman

President of Germany 1994–99. Herzog was born in 1934 in Landshut and studied at the University of Munich, the Free University of Berlin, and the College of Administrative Sciences at Speyer. He has held high office in protestant organisations and in the Christian Democratic Party (CDU). In the state of Baden-Württemberg he was Minister for Culture and Sport 1978–80 and Minister for the Interior 1980–83. He was a member of the Federal Committee of the CDU 1979–83. He was

Vice-President of the Federal Constitutional Court (FCC) 1983–87 and President of the FCC 1987–94. He was nominated as the CDU candidate for President of the FRG after Kohl withdrew his proposal to nominate Heitmann, a minister in the Saxony Land government, whose lack of popularity within the party and outside it called into question his suitability as presidential candidate.

Heuss, Theodor

First President of the Federal Republic of Germany and first leader of the Free Democratic Party (FDP). Heuss was born in Württemberg, in south-west Germany, in 1884. After a period as a journalist, he taught political science in Berlin (1920–33) and was elected to the Reichstag (the Parliament of the Weimar Republic) for the German Democratic Party 1924–28 and 1930–33. Having criticised Hitler in his books and journalism, Heuss was dismissed from his university post when the Nazis came to power. After the Second World War, Heuss helped to found the Liberal Party in south-west Germany, was the first Minister of Education for the Land of Württemberg-Baden, and a member of the Land Parliament. When a liberal party for West Germany was founded in 1948, he was elected as its first leader. He was an influential member of the Parliamentary Council, which drafted the Basic Law for the new Federal Republic. Coalition negotiations between the FDP and Adenauer's Christian Democrats led to an agreement that Heuss would be supported by both parties for the position of Federal President when the Federal Republic was founded in 1949. Heuss was a much-respected President, and enjoyed a good relationship with Adenauer. He was re-elected as Federal President in 1954 for a second term. He died in 1963.

[See also: Adenauer; Hitler; nazism*]

Heym, Stefan

Controversial writer from the former German Democratic Republic (GDR) and latterly social democratic politician. Heym was born 10 April 1913 in Chemnitz and studied at the Universities of Berlin and Chicago. In 1933 he fled the National Socialist regime to Czechoslovakia where he worked as a journalist until 1935. He left for the USA in 1935, working as a waiter as he edited an anti-fascist newspaper. He served in the American army 1943–45. He was co-founder of the newspaper: the *Neue Zeitung* in Munich in 1945. In 1950 he led the American delegation to the Second World Peace Congress in Warsaw. In 1952 he returned to what was now the GDR. He was a member of the executive board of the GDR Writers' Association but was expelled in 1979. After German unification he joined the Social Democratic Party (SPD) and was a Member of the Bundestag 1994–96. He died in 2001.

Hitler, Adolf

Chancellor and then President of the Weimar Republic; leader ('Führer') of the Nazi state – the Third Reich. Hitler was born in 1889 in Braunau (Austria). After failure to enter training courses for art and architecture, he served in the Bavarian army in the First World War, attaining the rank of corporal and being awarded the Iron Cross. After the war, he became employed in various tasks for the military, then joined and took over the National Socialist Workers' Party (Nazi Party). In 1923 he attempted, with General Ludendorff (one of the military rulers of Germany during the war), to seize control of the Bavarian government by an armed putsch. This failed, and he was sentenced to imprisonment, during which time he commenced writing his manifesto: *Mein Kampf* (My Struggle). The crises which weakened the Weimar Republic provided opportunities for both electoral advances and direct action by the Nazis, and in 1933 President Hindenburg was compelled to ask Hitler to form a coalition government. Hitler used this opportunity to manufacture an election victory with the aid of the Reichstag fire (allowing him to exclude communists – blamed for starting the fire – from the Parliament) and then to pass emergency legislation (the Enabling Acts) which in effect marked the end of democracy and the commencement of the dictatorial Third Reich. Exerting a form of totalitarian rule in Germany, which included a policy of violent discrimination against the Jewish population and, later, their transfer to concentration camps and their mass murder, Hitler was able to commence what he regarded as 'rectifications' of the Versailles Treaty, including reoccupation of the Rhineland by the German military, the annexation of Austria and then seizure of territory from Czechoslovakia and Poland. This led to the Second World War, in which Hitler, after initial successes in northern and western Europe, sought to defeat the USSR. The entry of the USA into the war in 1941 marked the beginning of Hitler's downfall. The German army was halted at Stalingrad and at El Alamein (North Africa), and Allied invasions of Italy (1943) and France (1944) led to the defeat of the German military, their unconditional surrender and the occupation of Germany in 1945. Hitler, who had been the target of assassination attempts (most notably the 'July plot' in 1944), committed suicide in his Berlin headquarters a few days before the surrender of German forces.

[See also: nazism*]

Home, Lord

British Prime Minister and leader of the Conservative Party 1963–64. Alec Douglas-Home was born in London in 1903 and was educated at Eton and

Oxford University. He was elected to the House of Commons in 1931, and became an aide to Chamberlain during pre-war negotiations with Hitler. He succeeded to the hereditary title of Earl of Home in 1951, and held several ministerial positions in Conservative governments before Macmillan appointed him as Foreign Secretary in 1960. When Macmillan announced his resignation as party leader and Prime Minister, he surprisingly recommended Lord Home as his successor. This led necessarily to Home resigning his peerage under the 1963 Peerage Act, and he was elected to the House of Commons in a by-election. Home never established his authority as Prime Minister, and was defeated in the 1964 general election. He resigned as party leader in 1965, and became Foreign Secretary for a second time in Heath's 1970 government. He returned to the House of Lords as a life peer in 1974. He died in 1995.

[See also: Heath; Hitler; Macmillan]

Honecker, Erich

General Secretary (i.e. leader) of the ruling communist party (the Socialist Unity Party: SED) in the German Democratic Republic from 1971 until his forced resignation in 1989. He was born in the Saarland in 1912. He joined the Communist Party of Germany (KPD) in 1929. Honecker was imprisoned during the Third Reich because of his underground political activities. In the Soviet zone of occupation, later the German Democratic Republic, he was leader of the communist youth organisation (the Free German Youth: FDJ) until 1955. He rose rapidly within the SED organisation, and was put in charge of the building of the Berlin Wall in 1961. As leader of the SED, he attempted to introduce a measure of economic modernisation, though remaining within the confines of a strictly controlled and planned economy. He was a loyal follower of the Soviet Union's policies, eagerly committing the

GDR to support of repression of reformist movements in other countries of the Soviet bloc. At Soviet insistence, he participated in the development of policies of détente in the 1970s, including signing of the Basic Treaty with the Federal Republic of Germany and the Helsinki Treaties. He made a long-awaited official visit to the Federal Republic in 1987. As events unfolded in the second half of 1989, Honecker maintained a stubborn refusal to adapt the policies of the regime in any way, even, in this case, rejecting the lead of Gorbachev and the Soviet Union Communist Party with their policies of glasnost and perestroika. Though he was still leader of the GDR when the state celebrated the fortieth anniversary of its foundation in October 1989, he was compelled by his colleagues (with the acquiescence of the USSR) to resign on 17 October 1989. After German reunification, he was charged with various offences, including the 'shoot to kill' orders which resulted in the deaths of many would-be escapees at the East German border. He escaped trial because of illness, and died of cancer in Chile in 1994.

[See also: Berlin Wall*; détente*; glasnost*; Helsinki Agreements*; nazism*; perestroika*; reunification of Germany*; Vergangenheitsbewältigung*]

Hume, John

Leader of the Irish Social Democratic and Labour Party (SDLP) since 1979. Born in 1937 in Londonderry, Northern Ireland, Hume studied at the National University of Ireland. He was appointed Research Fellow at Trinity College and then Associate Fellow at the Centre for International Affairs at Harvard. He was a founder member of the Credit Union in Northern Ireland and its President 1964–68. Opposed to violence, he was a civil rights leader 1968–69. Hume represented Londonderry in the Northern Ireland Parliament 1969–72 and the Northern Ireland Assembly 1972–73.

He was Minister of Commerce in the power-sharing executive of 1974 and again represented Londonderry in the Northern Ireland Convention 1975–76. He has been a Member of the European Parliament since 1979. He was a Member of the Northern Ireland Assembly 1982–86 and from 1998. He participated in the SDLP New Ireland Forum 1983–84. He has held many national and international posts, particularly concerning workers' issues, regional issues and civil rights.

Jenkins, Roy

Former senior British Labour Party politician, former President of the Commission of the European Community, and co-founder of the Social Democratic Party. Jenkins was born in Abersychan, Wales, in 1920. He was first elected to the House of Commons in 1948, and was appointed to several ministerial offices in Labour governments, including those of Home Secretary (1965–67 and 1974–76) and Chancellor of the Exchequer (1967–70). He was elected as deputy leader of the British Labour Party in 1970. Jenkins served as President of the EC Commission 1977–81. As one of the 'Gang of Four' he founded the Social Democratic Party in 1981, and became its first elected leader in 1982, though he gave way as leader to David Owen in 1983. He entered the House of Lords as Lord Jenkins of Hillhead in 1988. He served as Chancellor of Oxford University, and has written several well-received books, especially biographies of Asquith, Dilke and Gladstone. In 1998 he was Chairman of a Commission on Electoral Reform, which reported in October 1998.
[See also: Gang of Four*]

Jospin, Lionel

Prime Minister of France since 1997; leader of the Socialist Party 1981–87;

1995–97. Jospin was born in 1937 at Meudon (Seine-et-Oise). He graduated from the Institute of Political Studies and the National College of Administration in Paris and embarked on a career in the Foreign Ministry (1965–70) before taking up a university post in economics (1970–81). A protégé of Mitterrand, he joined the Socialist Party (PS) in 1972 and was advanced rapidly as one of a new cadre of leaders who Mitterrand hoped would keep the party loyal to him. From 1973 to 1975 Jospin was the party's National Secretary for Political Education before taking charge of Third World Relations (1975–79) and then International Affairs (1979–81). He was appointed First Secretary of the party in 1981, leading the party in a process of ideological transformation away from traditional socialism towards a new style of social democracy, which culminated in the party's 1985 Congress at Toulouse. As party leader he was forced to adopt a rather passive leadership role during the cohabitation period from 1986 and faced growing criticism from within the PS. He stood down in 1987, but later took up the party leadership again (1995–97). After Mitterrand's re-election as President in 1988, Jospin was rewarded with the prestigious post of Minister of State for Education, Research and Sport in Rocard's government, keeping education as the ministerial responsibilities were restructured. In 1997 he was appointed Prime Minister following the general election called by newly elected President Chirac, and which resulted in 'cohabitation' when the PS won that election.
[See also: Mitterrand; Rocard; cohabitation*]

Juan Carlos, King

King of Spain since 1975. Juan Carlos was born in Rome in 1938. He was the grandson of King Alfonso XIII, who abdicated in 1931. Invited by Franco to return to Spain from exile in 1960, he was nominated in 1969 by Franco as heir to the Spanish throne (bypassing his father, Don Juan). On Franco's death in 1975, Juan Carlos became King. Franco had believed Juan Carlos would be a reliable defender of the values of his authoritarian regime, but Juan Carlos proved to be a promoter of democracy, and sought to become a constitutional monarch on the model of the British and northern European monarchies. He bravely resisted the group of officers who attempted to engineer a military coup in February 1981. He has proved to be an integrative figure in the Spanish political system, characterised as it is by strong regional identities.

[See also: Franco; Spanish coup attempt*]

Karamanlis (Caramanlis), Konstantine

Prime Minister of Greece 1955–58, 1958–61, 1961–63, 1974–80; President of Greece 1980–85, 1990. Karamanlis was born in 1907 in Macedonia and graduated in law from the University of Athens in 1932. He was elected to Parliament in 1935. The dictator Ioannis Metaxas closed the Parliament in 1936 and offered Karamanlis a place in his government, but Karamanlis refused and stayed out of politics until after the Second World War. He was elected to Parliament again in 1946 and served in various ministerial positions until the mid-1950s, becoming popular particularly as Minister of Public Works 1952–54. During his first term as Prime Minister he formed the National Radical Union and won the elections of 1956. The defection of some of his party group to the opposition in 1958 led to his resignation, but he was again named Prime Minister after elections in May 1958. During this period he negotiated the establishment of an independent republic of Cyprus with Turkey. In spite of allegations of electoral fraud, his party

was successful again in 1961 and he resumed as Prime Minister, resigning in 1963 over a dispute with King Paul I over the respective powers of the monarch and the prime minister. Karamanlis left Greece for Paris where he stayed for ten years. After the military takeover in 1967, he issued statements calling for the re-establishment of democratic rule. In 1974, following the crisis between Turkey and Greece over Cyprus, Karamanlis was asked to return and form a civilian government. He negotiated a settlement to the war in Cyprus and introduced democratic reforms. He lifted the military junta's ban on free speech and the press and cancelled most of the martial law measures. He founded the New Democracy party which formed a majority government. He stepped down as Prime Minister to become President of Greece in 1980 and was again President in 1990.

[See also: Aegean Sea dispute*]

Kekkonen, Urho

President of Finland 1956–81. Kekkonen was born in Pielavesi in 1900. He studied law at Helsinki University, then was employed as a civil servant. He entered the Finnish Parliament in 1936 as a representative of the Agrarian Party, and became a minister in the coalition government. After the Second World War he helped to negotiate a treaty of friendship with the USSR in 1948. He became Prime Minister in 1950, and served, with one interruption, until 1956. He was a proponent of a policy of co-operation with the USSR, which has acquired the label: 'Finlandisation'. He resigned as President on grounds of ill-health in 1981. He died in 1986.

[See also: Finlandisation*]

Kelly, Petra

Leading member of the West German Green Party in its early years. Kelly was born in Günzburg in 1947. She studied political science at university in the USA. She then was employed by the European Community as an administrator. She was a member of the SPD 1972–78, but resigned in protest at the moderate and compromising policies of the Schmidt government. She became involved in the feminist, peace and ecological movements in Germany, and played a leading part in establishing the Green Party in West Germany, including campaigning vigorously in the 1980 and 1983 Bundestag elections. She was elected to the Bundestag in 1983 and 1987, and was involved in the collective leadership of the party within and outside the Bundestag. She was associated with the 'fundamentalist' wing of the Green Party, rejecting any idea of forming coalitions with established parties, though she came to oppose several of the party's organisational tenets, such as rotation of office, and came to view the party's organisation as primitive and amateurish. Her views and her obvious charisma (which led to her being seen by the media as the personification of the Green movement) led to her increasing unpopularity within the Green Party. She committed suicide with her partner, the former General Gerd Bastian, in 1992.

Kennedy, Charles

Leader of the British Liberal Democratic Party since 1999. Kennedy was born in Fort William in 1959. He studied at Glasgow University and commenced a career in broadcasting before being elected for the Social Democratic Party for the constituency of Ross, Cromarty and Skye in 1983. In 1988 he agreed to support the merger of the SDP with the Liberals. In 1999, following the resignation as party leader of Paddy Ashdown, Kennedy was elected leader by a vote of the party membership.
[See also: Ashdown]

Kiesinger, Kurt Georg

Chancellor of the Federal Republic of Germany 1966–69. Kiesinger was born in Württemberg in 1904, and qualified as a lawyer. He was employed in the German Foreign Office during the Second World War. He was elected to the Bundestag as a Christian Democrat in 1949, but resigned his seat in 1958 to become Prime Minister of Baden-Württemberg. When Erhard was compelled to resign as Chancellor in 1966, Kiesinger was chosen to take his place at the head of a 'grand coalition' between the Christian Democrats and the Social Democrats (SPD). That coalition was responsible for several achievements, including the stabilisation of the economy, some improvements in relations with Eastern European states, and the preservation of a democratic regime challenged by extremists from the left-wing student movement and the radical right-wing National Democratic Party. Though his party secured the largest share of votes in the 1969 federal election, Kiesinger had to make way for Chancellor Brandt who led a coalition between the SPD and Free Democratic Party. Kiesinger was leader of the CDU 1967–71 and was again a Member of the Bundestag from 1969 to 1980. He died in 1988.
[See also: Brandt; Erhard; grand coalition*]

Kinnock, Neil

Leader of the British Labour Party 1983–92. Kinnock was born in Tredegar in 1942. He engaged in socialist political activity while a student, and was elected to the House of Commons in 1970. He was elected to succeed Michael Foot as party leader. Though he, like Foot, had a left-wing reputation, being among other things a staunch supporter of the Campaign for Nuclear Disarmament, Kinnock realised that for Labour to win general elections in future it would have to discard many of its ideological attitudes. He thus introduced measures of organisational and policy reform. Defeated in the 1987 general election, Kinnock had high hopes of winning in 1992. When Labour was defeated again, even though more narrowly than in the 1980s, Kinnock resigned as party leader. He became a Commissioner of the European Union in 1994, and survived the scandals that led to the resignation of Santer and his fellow Commissioners in 1998, being reappointed with the responsibility of reforming the administration, financial control and practices of the Commission.

[See also: Foot; Santer; Smith; Campaign for Nuclear Disarmament*; Clause Four*]

Kohl, Helmut

Chancellor of the Federal Republic of Germany 1982–98; leader of the Christian Democratic Union (CDU) 1973–98; Prime Minister of Rhineland-Pfalz 1969–76. Kohl was born in 1930 in Ludwigshafen, and was awarded his doctorate in political science from Heidelberg University in 1958. He joined the CDU in 1946, and held numerous party offices at local and Land levels. He was chancellor-candidate in the 1976 Bundestag election, but, though securing the highest vote-share for the Christian Democrats since Adenauer's absolute majority of votes in 1957, this was insufficient to defeat the Social Democrat–Free Democrat (FDP) coalition. He became Chancellor when the FDP withdrew from that coalition in 1982, and supported Kohl in the first ever successful use of the constructive vote of no confidence, which dismissed Helmut Schmidt from the office of Chancellor. Though Kohl had successes in politics prior to 1990, and led his coalition to election victories in 1983 and 1987, his place in history will be based mainly upon his leading role in promoting the reunification of Germany in 1990. His ten-point plan of 28 November 1989 referred to the possibility of reunification. However, his negotiations with the government of the GDR in December 1989 and February 1990; his personal popularity in the GDR in early 1990 and his successful sponsorship of the Christian Democrat-led electoral 'Alliance for Germany' in the first free elections to the GDR People's Chamber in March 1990; his promotion of economic and monetary union of the two German states; and his role in negotiations with other states (especially the USSR) to lay the diplomatic foundations for German reunification will all be seen as great personal achievements. Following German reunification, he led his coalition to a narrow victory in the 1994 Bundestag election, a victory which owed much to his personal popularity. He was unable to capitalise on that popularity in the 1998 election, following which some experts stated that he should have made way for a replacement chancellor-candidate well before that election campaign got under way. Immediately after the election result was known on 27 September 1998 he announced his intention to resign as leader of the CDU, and later that year was replaced by his protégé, Wolfgang Schäuble. In 1999 revelations of secret donations to the CDU led to a scandal, in which Kohl was centrally involved.

[See also: Adenauer; Schmidt; constructive vote of no confidence*; reunification of Germany*]

Kreisky, Bruno

Chancellor of Austria 1970–83. Kreisky was born in Vienna in 1911. He studied law at university, and became active in politics as a socialist. He was imprisoned following the socialist uprising in Austria in 1934, and was again briefly imprisoned in 1938 after the Nazis took over Austria. He emigrated to Sweden later in 1938, returning to Austria after the end of the war. After periods in the diplomatic service and as a civil servant, he was appointed Austrian Foreign Minister in 1959, a position he retained until 1966. In 1967 he became leader of the Social Democratic Party (the SPÖ). Though head of a minority government in 1970, Kreisky's personal popularity contributed to his party's successes in elections in 1971, 1975 and 1979, where in each case it secured an absolute majority of seats. As leader of the government of a neutral state, Kreisky was able to play a role (with others such as Olaf Palme) in mediation in several international conflicts, especially in the Middle East. He resigned as Chancellor following the loss of a parliamentary majority in the 1983 elections.

[See also: Palme; nazism*]

Krenz, Egon

The last leader of the communist regime in the German Democratic Republic. Krenz was born in 1937 in Pomerania, now part of Poland. Krenz developed a career within the Socialist Unity Party (the SED) which he joined in 1955, becoming leader of the Free German Youth in 1974. He was long regarded as the probable successor to Honecker, and when Honecker was compelled to resign his offices in October 1989 because of manoeuvres initiated by Krenz and others, Krenz took over as party General-Secretary and head of state. In his short period as leader, he attempted to introduce concessions on issues such as freedom to travel, but these reforms were always too little to satisfy the growing numbers of discontented East Germans. The opening of the border on 9 November 1989 (the 'fall of the Berlin Wall') seemed to result from a misunderstanding rather than

a considered policy decision. Krenz resigned his offices in December 1989. In 1999 he was sentenced to a term of imprisonment for his implication in fraud.

[See also: Honecker; reunification of Germany*]

Lafontaine, Oskar

Former leader of the German Social Democratic Party (SPD) and the SPD's chancellor-candidate in the 1990 Bundestag election. Lafontaine was born in Saarlouis (Saarland) in 1943 and studied physics at university. He joined the SPD in 1966, and was elected to the Saarland legislature in 1970. He became lord mayor of Saarbrücken in 1976 (at the time, he was the youngest city leader in West Germany). In 1985 he became Prime Minister of the Saarland after the SPD's first post-war election victory in the Saarland parliamentary elections. He became a deputy leader of the SPD in 1987. He was unable to revive the fortunes of the SPD in the 1990 all-German Bundestag election: the SPD only secured 33.5 per cent, its worst showing for thirty years. In that campaign, Lafontaine was stabbed in the neck by a deranged person, who inflicted a serious wound. Lafontaine's sceptical stance vis-à-vis German reunification, especially concerning its likely costs, is thought to have been a factor in that 1990 election defeat. In 1995, Lafontaine successfully challenged the incumbent party leader, Scharping, for the party leadership. This meant that when the SPD came to power in the 1998 Bundestag election, Lafontaine could take much of the credit, and could demand an important government post; Schröder appointed him as Finance Minister. However, Lafontaine's traditionalist social democratic views were at odds with the more modernistic policies pursued by Chancellor Schröder and the two were frequently in conflict. Lafontaine unexpectedly announced his resignation from government and party offices on 11 March 1999.

[See also: Scharping; Schröder; reunification of Germany*]

Lambsdorff, Otto Graf

Leader of the German FDP 1988–93. Lambsdorff was born in Aachen in 1926. He served in the Second World War, and was seriously wounded in the closing days of that conflict. Following study of law at university, after the war was over he practised as a lawyer, then worked in the banking and insurance sectors. He joined the FDP in 1951, and became a member of the party executive in 1972, the year of his first election to the Bundestag. After a period as economics spokesman for his parliamentary party group, he became Minister of Economics in the Schmidt government in 1977. His strongly liberal and free-enterprise attitude to the economy led to conflicts with Schmidt and eventually to the termination of the SPD–FDP coalition in 1982. He remained as Economics Minister in the Kohl government, but resigned in 1984 because of his implication in the Flick Affair. As party leader, he decided to remain outside the government, and led his party to an excellent result in the 1990 Bundestag election.

[See also: Kohl; Schmidt; Flick Affair*; 'Wende'*]

Laval, Pierre

Prime Minister of the Vichy government in war-time France, and executed for treason in 1945, Laval bore the brunt of recriminations against the Vichy regime which had collaborated with Nazi Germany. Born in the Auvergne in 1883, Laval studied science at Lyons and law in Paris. He founded a law practice and a radio and press empire, which funded his political activities. A socialist, he was elected to the Parliament of the French Third Republic in 1914. More interested in his constituency than in ideology, when the Socialist and Communists split in 1920, Laval continued as an independent and was elected to the Senate in 1927. He was Minister and Prime Minister in a series of governments 1925–35, moving progressively to the right of the political spectrum in reaction to the success of the left-wing Popular Front and through his increasing attraction to fascism. Convinced that Bolshevism posed the main threat to European civilisation, Laval tried actively to promote Franco-German relations. He joined Marshal Pétain's right-wing Vichy government, first as Deputy Prime Minister (1940), then as Prime Minister (1942–44). After the armistice with Germany on 22 June 1940, Laval masterminded the suspension of the 1875 constitution and the transfer of full powers to Pétain on 10 July 1940, ending the Third Republic. As Prime Minister, Laval made growing concessions to Hitler, including the authorisation of French labour for the Nazi war effort and the deportation of Jews. After the fall of the Vichy regime, he was executed after a notional trial on 15 October 1945.

[See also: Hitler; nazism*; Vichy regime*]

Lemass, Sean Francis

Irish revolutionary and Prime Minister of Ireland 1959–66. Lemass was born in 1899 in Dublin and took part in the Irish independence movement that culminated in the Easter Week Rebellion in 1916. When the rebellion collapsed he was arrested by the British forces, but his young age saved him from imprisonment or execution. Lemass joined the Irish Republican Army (IRA) and was again arrested for revolutionary activities. He was kept in prison until July 1921 when a truce was declared. When civil war broke out in July 1922, Lemass fought with the IRA, was captured, but managed to escape. Recaptured in December 1922 he stayed in prison until the Republicans were defeated in the spring of 1923. Lemass resigned from the Sinn Féin party and joined de Valera's new Fianna Fail (FF) party. In 1924 he was elected to the Irish Parliament. In 1932, he became de Valera's Minister of Industry and Commerce. In 1939 he became Minister of Supplies, a post he kept until 1945. After the Second World War he was Deputy Prime Minister until Fianna Fail was defeated in the 1948 elections. Lemass then worked for the party newspaper: the *Irish Press* until FF returned to power in 1951 and he again became Deputy Prime Minister and Minister of Industry and Commerce. When, in 1959, de Valera resigned as Prime Minister to become President, Lemass was his successor. He negotiated with Northern Ireland in the hope of reuniting the country. In 1965 he arranged a free trade pact with Britain. He resigned as Prime Minister in 1966 but remained in Parliament until his retirement in 1969. Lemass died in 1971.

[See also: Irish Republican Army*]

Leone, Giovanni

Prime Minister of Italy June–November 1963; June–December 1968; President of Italy 1971–78. Giovanni Leone was born in 1908 in Naples. He studied at the University of Naples, then became a Professor of Law there. He began a long parliamentary career as a Christian Democrat (DC) representative with his election to the Constituent Assembly in 1946. He was Vice-President of the Chamber of Deputies 1948–49 and its President 1955–63. After his first premiership, he became a life senator in 1967. He was elected President of Italy in 1971 as a compromise candidate after 23 ballots. His presidency coincided with a period of terrorist campaigns in Italy. He was forced to

resign his presidency through his implication in a corruption scandal: the first Italian president to suffer this disgrace. He died in 2001.

Le Pen, Jean-Marie

Leader of the radical right-wing National Front party in France. Born in 1928 at La Trinité-sur-Mer (Morbihan), Le Pen studied in Paris, graduating in law and political science. Violently anti-Marxist, he was a student leader 1949–51 and was often in trouble with the police for taking part in fights. In 1953 he joined the Foreign Legion and went to Indo-China as a parachutist, where he worked as a political journalist for the military's press. He returned to his studies and his activities in student politics in 1954. In 1956 he was elected as a Poujadiste (reactionary, anti-taxation party) Deputy and gained a reputation as a charismatic speaker. He rejoined his former regiment 1956–57. In 1957 he was accused of torturing a young Algerian arrested by the parachutists, but was not prosecuted. Back in France, Le Pen lost an eye in a fight at an electoral meeting trying to defend a Muslim friend. In late 1957, he left the Poujadistes and sat first as an independent in the National Assembly, then, from 1958 to 1962, with the conservative party group Independents and Peasants. Le Pen was sued for allegedly pro-Nazi statements. He actively supported the presidential campaign of the right-wing candidate Tixier-Vignancourt in 1965. In 1972 he launched his own party, the far right Front National (FN), on a platform of nationalism, morality, anti-communism and law and order. He and his family survived a bomb attack at their home in 1976. After a disastrous return of 0.74 per cent of the vote at the presidential election of 1974, the FN made little impact until the 1980s, when it made a credible showing at local and European elections and Le Pen became a media

117 BIOGRAPHIES

celebrity. Le Pen was returned to Parliament for the FN in 1986, where he was an outspoken advocate of the repatriation of immigrants and tougher policing, but was damaged by a very public and acrimonious divorce and by his comments which played down the Holocaust. In 1987, a cheap joke he made about gas ovens resulted in the one FN Deputy in Parliament leaving the party and the RPR ruling out any future local or national electoral alliance with the FN.

[See also: Poujade; Holocaust*; immigration*; nazism*]

Lubbers, Ruud

Prime Minister of the Netherlands 1982–86 and 1989–94. Lubbers was born in Rotterdam in 1939. After studying economics, he managed the family machinery production business. A Christian Democrat, he served as Economics Minister 1973–77. In 1982 he became the youngest ever Netherlands Prime Minister. He played a significant role in bringing about the Maastricht Treaty in December 1991, since the Netherlands held the presidency of the Council of Ministers at the time.

[See also: Maastricht Treaty*]

Lübke, Heinrich

President of the Federal Republic of Germany 1959–69. Lübke was born in Enkhausen, Westphalia in 1894. Having studied engineering, his employment before the Second World War included that of director of the German Farmers' Association. During the war he was engaged in the design of buildings for war purposes, including the factories which produced the V–1 'flying bombs' in Peenemunde (an activity which was used by his opponents to attack Lübke during his presidency). After the war he was active in founding the CDU, and served first in the Land government of North Rhine-Westphalia, then in the

federal government, as Minister for Food and Agriculture. When Adenauer decided that he himself would not seek the presidency in 1959, and when other leading CDU politicians such as Erhard also refused to be candidates, Lübke was chosen. He was criticised during his presidency for his blunders in public speaking, although it was subsequently suggested that these might have been caused by advancing illness. He used his second term as President (1964–69) to promote the idea of a 'grand coalition' of the CDU–CSU and SPD, an idea which became reality in 1966. Lübke died in 1972.

[See also: Adenauer; Erhard; grand coalition*]

Macmillan, Harold

British Prime Minister and leader of the Conservative Party 1957–63. Macmillan was born in London in 1894 and educated at Eton and Oxford University. He served and was wounded in the First World War. While directing the family publishing firm, he entered the House of Commons in 1924. He held various posts in Churchill's war-time government, and in the post-war Conservative governments of Churchill and Eden, including the post of Foreign Secretary in 1955 and then Chancellor of the Exchequer. On Eden's retirement, Macmillan became Prime Minister. He is particularly remembered for presiding over a period of economic growth in the late 1950s, coining the phrase: 'you've never had it so good'; for his acceptance of the decline of British power in its former African possessions, where he used the phrase: 'the winds of change' to describe the process of African states asserting their independence; and for making an unsuccessful attempt to take the United Kingdom into the European Economic Community. Though he won the general election of 1959 with a large majority, illness and a series of debilitating political crises (including the Profumo scandal) persuaded him to resign in 1963, before the 1964 general election, handing over as Prime Minister and leader to Lord Home. He became the Earl of Stockton in 1984, and died in 1986.

[See also: Churchill; Eden; Home; Profumo Affair*]

de Maizière, Lothar

Prime Minister of the German Democratic Republic following the first (and only) free elections to the People's Chamber (Volkskammer) in 1990. De Maizière was born in Nordhausen in 1940. He studied music and law, and joined the East German CDU (a party within the block-party arrangement of GDR parties, under the dominance of the communist party, the SED). As a lawyer, he defended several dissidents prior to the collapse of the communist regime in 1989. He was active in church affairs and held high office within the East German Protestant church. During the political turbulence following Honecker's resignation in 1989, de Maizière was elected in November 1989 as Chairman of the GDR–CDU when the previous Chairman, associated with the years of CDU subservience to the SED, had to resign. He led the CDU-dominated electoral 'Alliance for Germany' to victory in the 1990 elections to the People's Chamber, becoming Prime Minister after that election. He enthusiastically pursued negotiations with the government of the Federal Republic and with foreign governments, leading to economic and monetary union, then to political fusion, with the FRG. Following reunification he served briefly in Kohl's government as a minister without portfolio, and was elected to the Bundestag in December 1990. However, as with many other prominent East German politicians, accusations of association with the GDR secret police (the Stasi) proved to be

such a political embarrassment to de Maizière that he resigned from his party offices, his political career at an end.

[See also: Honecker; Kohl; reunification of Germany*; Stasi*]

Major, John

Prime Minister of the United Kingdom and leader of the Conservative Party 1990–97. John Major was born in 1943 in Carlshalton, Surrey. He entered a career in banking, combining this with local government activities in London. He became an MP in 1979. He rose rapidly within the ranks of the Thatcher government, serving as Foreign Minister and then Chancellor of the Exchequer in 1989. In 1990 he persuaded Mrs Thatcher to allow Britain to join the European Exchange Rate Mechanism, which limited currency fluctuations. However, Britain had to abandon its membership of that currency system in 1992. Though he had, somewhat surprisingly, led the Conservatives to victory in the 1992 general election, his small majority in the House of Commons soon eroded. This meant that he could not afford to offend either the pro-European or the 'euro-sceptic' wings of his party, which gave the impression of indecisive leadership. He was unable to prevent the Conservative Party suffering a heavy defeat in the 1997 general election. Major took responsibility for that defeat, and resigned as party leader shortly afterwards.

[See also: Thatcher; Exchange Rate Mechanism*; euro-sceptic*]

Makarios, Archbishop

President of the Republic of Cyprus 1959–77. Makarios was born as Mihail Mouskos in Cyprus in 1913. He became a priest of the Orthodox church in 1946, a bishop in 1948, and archbishop in 1950. He was a leader of the Enosis movement in Cyprus, which sought to link Cyprus to Greece. The British colonial authorities arrested Makarios and deported him to the Seychelles in 1956. He returned to Cyprus in 1959 and became Prime Minister in the government which combined Greek and Turkish Cypriot leaders. Ousted by a military coup in 1974, he returned as Prime Minister of the Greek part of Cyprus in 1975 and held that office until his death in 1977.

[See also: Colonels' coup*; Enosis*]

Marchais, Georges

Leader of the French Communist Party. Born into a working-class background at La Hoguette (Calvados) in 1920, Marchais was a skilled mechanic in the aeronautics industry. Later, his political career was dogged by controversy over his war-time record: Marchais denied the allegation that he worked voluntarily at the German Messerschmidt factory in Neu-Ulm before the introduction of compulsory labour regulations in 1943. After the Second World War, he became involved in trade union activity and in 1947 joined the French Communist Party (PCF). In 1956, he became Secretary of the Seine-South federation of the party and joined the Central Committee and Political Bureau in 1959. In 1961, he was made responsible for party organisation and in 1972 became leader of the PCF. He stood in the presidential elections of 1981, losing to his socialist rival Mitterrand. Throughout the 1960s, Marchais was known as a plain-speaking pro-Soviet. Controversially, he did not see the social unrest of May 1968 as an opportunity for socialist revolution. Instead he criticised the student leader Daniel Cohn-Bendit as a 'German anarchist' and saw the groups taking part in the protest as 'false revolutionaries' and splinter groups. Marchais led the PCF to assert the legitimacy of the Soviet Union's invasion of Czechoslovakia. In 1972

Marchais signed the historic Common Programme for the alliance of the left with the Socialist Party (PS) and left-wing Radicals, and later joined a coalition governmnent with the PS (1981–84). During the 1970s, Marchais presented the PCF as 'eurocommunist', adopting a specific French path to communism in place of the model of the Soviet Union. Under eurocommunism, the PCF dropped some aspects of Marxist–Leninist doctrine, accepted full democratic rights as understood in Western countries, and acknowledged the principle of pluralism in free elections and a multi-party system, social and religious life. However, when electoral gains in support fell in favour of the Socialists rather than the Communists, Marchais withdrew the PCF from the co-operation with the PS and turned the party back to a more pro-Soviet line, particularly on world issues such as the Soviet intervention in Afghanistan and on events in Poland. As the PCF's electoral support declined rapidly from 1981 to 1986, Marchais' support within the party crumbled. He was accused of authoritarianism and dissident 'renovators' began to contest the leadership from the late 1980s.

[See also: Mitterrand; eurocommunism*]

Martens, Wilfried

Prime Minister of Belgium 1979–81, 1981–92 and prominent European christian democrat. Martens was born in 1936 at Sleidinge. He studied at Louvain University and in 1960 became a lawyer at the Court of Appeal in Ghent. He was a leader of the Flemish People's Movement before becoming a christian democrat. He joined the Christian People's Party (CVP) in 1962 and was President of its youth organisation 1967–71. He was adviser to the Harmel cabinet (1965), the Vanden Boeynants cabinet (1966) and with the Ministry of

Community Relations in 1968. He was President of the CVP 1972–79, a Member of Parliament 1974–91 and a Member of the senate 1991–94. His first term as Prime Minister ended in his resignation in April 1981 when the Socialists in his government refused to accept Martens' economic plan to beat Belgium's rising unemployment and budgetary problems. In 1976 he was co-founder of the European People's Party (EPP). During his second term as Prime Minister (1981–92), he introduced legislation promoting regional autonomy in Belgium, but had difficulties in getting the bill through Parliament. His government collapsed in 1991 and he became Minister of State in 1992. He became the EPP's President 1990–99 and also acted as President of the EPP party group in the European Parliament 1994–99. From 1993 to 1996 he was President of the European Union of Christian Democrats.

Mauroy, Pierre

The first Socialist Prime Minister of the Fifth Republic (1981–84). Mauroy was born in 1928 at Cartignies. He was General-Secretary of the Socialist Party's (SFIO) Young Socialists 1950–58. A secondary school teacher from 1952, he was a branch General-Secretary of the main teacher's union FEN 1955–59. In 1966, he became Deputy General-Secretary of the Socialist Party, but party leader Guy Mollet backed Savary rather than Mauroy to succeed him as leader of the newly formed Socialist Party (PS) in 1969. Mauroy backed Mitterrand's successful challenge to the party leadership in 1971 and was rewarded with the party position of National Co-ordination Secretary. An experienced and committed socialist, he successfully integrated the different and sometimes conflicting factions within the party, particularly the Christian and secular tendencies. Mauroy clashed with Mitterrand after the left's defeat in the

1978 elections and was ousted from the ranks of the party leadership at the party congress of 1979. However, in 1980, he was appointed as director of Mitterrand's presidential election campaign. Mauroy was appointed Prime Minister in 1981 and headed three successive governments. The second of these included four Communist ministers and carried through the major reforms of the Mitterrand presidency. Mauroy resigned in 1984 after a disagreement with Mitterrand over secondary school policy, but continued to promote the unity of the left. In 1988, Mauroy succeeded Jospin as First Secretary of the PS (a post he held until 1992) in spite of Mitterrand's preference for the moderniser Fabius.

[See also: Fabius; Jospin; Mitterrand; Mollet]

Mendès France, Pierre

A controversial figure whose political career spanned three Republics, Mendès France was Prime Minister in the Fourth Republic from June 1954 to February 1955. Born in Paris in 1907, Mendès France was a brilliant student who became the youngest lawyer in France at age 19. He later graduated in politics and took a doctorate in law at 21. Politically active from an early age, he joined the Radical Party at 16. In 1932 he became the youngest Deputy in the Parliament and in 1938, as Under-Secretary of State for the Treasury, the youngest member of a government in the Third Republic. Falsely charged with desertion during the Second World War, he escaped from prison to England, joined General de Gaulle's Free French air force and served with a bomber squadron 1942–43. He worked with de Gaulle in Algiers as 'minister' of finance in what was to become the Provisional Government of France in May 1944. In 1944 he led the French delegation to the 1944 Bretton Woods conference on international monetary issues and participated in the creation of the World Bank. In September 1944, after the liberation of Paris, he was named by de Gaulle as Minister of the National Economy. Dynamic and stubborn, he pursued unpopular anti-inflationary measures and currency reform, but was opposed by Finance Minister René Pleven. De Gaulle opted to support Pleven and Mendès France resigned in May 1945. He took a principled stance, refusing a ministerial post in 1946 as he believed he would not be permitted sufficient autonomy to carry out his duties, and instead accepted numerous national and international economic assignments. During his short premiership (1954–55), Mendès France launched a radical programme. Serving also as Foreign Minister, he brought the war in Indo-China to a close; he resolved an explosive situation in Tunisia by granting its autonomy; allowed a vote in the National Assembly to decide an entrenched controversy over the European Defence Community (the vote went against the project, which was dropped); and helped to negotiate the terms for German rearmament and entry into NATO. His bold handling of controversial issues mobilised various forces against him and he was voted out of office in February 1955, ostensibly over his Algerian policy. From 1955 to 1957 he tried to renovate the Radical Party, but failed, and resigned as leader. After serving briefly as Minister without Portfolio (1956) in Guy Mollet's government, he remained in an opposition role for the next twenty-five years. Mendès France opposed both the institutional framework of the Fifth Republic and the way in which de Gaulle came to power at the head of the new Republic, which he saw as illegitimate. During the Fifth Republic, Mendès France associated briefly with left-wing groups but was politically active largely on the basis of his personal experience and reputation. During the 1970s, he devoted his attention to trying to broker an agreement between Israel and the Palestinians. Mendès France supported Mitterrand in the presidential elections of 1981. He died in October 1982.

[See also: de Gaulle; Mitterrand; Mollet; Algerian conflict*; European Defence Community*]

Mitterrand, François

Leader of the French Socialist Party and President of France 1981–95. Mitterrand was born in Jarnac (in the Charante region) in 1916. He studied law, and worked in law and publishing. In the Second World War he became a prisoner-of-war in 1940, but escaped via Algeria to London. He served in de Gaulle's provisional government until 1946, then became a member of the National Assembly, serving in various capacities in eleven different governments during the Fourth Republic. He played a leading role in various efforts to reorganise the Socialists, and in 1971 became leader of the newly formed Socialist Party, remaining leader until 1981. He was the losing candidate in the second round of voting in the presidential elections of 1965 and 1974 (against de Gaulle and d'Estaing). He defeated d'Estaing in 1981 to become the first Socialist President of the Fifth Republic, and was re-elected in 1988. In his second term he twice had to govern under conditions of cohabitation, with a prime minister from the right wing as a consequence of the outcome of elections to the National Assembly. Mitterrand had to confront rumours that he had collaborated with the Vichy regime during the war and of corruption within the ranks of his own party. He died in 1996.

[See also: de Gaulle; Giscard d'Estaing; cohabitation*; Vichy regime*]

Modrow, Hans

Head of government of the GDR
1989–90. Modrow was born in West
Pomerania in 1928. He joined the SED
in 1949, involving himself at first
especially in its youth organisation (the
Free German Youth), in which he
became a full-time employee, moving
then to a staff position in the SED. He
became head of the party organisation
in Dresden in 1973, but was always
regarded as something of an outsider in
the party, and failed to attain positions
within the party that his experience and
qualifications would seem to have
deserved. This was associated with a
reputation in Dresden for resistance to,
and criticism of, some policies of the
SED central committee in Berlin. Thus
when the SED came under pressure
during the citizen movement protests in
Autumn 1989, Modrow was seen as a
potential reformer who could rescue the
party, and Krenz persuaded him to take
the post of Prime Minister. This post he
retained until the first democratic
elections for the Volkskammer in March
1990, but during his period in office he
was seen as too reactionary for the
times, being opposed by the Round
Table and by other parties within and
outside his coalition government.
Following the reunification of Germany,
Modrow became a Member of the
Bundestag for the PDS. Accusations of
electoral manipulation in Dresden in
1989 led to his trial and conviction in
1993. He later became Honorary
Chairman of the PDS.
  [See also: Krenz; reunification of
Germany*; Round Table*]

Mollet, Guy

Secretary-General of the Socialist Party
(SFIO) 1946–69 and Prime Minister of
France 1956–57, Mollet played a key
role in the transition between the
French Fourth and Fifth Republics.
Mollet was born into a working-class

family in Flers (Normandy) in 1905 and
was educated through a state
scholarship. He joined the Young
Socialists in 1921 and the SFIO proper
in 1923. A school teacher, Mollet helped
to found the union, the General
Federation of the Teaching Profession.
During the Second World War he
worked with the resistance and was a
German prisoner-of-war 1940–41.
Elected Secretary-General of the SFIO in
1946, he brought ideological and
strategic change to the party. He was
elected to the first National Assembly of
the Fourth Republic in 1946 and
appointed Minister of State in Léon
Blum's government 1946–47, a post he
returned to under Pleven in 1950 before
becoming Deputy Prime Minister
1950–51. After the parliamentary
elections of 1956, Mollet became Prime
Minister of a coalition government
comprising mainly Socialists and
Radicals. His programme featured
stabilising the situation in Algeria and
social welfare reforms, but mounting
problems led to his resignation in 1957.
In 1958 Mollet was instrumental in
bringing de Gaulle's Fifth Republic into
being, believing that this was the only
way France could avoid a military
dictatorship. Mollet was appointed
Minister of State in de Gaulle's
government, and helped to draw up the
new constitution of the Fifth Republic,
but moved the Socialists into opposition
in 1959. By 1965, Mitterrand had
emerged as the leading individual on
the left of the political spectrum. When
the Socialists formed a new party (PS)
in 1969, Mollet resigned as
Secretary-General and devoted himself
instead to his socialist research institute
OURS. He died in 1975.
  [See also: de Gaulle; Algerian
conflict*; resistance groups*]

Monnet, Jean-Marie

The key thinker behind French post-war
economic planning and the visionary

123 BIOGRAPHIES

strategist behind European integration, Jean Monnet never held elected office, nor did he follow a regular civil service career path. Monnet was born in Cognac in 1888, was apprenticed in London to learn English, and at 18 became an international salesman for his father's wholesale brandy co-operative. Unfit for service in the First World War, he helped to initiate the creation in 1916–18 of eight Allied Executives co-ordinating scarce supplies of commodities and pooling transport. After the war, he became Deputy Secretary-General of the new League of Nations and was concerned with rehabilitation programmes. In 1938, Monnet was co-opted by the Prime Minister, Edouard Daladier, to help with preparations for the Second World War. He negotiated aeroplane orders with the neutral USA and took a leading role in Anglo-French co-ordination. Sent to the British Supply Council in Washington by Churchill, by 1941 Monnet was acting as an adviser to Beaverbrook and Roosevelt, promoting war production. Sent to Algiers to advise the Allies in North Africa, Monnet helped de Gaulle to gain control of the French committee of national liberation. Back in France, in 1946 Monnet took charge of the new, independent General Planning Commission attached to the Prime Minister, where he devised the 'Monnet Plan' on investment priorities for economic reconstruction through American funding. The plan was intended to modernise France's economic capacity, to be responsive to changing economic needs and to integrate affected interests, including the trade unions. It provided the foundations for French economic co-operation and competition with Germany. In 1950, Monnet turned his attention to European integration, preparing a plan for the future European Coal and Steel Community (ECSC), which was promoted by the French Foreign Minister Robert Schuman. Monnet chaired the conference which produced the Treaty

of Paris (18 April 1951) formally establishing the ECSC. He also participated in plans for a European Defence Community (EDC), abandoned when the French National Assembly refused to ratify it. In spite of this setback, Monnet and the Belgian Foreign Minister Spaak managed to maintain the momentum towards European economic integration. In 1955, Monnet presented Spaak with plans for a European Atomic Energy Community. Together with Dutch proposals for a Common Market, this proposal culminated in the Rome Treaties of 1957, which established the EEC and EURATOM. De Gaulle's return to power in 1958 restored a nationalist mentality to French politics and undermined Monnet's internationalist stance and his personal influence in France. In 1959 he persuaded the USA to co-found the OECD. Monnet died in 1979.

[See also: Churchill; de Gaulle; Schuman; Spaak; European Coal and Steel Community*; European Defence Community*; European Free Trade Association*]

Moro, Aldo

Prime Minister of Italy 1963–68, 1974–76, Moro was kidnapped and murdered by Red Brigade terrorists in 1978. Moro was born in 1916 in Maglie and studied at the University of Bari, where he took part in Catholic student politics and gained a PhD in law in 1940. After the Second World War, Moro joined the Christian Democratic party (DC) and was elected to Italy's Constituent Assembly in 1946. Moro took part in the drafting of the constitution which established the Republic of Italy in June 1946. In 1948 he was elected to the Chamber of Deputies and became a leading member of the DC party group. He served as Under-Secretary of State in de Gasperi's government in May 1948. In 1955 he became Minister of Justice and carried out a reform of the prison system.

He was appointed Minister of Education in May 1957 and in 1959 became leader of the DC. In 1963 he formed a centre-left government which he successfully steered and reorganised until June 1968, when the Socialists refused to take part. He then took the post of Foreign Minister until he again formed a coalition government with the Republican Party. From February 1976 he maintained a minority government in power until July 1976. He then became President of the DC and it was anticipated that he might be chosen as President of the Republic. However, on 16 March 1978, he was kidnapped by Red Brigade terrorists, 'tried' and killed. His body was found in Rome on 9 May 1978.

[See also: de Gasperi; Red Brigades*]

Mussolini, Benito

Fascist dictator of Italy. Born in 1883 in the Romagna, Mussolini became a socialist agitator in his youth. He fought in the First World War, then became a representative of an ex-servicemen's association. In 1919 he began to promote fascist beliefs, based on radical nationalism and authoritarian rule, and engaged in terrorising his former socialist allies. He became Prime Minister of Italy following his 'March on Rome' by his blackshirted fascist supporters, but soon turned this post into that of a dictator (Il Duce). He then developed a policy of overseas expansion, to rival Hitler's territorial ambitions in Europe. The invasion of Abbysinia was followed by engagement on the side of General Franco in the Spanish civil war, then the occupation and annexation of Albania. He entered into a pact with Hitler (the Axis pact). Joining in the Second World War once France had collapsed, Mussolini's military advances in Greece and North Africa were soon followed by serious defeats. He was forced to resign from his position as head of the government in 1943 and was then imprisoned. A

daring glider rescue from this imprisonment by German troops permitted Mussolini to set up a puppet regime in German-occupied Italy, but as the war came to an end in April 1945 Mussolini was caught by partisans when attempting to escape to Switzerland, and was summarily hanged.

[See also: Franco; Hitler; Spanish civil war*]

Ollenhauer, Erich

Leader of the West German Social Democratic Party (SPD) 1952–60. Born in Magdeburg in 1901, Ollenhauer joined the SPD in 1916 and became a member of the party's paid staff. He was a member of the SPD contingent on the Parliamentary Council which drafted the Basic Law, was elected to the Bundestag in 1949, and, following the death of Schumacher, became party leader in 1952. He was the SPD chancellor-candidate in the 1953 and 1957 Bundestag elections. His failure in the 1957 election (when Adenauer secured an absolute majority of votes and seats) and his discomfiture with the 1959 Bad Godesberg SPD reform programme led to his resignation as party leader in 1960. He died in 1963.

[See also: Adenauer; Schumacher; Godesberg Programme*]

Paisley, Ian

Leader of the Democratic Unionist Party (Northern Ireland). Paisley was born in Armagh in 1926. After a theological education, he was ordained as minister in 1946 and became involved in Unionist politics. He was a member of the Northern Ireland Parliament at Stormont 1970–72, and of the Northern Ireland Assembly 1973–74. He has been an MP in the House of Commons since 1970 and was elected to the new Northern Ireland Assembly in 1998. He was elected leader of his party in 1979. Paisley has a reputation as an intemperate orator, an uncompromising opponent of Northern Ireland political Catholicism and nationalism, a propagator of fundamentalist Protestantism and a bitter critic of the British government whenever proposals for a compromise settlement in Northern Ireland are mooted. Paisley opposed the Sunningdale Agreement in 1972, for instance. His behaviour in the House of Commons has resulted in his exclusion on several occasions.

[See also: Good Friday Agreement*; Stormont*]

Palme, Olaf

Prime Minister of Sweden 1969–76 and 1982 until his assassination in 1986. Palme was born in Stockholm in 1927. He studied law, but began a career in politics within the organisation of the Swedish Social Democratic Labour Party. He was elected to the Swedish Parliament in 1957 and from 1963 was appointed to several governmental positions, before becoming party leader and Prime Minister in 1969. While out of office between 1976 and 1981, he was a member of several international commissions concerned with third-world development and disarmament. His government undertook several important constitutional reforms in Sweden, including making the Swedish Parliament unicameral and eliminating almost entirely the political role of the monarch. He was killed by gunfire from an unknown assailant in Stockholm in February 1986.

Papandreou, Andreas

Prime Minister of Greece 1981–89 and 1993–96. Papandreou was born in Chios in 1919, the son of the former Prime Minister Georgios Papandreou. He studied law at the University of Athens and became a Trotskyist critic of the dictatorship of Ioannis Metaxas. Arrested

and tortured in 1939, he left in 1940 for the USA, where he studied at Columbia University and received a doctorate from Harvard in 1943. Papandreou took US citizenship, served in the US navy and began an academic career in economics. He returned to Greece in 1959 and became Director of the Centre of Economic Research. He renounced his American citizenship in January 1964 and was elected to Parliament as a representative of his father's Centre Union Party. When Georgios Papandreou became Prime Minister in 1964, his son Andreas became his chief adviser. Andreas was an outspoken critic of the King and the military and was forced to step down in November 1964 on charges of corruption. He was reinstated in the Spring of 1965, but fell with his father's government in July 1965. When the military staged a coup in April 1967, Andreas Papandreou was charged with high treason and was kept in solitary confinement until he was released in an amnesty in December 1967. He went into exile as an opponent of the junta, again working as an academic. He founded the anti-junta Panhellenic Liberation Movement in 1968. Papandreou returned to Greece in 1974 when the military government fell. He refused to lead his father's former party, the Centre Union Party, and instead founded the Panhellenic Socialist Movement. For the rest of the 1970s, Papandreou vigorously attacked the Karamanlis government. In the elections of 1981, his Panhellenic Socialist Movement beat Rallis' New Democratic Party and Papandreou became Prime Minister. His government introduced a series of socialist reforms. In 1988 his government's popularity fell and he was accused of corruption and the misuse of power. He stepped down in 1989 after electoral defeat. Once his parliamentary immunity was lifted, Papandreou was charged with corruption, but was acquitted in January 1992. He led his party to an election victory in 1993, but his health deteriorated from 1995, and he resigned as Prime Minister in January 1996. He died later that year.

[See also: Karamanlis]

Pétain, Marshal [See: Vichy regime*]

Pflimlin, Pierre

Prime Minister of France 1958. Pflimlin was born in Roubaix in 1907. He was educated in Mulhouse (in Alsace) and universities in Paris and Strasbourg and qualified as a lawyer. He was a prisoner-of-war in 1940, and on release joined the resistance. Elected to the National Assembly in 1946 as a Republican Party deputy, he became a minister in many of the – usually short-lived – cabinets of the Fourth Republic. After his very brief term as last Prime Minister of the Fourth Republic (except for de Gaulle himself), Pflimlin served in de Gaulle's Fifth Republic government in 1962. He served as mayor of Strasbourg from 1959 until 1984, and was a Member of the European Parliament 1979–89, holding the office of President of the Parliament 1984–87. He was an enthusiastic supporter of European integration. He died in 2000.

[See also: de Gaulle; Algerian conflict*; resistance groups*]

Pöhl, Karl Otto

President of the German Federal Bank (Bundesbank) 1980–91. Pöhl was born in Hanover in 1929. After an early career as a journalist, he became Vice-President of the Bundesbank in 1977, and became President in 1980. Though a member of the Social Democratic Party, he resisted several measures of the SPD–Liberal coalition designed to decrease unemployment through state expenditures. Pöhl is particularly remembered for his criticism in 1990 of the plan by the Kohl government for an exchange rate of 2:1

(and parity for some transactions) when the German Democratic Republic and the German Federal Republic entered into a Treaty of Economic and Monetary Union. Pöhl warned that such a generous exchange rate would prove to be inflationary and would damage the East German economy.

[See also: Kohl; Bundesbank*]

Pompidou, Georges

Prime Minister, then President, of the Fifth French Republic. Pompidou was born in the Auvergne in 1911. After studying classics, he became a secondary school teacher. Involved in the resistance during the Second World War, he joined de Gaulle's staff in 1944, and held various political appointments before entering banking in 1955. He returned to politics when the Fifth Republic was established in 1958, and was principal negotiator of the Évian Agreements, ending French involvement in the Algerian struggle for independence. De Gaulle made Pompidou Prime Minister in 1962. In 1968, Pompidou played a major role in calming the riots and protests initiated by the students and workers. De Gaulle held Pompidou responsible for what he saw as unwise concessions to the workers and dismissed him as Prime Minister that same year. However, following de Gaulle's sudden resignation as President in 1969, Pompidou was elected as de Gaulle's successor. Pompidou set about extending the powers of the president into economic and other domestic policy areas, in a drive to modernise the French economy, especially in relation to its infrastructure. He died in office in 1974.

[See also: de Gaulle; Évian Agreements*; resistance groups*]

Poujade, Pierre-Marie

Born in 1920 in Saint-Céré (Lot), Poujade was a political activist who challenged processes of modernisation in France. Brought up as a monarchist, he at first supported the Vichy regime. However, by 1942 Poujade was disillusioned by Vichy's subservience to the Germans and tried to leave France for Spain. He was arrested but was freed in 1943. After the war he went back to Saint-Céré and set up a wholesale book business. By the early 1950s such small businesses, a strong feature of France's economy, were threatened by the rise of big business. In 1953, Poujade began to organise demonstrations against the way the complicated tax system was implemented with respect to smaller businesses. In 1954 he formed the pressure group, the Union for the Protection of Businesses and Craftsmen, (UDCA), which soon took on a wider protest role, attacking aspects of modernisation including foreign influences in France, republicanism, bureaucracy, the dominance of Paris and urbanisation. In 1955 Poujade formed a political party, the Union and Fraternity of the French (UFF) and conducted major rallies throughout France. In the 1956 elections, the UFF gained 52 seats in the National Assembly. However, the party was organisationally and electorally unstable, and did not survive the transition to the Fifth Republic in 1958 as a credible political force. Poujade remained a wild card in French politics until the mid-1960s, when he became reconciled to the Fifth Republic and even became adviser to Pompidou on small businesses. He launched a further party (UDI) for the 1979 European elections, but it was not successful. In 1981, he supported Mitterrand's candidacy for the presidential elections.

[See also: Mitterrand; Vichy regime*]

Prodi, Romano

Prime Minister of Italy 1996–98 and President of the European Commission.

Born in 1939 in Scandiano, Prodi studied at the Catholic University of Milan. He became Professor of Economics and Industrial Policy at the University of Bologna in 1971. He was Minister of Industry 1978–79. During the 1980s and 1990s he held high-ranking posts related to economic and industrial research and has published widely on such issues. In 1995, following the public collapse in confidence in the traditional parties, he founded the Olive Tree, a coalition of centre-left parties, and after the electoral success of the coalition he became Prime Minister 1996–98. In 1999 he became President of the European Commission.

[See also: Tangentopoli*]

Rau, Johannes

President of the Federal Republic of Germany from 1999, and Prime Minister of North Rhine-Westphalia (NRW) 1978–97. Rau was born in Wuppertal in 1931. He went into a career in the book trade. He joined the Social Democratic Party in 1957, and was elected to the NRW Land Parliament in 1958. After serving as lord mayor of his home town, Wuppertal, he became a minister in the NRW Land government from 1970 until his election by his party in 1978 as NRW Prime Minister. He led his party to a series of electoral successes in NRW, making what had previously been a marginal Land for his party into one which provided the SPD with absolute majorities. He was SPD chancellor-candidate in the 1987 federal election, but was unable to attract many additional votes to his party. He served in several senior positions in the national SPD organisation, becoming a deputy chairman in 1982. He ran as SPD candidate for the office of federal president in 1994, but without success. However, in 1999, supported by the large number of SPD Members of the Bundestag elected in 1998, Rau was elected President of the republic on the second ballot. Rau has always had close links to the Protestant church in West Germany.

Robinson, Mary

Former President of Ireland and UN High Commissioner for Human Rights. Robinson was born in 1944 in County Mayo, Ireland. She studied law at Trinity College, Dublin and Harvard University. She then practised as a lawyer and became a professor at Trinity College. She was a member of the Irish Senate 1969–89. In 1990 she was elected as President of Ireland and served until 1997. As President, she lent her support to several measures promoting a more liberal society in Ireland. She was then appointed as UN Commissioner for Human Rights, in which role she has been involved in various crises all over the world, for example in East Timor.

Rocard, Michel

French Prime Minister 1988–91, Rocard was born in 1930 at Courbevoie (Seine). He studied at the Institute of Political Studies in Paris and at the National College of Administration. He pursued a dual career as an inspector of finances and in the 'new left' in politics, using the pseudonym Georges Servet for his political activities until the mid-1960s. Rocard was National Secretary of the Association of Socialist Students 1955–56. The group was allied to the Socialist Party (SFIO), but Rocard split with the party over the Mollet government's Algerian policy. In 1958, he became a member of the Autonomous Socialist Party (PSA) which joined with the Unified Socialist Party (PSU) in 1960. He was National Secretary of the PSU 1967–73, the youngest leader of an organised political party. Opposed to violence, he did not join the street protests of 1968, but later became spokesman of that movement. In 1974 Rocard supported Mitterrand's

presidential campaign and joined the new Socialist Party (PS) later that year, following the party's integration of the bulk of the non-communist left of the party spectrum. He soon became the leading voice of the new left or 'realist' social democracy within the PS and the only serious rival to Mitterrand for the party's leadership. Popular with the public in the late 1970s, in the 1980s he had to contend with a new generation of 'Mitterrandists', particularly Fabius and Jospin. Rocard was Minister of the Plan 1981–83 and Minister of Agriculture 1983 but resigned in 1985 in protest over the PS's tactical decision to introduce proportional representation for the 1986 parliamentary elections. He distanced himself from the party to prepare his candidacy for the presidential elections of 1988, but withdrew when Mitterrand declared he would stand. Rocard became Prime Minister of France (1988–91). He was Secretary of the Socialist Party 1993–94 and has been a Member of the European Parliament since 1994.

[See also: Fabius; Jospin; Mitterrand; Mollet; Algerian conflict*]

Rohwedder, Detlev

Head of the Treuhandgesellschaft (Trustee Agency) responsible for privatisation and restructuring of East German business enterprises following reunification. Rohwedder was born in Gotha in 1932. He studied law at the Universities of Mainz and Hamburg, then was employed by various business companies. He joined the SPD in 1969, and that same year was appointed as the chief civil servant (State Secretary) in the Ministry of Economics when the SPD–FDP coalition was formed. He retained that post until 1978. In 1990 he was appointed Chairman of the Treuhandgesellschaft. In 1991 he was assassinated by a bomb set by the Red Army faction.

[See also: Treuhandanstalt*]

Salazar, Antonio

Prime Minister of Portugal 1932–68. Salazar was born in Santa Comba Dao in 1889. He studied economics and finance at university, and became a professor of economics in 1916, before entering politics. He was elected to Parliament in 1921 and became Minister of Finance in 1926 and again from 1928. He ruled as a dictator. He maintained Portugal's neutral stance in the Spanish civil war and the Second World War, though he gave support to Franco. He set himself firmly against the introduction of steps towards autonomy for Portugal's overseas colonies. He reluctantly agreed to allow a multi-party system to develop after the Second World War, though the secret police kept opposition activities in check. He survived a number of attempts to overthrow him and his regime by communists and elements of the military. He retired on grounds of ill-health in 1968 and died in 1970.

[See also: Armed Forces Movement*]

Santer, Jacques

Prime Minister of Luxembourg 1984–89 and 1989–94 and President of the European Commission 1994–99. Born in 1937 in Wasserbillig, Santer studied at the Universities of Paris and Strasbourg and at the Paris Institute of Political Studies. He became an advocate at the Luxembourg Court of Appeal 1961–65. He worked with the Ministry of Labour and Social Security 1963–65 and was a government attaché 1965–66. He was President of the Christian Social Party 1974–82. He was Secretary of State for Cultural and Social Affairs 1972–74. He was a member of the Luxembourg Chamber of Deputies 1974–79 and of the European Parliament 1975–79, becoming its Vice-President in 1975–77. He then returned to Luxembourg politics, acting as Minister of Labour, of Finance and of Social Security 1979–84.

While Prime Minister he was simultaneously Minister of State and of Finance 1984–89 and Minister of State, of Cultural Affairs and of the Treasury and Financial Affairs 1989–94. Santer became President of the European Commission in 1994 but a series of scandals led to his resignation, together with his Commission team, in 1998.

Scalfaro, Oscar

President of Italy 1992–99, Scalfaro promoted the ongoing process of constitutional reform in Italy during the 1980s. Born in 1918 in Novara, Scalfaro studied at the Catholic University of Milan. He was elected Christian Democratic (DC) deputy for Turin-Novara-Vercelli in 1948. He played a leadership role in the DC, acting as Secretary, then Vice-Chair of the parliamentary party group and participating in the party's national council. During de Gasperi's leadership, Scalfaro joined the DC central office. He was Under-Secretary of State at the Ministry of Labour and Social Security in the Fanfani government, Under-Secretary in the Ministry of Justice and Under-Secretary at the Ministry of the Interior 1959–62. He was Minister of Transport and Civil Aviation in the Moro, Leone and Andreotti governments, Minister of Education in the second Andreotti government, and Minister of the Interior 1983–87. In April 1987 he tried to form a government, but was not successful. He became President of the Republic on 28 May 1992.

[See also: Andreotti; de Gasperi; Leone; Moro; Tangentopoli*]

Scharping, Rudolf

Former leader of the German Social Democratic Party and chancellor-candidate in the 1994 Bundestag election. Scharping was born in Niederelbert in 1947. After studying law, politics and sociology at the

University of Bonn, he became an assistant to two Members of the Bundestag (1969–75) and was Land Chair of the Young Socialists 1969–74, and Deputy Chair of the federal Young Socialists 1974–76. He was elected to the Rhineland-Pfalz Land Parliament in 1975, remaining a Member until 1994. He served as Chair of the Land parliamentary party from 1985 to 1991, Chair of the Rhineland-Pfalz SPD 1985–94 and Minister-President 1991–94. Elected to the Bundestag in 1994, he became leader of the SPD Bundestag party group, a post he held until the 1998 election. He was elected leader of the SPD in 1993 but his failure to win the 1994 Bundestag election and poor Land election results after that election led to a successful challenge by Lafontaine at the 1995 party conference. Following the 1998 election, as a result of which the SPD formed a government with the Greens, Scharping was unsuccessful in his efforts to retain the leadership of the parliamentary party, and instead was persuaded to become Minister of Defence.

[See also: Lafontaine]

Scheel, Walter

Foreign Minister of the Federal Republic of Germany, leader of the Free Democratic Party (FDP) and federal President. Scheel was born in 1919 in Solingen. He served in the German air force during the Second World War, afterwards pursuing a business career. He joined the FDP and entered local politics before his election to the Bundestag in 1953. He was one of the group of young FDP members whose campaign in North Rhine-Westphalia in 1956 resulted in the termination of the Land governing coalition of the FDP and CDU, and its replacement by a coalition with the SPD, in protest at Adenauer's proposed electoral system changes. He became a deputy leader of the FDP in 1958, and was elected as leader in 1968,

taking the FDP into coalition with the SPD after the Bundestag election of 1969. As Foreign Minister in the Brandt government, Scheel played a significant role in Brandt's Ostpolitik. Scheel resigned as Foreign Minister and leader of his party in 1974 on health grounds, and was elected as federal President that same year, serving one term (1974–79).

[See also: Adenauer; Brandt; Grabenwahlsystem*; Ostpolitik*; Young Turks' revolt*]

Schmid, Carlo

Prominent politician in the West German Social Democratic Party after the Second World War. Schmid was born in 1896 in Perpignan, in southern France. He was a lawyer by training, becoming a professor of law and then of political science. He served as Minister of Justice in the Land of Württemberg-Hohenzollern 1947–50, and as a member of the SPD delegation to the Parliamentary Council which drafted the Basic Law 1948–49. As a member of the Praesidium of the SPD Schmid had great influence on the drafting and adoption of the Godesberg Programme. He was a Member of the Bundestag 1949–72, and played a leading role in the parliamentary party of the SPD and in Bundestag committees, as well as acting as a Vice-President of the Bundestag 1949–66 and 1969–72. He served as Minister responsible for co-ordination with the Länder in the grand coalition (1966–69). He was also author of several distinguished books on political and historical topics, and did much to foster Franco-German relations. He died in 1979.

[See also: Godesberg Programme*; grand coalition*]

Schmidt, Helmut

Chancellor of the Federal Republic of Germany 1974–82. Born in Hamburg in 1918, Schmidt served in the German army in the Second World War and was awarded the Iron Cross. He then attended Hamburg University, and joined the Social Democratic Party (SPD) in 1946. He was employed as a manager by the city government after graduation. First elected to the Bundestag in 1953, he resigned in 1962 to become a minister in the Hamburg Land government, where his actions during the severe 1962 flooding of the city were praised. He returned to the Bundestag in 1965, and, following service as Chairman of the SPD parliamentary party group during the 'grand coalition', became Minister of Defence in the Brandt coalition in 1969. When Schiller resigned in 1972 as Finance and Economics Minister, Schmidt took those ministries, then served as Finance Minister after the Bundestag election in 1972 until 1974. In 1974 he was the undisputed successor as Chancellor, after Brandt resigned that office in the wake of the Guillaume scandal. As Chancellor, Schmidt was effective and efficient, but, with Brandt remaining as party leader, was not successful in integrating the various factions in the SPD. In particular, the hostile attitudes of his own left wing towards defence and economic policies led to a breach within the coalition. The FDP's decision to support Kohl (the leader of the CDU) in a constructive vote of no confidence against Schmidt in October 1982 led to the replacement of Schmidt's government by a coalition of Christian Democrats and the FDP. Schmidt in political retirement took on a role as elder statesman, and from 1983 became involved in the editorship of the news weekly: *Die Zeit*.

[See also: Brandt; Kohl; constructive vote of no confidence*; grand coalition*; Guillaume Affair*]

Schönhuber, Franz

Co-founder and former leader of the German Republican party. Schonhüber was born in Trostberg (Bavaria) in 1923. In the Second World War he served as a member of the Waffen-SS (the military arm of the SS). After the war he commenced a career in journalism, which led to an important post with the Bavarian broadcasting service, including having his own talk-show, but was dismissed because of public and media reaction to his memoirs (published in 1981) in which he defended the Waffen-SS and the 'idealism' of its members. In 1983 he was a co-founder of the Republican party, a breakaway party of former CSU politicians, which soon developed a radical right-wing identity and anti-foreigner rhetoric once Schönhuber became Chairman. The Republicans had surprising successes in the Berlin Land election and European parliamentary election of 1989 (Schönhuber himself serving as an MEP until 1994) and in the Baden-Württemberg Land election in 1992. Schönhuber lost the chairmanship of the Republicans in 1994 and resigned from the party in 1995. He remained active in far-right political circles, and was a candidate for the German People's Party (DVU) in the 1998 Bundestag election.

[See also: xenophobia*]

Schröder, Gerhard

Chancellor of the Federal Republic of Germany since 1998 and leader of the Social Democratic Party (SPD) since 1999. Schröder was born in 1944 in Mossenberg, near Detmold. He studied law at the University of Göttingen. He joined the SPD in 1963, and in 1986 became leader of the SPD parliamentary group in the Lower Saxony Land Parliament. In 1989 he was elected to the Praesidium of the SPD, and in 1990 he became Minister President of Lower Saxony, winning the elections in 1994 and 1998 also. Though he had lost to Scharping in the membership ballot for the post of party leader in 1993, his electoral successes in Lower Saxony made him the obvious choice to be chancellor-candidate for the 1998 Bundestag election. He led his party to an overwhelming electoral victory in that election, and formed a coalition with the Greens. In 1999 he replaced Lafontaine as party leader, after Lafontaine resigned from his governmental and party positions.

[See also: Lafontaine; Scharping]

Schumacher, Kurt

Leader of the Social Democratic Party of West Germany after the Second World War. Schumacher was born in Prussia in 1895. His wounds in the First World War resulted in the amputation of an arm. He studied law and political science at university. He then involved himself in socialist politics in the Weimar Republic, being elected to the Reichstag in 1930. He spent much of the Hitler period in concentration camps. Involving himself in the revival of the SPD even before the Second World War had ended, Schumacher became a leading politician in the British zone of occupation. He vehemently opposed the scheme in the Soviet occupation zone to merge the SPD and the Communist Party, rejecting it for the western zones. He was elected leader of the West German SPD in 1946. The result of the Bundestag election in 1949 meant that the SPD was in opposition, and Schumacher, as leader of the opposition, criticised many of Adenauer's policies, especially concerning the market economy and Adenauer's preference for western integration rather than the pursuit of German reunification. Schumacher died in 1952.

[See also: Adenauer; Hitler]

Schuman, Robert

Schuman held high office in France, but is best known for his work for European integration. Schuman was born in Luxembourg in 1886, grew up in Metz (then German) and studied law at Bonn, Munich and Berlin. When Alsace-Lorraine was returned to France in 1918, Schuman entered French politics, being elected to Parliament in 1919 as a christian democrat. In 1940 he was appointed Under-Secretary of State for Refugees in Reynaud's war cabinet. After briefly supporting Pétain, Schuman resigned from the Vichy government and forged links with the resistance instead. After the Second World War Schuman joined the new christian democratic party: the Mouvement Républicain Populaire (MRP) and was re-elected to Parliament. He was Minister for Finance in the governments of Bidault (1946) and Ramadier (1947). He became Prime Minister (1947–48) under conditions of financial crisis and industrial unrest. From 1948 to 1953 Schuman was Minister for Foreign Affairs in ten successive governments, faced with the task of restraining Germany in the context of European co-operation. In May 1950 he adopted Monnet's plan to merge the French and German coal and steel industries. This 'Schuman Plan' led to the creation of the European Coal and Steel Community (ECSC) and eventually the EEC. His close association with the failed 'Pleven Plan' for a European Defence Community ended his spell as Foreign Minister in 1953. Schuman died in 1963.

[See also: Monnet; European Coal and Steel Community*; European Defence Community*; Vichy regime*]

Smith, Iain Duncan [See: Duncan Smith, Iain]

Smith, John

Leader of the British Labour Party from 1992 until his death in 1994. John Smith was born in 1938, and qualified as a lawyer. He became an MP in 1970, and held office in the Wilson and Callaghan governments. Having held various senior posts in the opposition's 'shadow cabinet' from 1979 onwards, he was elected as party leader in succession to Neil Kinnock, following Kinnock's resignation after the election of 1992. Smith continued and developed some of the processes of reform of the Labour Party's policies, image and organisation which had commenced under Kinnock's leadership, and which were continued by Tony Blair.

[See also: Blair; Callaghan; Kinnock; Wilson]

Soares, Mário

Prime Minister of Portugal three times 1976–85; President of Portugal 1986–96. Soares was born in 1924 in Lisbon. His father was João Soares, a liberal who had served in the republican government overthrown by a military coup in 1926. Mário Soares studied at the University of Lisbon, where he founded the United Democratic Youth Movement in 1946, and, later, at the Sorbonne in Paris. An active opponent of Salazar's dictatorship, Mário Soares was jailed 12 times on political grounds. He was first arrested for anti-government activities in 1947. In 1958 Soares was active in the unsuccessful presidential campaign of the opposition candidate General Delgado. When Delgado was murdered in Spain in 1965, Soares acted as the lawyer for his family and attracted international attention by revealing how Salazar's secret police were implicated in the crime. He was deported to São Tomé March–November 1968 and went into exile in France during the early 1970s. In West Germany in 1973, he founded the Portuguese Socialist Party and was its Secretary-General until 1986. Soares represented the Portuguese Socialists at various European socialist congresses and was the Portuguese representative to the International

League of Human Rights. After the coup of April 1974, Soares returned to Portugal. As Minister of Foreign Affairs 1974–75, he led negotiations on the independence of the Portuguese overseas colonies of Guinea-Bissau, Mozambique and Angola. He was Vice-President of the Socialist International 1976–86 and its honorary president thereafter. The Socialists won a majority in the Constituent Assembly elections in 1975, but a tense period followed when the leftist military at first refused to acknowledge the result. In further elections of April 1976, the Socialists again won a majority of seats and Soares became Prime Minister until 1978, and again 1983–85. During his period in office he pursued negotiations leading to Portuguese membership of the European Community and signed the Treaty of Accession in 1985. In 1986 he became President of Portugal. He has held numerous other national and international positions.

[See also: Salazar; Armed Forces Movement*]

Soustelle, Jacques

Leading member of the French 'Secret Army' opposed to de Gaulle's Algerian policies. Soustelle was born in 1912. He worked closely with de Gaulle during the Second World War and its immediate aftermath. He was General Secretary of the RPF, de Gaulle's party after the war. He served as Governor of Algeria, but his intemperate statements concerning Algeria led to his recall in 1956. He supported the recall of de Gaulle and the creation of the Fifth Republic, serving in de Gaulle's first government. After his exclusion from the government following riots in Algeria in 1960, Soustelle joined the leadership of the 'Secret Army', and was exiled in 1962, only returning to France when pardoned after the 1968 student riots.

[See also: de Gaulle; Algerian conflict*; May Events*]

Spaak, Paul-Henri

Prime Minister of Belgium 1938–39, March 1946, 1947–49, and leading international politician. Spaak was born into a wealthy family of political activists in 1899 in Schaerbeek. He spent two years as a German prisoner-of-war during the First World War. After the war, he graduated in law from the Université Libre de Bruxelles. He joined the Socialist Party in the 1920s and in 1932 he was elected to the Belgian Chamber of Deputies, where he led the Socialists' left faction. He served in ministerial posts in 1935–36 before becoming Prime Minister in 1938. When Germany occupied Belgium, he fled to London and acted as Foreign Minister in the Belgian government-in-exile. After the liberation, Spaak returned to Belgium as Deputy Prime Minister, but also took an active role in European and international politics. Leading the Belgian delegation to the United Nations (UN) Conference in 1945, he helped to draft the UN charter and served as the first President of the United Nations General Assembly in 1946. Spaak promoted the formation of the Benelux customs union between Belgium, the Netherlands and Luxembourg and later played a leading role in the creation of the European Common Market in March 1957. He was Secretary-General of the North Atlantic Treaty Organisation (NATO) 1957–61, after which he returned to Belgian politics as Foreign Minister. He welcomed Britain's first application to join the EEC and was angered by the French veto on British membership in 1963. He worked to ease tense relations between Belgium and its former colony, the African Congo. When he retired from politics in 1966, Spaak continued to work as a commercial international adviser. He died in 1972.

[See also: de Gaulle; Benelux*]

Spring, Dick

Irish Foreign Minister and leader of the Irish Labour Party. Spring was born in Tralee in 1950. He studied and practised law before entering the Irish Parliament in 1981. He served as Deputy Prime Minister in coalition governments in 1982–87 and 1993–97; in the second of those coalitions he was Foreign Minister. He was leader of the Irish Labour Party 1982–97.

Springer, Axel

German publisher and media entrepreneur. Springer was born in Altona, near Hamburg, in 1912. In the period immediately after the Second World War he began his career as a newspaper publisher, founding a number of newspapers and magazines, including in 1952 the enormously successful *Bild* tabloid daily paper, and acquiring the respected *Die Welt* newspaper in 1953. The student movement which developed in the late 1960s targeted Springer as a 'monopoly capitalist' because of his ownership of a large share of the newspaper and magazine markets. Among other incidents such as blockades of distribution centres to prevent circulation of his publications, a bomb attack on the Hamburg headquarters of the Springer companies in 1972 wounded 17 people. Springer was unremitting in his critiques of the left-wing-dominated student movement, promoted the idea of German reunification and the illegitimacy of the GDR regime, and defended his position in the publishing market against those who claimed his dominance should be weakened by new legal constraints. Springer expanded into broadcasting, including involvement in the Sat–1 commercial television channel. He was generous in his contributions to charities, including to various charitable causes in Israel. He died in 1985.

[See also: May Events*]

Steel, David

Leader of the British Liberal Party 1976–88, when it merged with the Social Democratic Party to become the Liberal Democratic Party. Steel was born in Kirkcaldy, Scotland, in 1938. Following study at Edinburgh University, Steel became a journalist, then was elected to the House of Commons in a by-election in 1965. He became well known following the success of his 1967 Private Member's bill to reform legal restrictions on abortion. After serving as chief whip of his party, he was elected leader in 1976 following the resignation of Thorpe (Grimond, the former leader, serving as interim leader). In 1977 he took his party into an alliance with Callaghan's Labour government that was less than a formal coalition, and seemed to bring little counter-rewards to the Liberal Party in return for guaranteeing Callaghan a majority in the House of Commons. This move was criticised within and outside Steel's own party ranks. It resulted in electoral defeats for his party before and after the dissolution of that alliance in 1978. In 1983 he succeeded Roy Jenkins as leader of the Liberal–SDP electoral alliance. He decided not to seek leadership of the Liberal Democrat Party at the time of the merger between the Liberals and the SDP in 1988. In 2000 he became the first Speaker of the new Scottish Parliament in Edinburgh.

[See also: Callaghan; Grimond; Jenkins; Thorpe; Lib–Lab pact*]

Stoiber, Edmund

Leader of the Christian Social Union in Germany and Prime Minister of Bavaria. Stoiber was born in Oberaudorf in 1941. He studied law at Munich University and became a civil servant in the Bavarian Land government. He has been a Member of the Bavarian Land Parliament since 1974. He served as General-Secretary of the CSU 1982–86.

He was appointed Interior Minister in the Bavarian government in 1988, and served until 1993, when he became Prime Minister of Bavaria. He has been leader of the CSU since 1999. He became the chancellor-candidate for the 2002 Bundestag election on 11 January 2002, following the announcement by Merkel that she would not seek that position herself.

Stoph, Willi

Head of the government (in effect, Prime Minister) of the German Democratic Republic 1964–73 and 1976–89. Stoph was born in Berlin in 1914. He joined the Communist Party of Germany in 1931. After military service in the Second World War, he made a career within the communist Socialist Unity Party (SED) in the Soviet zone of occupation, then in the GDR. He served as head of state 1973–76. He represented the GDR in talks with Brandt in Erfurt and Kassel in 1970, as a prelude to later steps towards improving relations between the two German states. He was dismissed as Prime Minister in November 1989 during the last days of the communist regime, and was succeeded in that office by Hans Modrow. Court cases following reunification against Stoph on grounds of corruption in office and responsibility for the 'shoot-to-kill' orders concerning would-be escapees from the GDR were later dropped, mainly on grounds of his age and state of health.

[See also: Brandt; Modrow; German question*; Ostpolitik*]

Strauss, Franz Josef

Leader of the CSU, Prime Minister of Bavaria and Minister in the governments of Adenauer and Kiesinger. Strauss was born in Munich in 1915. Following university studies of history and economics, and from 1943 military service in the Second World War, he was one of the founders of the CSU in 1945 and became its General Secretary in 1949, then its Deputy Chairman in 1952. He was elected as Chairman in 1961, a post he retained until his death, and was largely responsible for consolidating, then expanding, the party within Bavaria and in its relations with the CDU. He was elected to the Bundestag in 1949, and was appointed to Adenauer's government in 1953, becoming Defence Minister in 1956. Forced to leave the government because of his responsibility for the improper imposition of sanctions on the magazine *Der Spiegel* in 1962, he was kept out of the Erhard government by FDP insistence. In the grand coalition led by Chancellor Kiesinger, Strauss became Finance Minister (1966–69). Strauss was the unsuccessful chancellor-candidate of the Christian Democrats in the 1980 Bundestag election. When the Christian Democrats returned to government in 1982, the insistence of the FDP that Strauss should not displace Genscher as Foreign Minister effectively kept Strauss out of the cabinet, as he would accept no other position. He instead remained Prime Minister of Bavaria, a post he had taken in 1979. Strauss was seen as being on the right of the Christian Democrats, and his various independent initiatives in foreign policy (such as his visit to China in 1972) and in German–German relations (his unauthorised promises of credits to the GDR government on a visit in 1983) earned him publicity, but were also grounds for criticism and concern even within his own party. He was also involved in scandals concerning possible improper dealings with the arms trade. Strauss died in 1988.

[See also: Adenauer; Erhard; Kiesinger; Spiegel Affair*]

Suárez González, Adolfo, Duke of

Prime Minister of Spain 1976–81 during the transition to democracy in Spain and leader of the Union of the

Democratic Centre (UCD) 1977–82. Born in 1932 in Cebreros in the Province of Avila, Suárez studied at the University of Salamanca and received a doctorate from the University of Madrid. He became governor of Segovia in 1969, then took high-ranking positions in radio and television and in tourism. He was involved with the Falange until 1975, when he founded the UCD and became its leader. He was appointed Prime Minister by King Juan Carlos in 1976 and his post-Franco government effected the transition to democracy in Spain. It allowed the formation of political parties and organised free elections. Suárez' UCD won the elections of 1977 and 1979 but then his popularity fell over his handling of the economy and the issue of Basque terrorism. He resigned in January 1981, nominating Calvo Sotelo as his successor. The King named him Duke of Suárez later that year. In 1982 he left the UCD to form and lead another party, the Democratic and Social Centre (CDS) but the party was not an electoral success and he stepped down as leader in 1991. He was President of the International Liberals 1988–91.

[See also: Franco; Juan Carlos, King]

Thatcher, Margaret

British Prime Minister and leader of the Conservative Party. Born Margaret Roberts in Grantham in 1925, she studied chemistry at Oxford University, then qualified as a lawyer. She was first elected to the House of Commons in 1959. As well as holding various posts within the Conservative 'shadow cabinets' 1967–70 and from 1974, she was Minister of Education in Heath's government 1970–74. She replaced Heath as party leader in 1975, and became Prime Minister following the 1979 general election. She led her party to victories in the 1983 and 1987 elections also. Her policy strategy became increasingly right wing, emphasising market forces and national sovereignty. This strategy, revealed in policies which limited trade union power, promoted the return of state-owned commercial activities, such as the telephone service and power supply, to private ownership, restricted local government autonomy and defended British interests in negotiations within the European Community (EC), was given the label: 'Thatcherism'. She became extremely popular as a result of the successful outcome of the Falklands War, overturning Argentinean invasion of the Falkland Islands in 1982. However, her increasingly strident criticism of the EC and the unpopularity of policies such as a new system of local government taxation (the 'poll tax') led to growing discontent with her leadership within her own party. After an unsuccessful challenge to her in a leadership election in November 1989, another challenge was mounted in 1990. Thatcher narrowly failed to obtain sufficient votes on a first round of balloting to win that election, and was persuaded not to remain in the contest for a second round, since it was almost certain she would be defeated. She entered the House of Lords in 1992.

[See also: Heath; Falklands War*; poll tax*]

Thorez, Maurice

Leader of the PCF 1930–64. Thorez was born in 1900 in Noyelles-Godault. He was a founding member of the PCF in 1920. He was elected to the French Parliament in 1932, and in 1936 agreed to participate in the 'Popular Front' government led by Blum. He refused to fight in the Second World War and deserted from the army, at a time when the USSR was still linked to Nazi Germany by the Treaty between Germany and the USSR. Thorez went to

Moscow, and only returned to France after its liberation. Apart from a brief period when Thorez was a member of a coalition government (1946–47) he and his party took a stance of uncompromising opposition to the Fourth Republic regime, using links to the trade unions to promote strikes. He was a convinced supporter of Stalin, and ensured that the PCF kept rigidly to a Stalinist political programme and Stalinist organisation of the party itself. He died in 1964.

[See also: nazism*; popular front*]

Thorn, Gaston

Prime Minister of Luxembourg 1974–79 and a leading European liberal, President of the European Commission 1981–84. Thorn was born in 1928 in Luxembourg and studied at the Universities of Montpellier, Lausanne and Paris. He became President of the Luxembourg National Union of Students. A Member of the Luxembourg Parliament since 1959, he was also a Member of the European Parliament 1959–69, where he was Vice-President of the Liberal group. He became President of the Democratic Party of Luxembourg in 1961. Prime Minister and Minister of State 1974–79, from 1969 to 1980 he also held ministerial responsibility (often overlapping) in foreign affairs and foreign trade; physical education and sport; national economy and the middle classes; and justice, as well as acting as Deputy Prime Minister 1979–80. In tandem with his national political career, he was a leading figure in the Liberal International and in European politics. He was President of the Liberal International 1970–82; President of the 30th Session of the UN General Assembly 1975–76; President of the Federation of Liberal and Democratic Parties of the European Community 1976–80; and President of the European Commission 1981–84.

Thorpe, Jeremy

Leader of the British Liberal Party 1967–76. Thorpe was born in London in 1929. Educated at Oxford University, he became a lawyer before becoming an MP in 1959. He remained in the House of Commons until 1979. He was elected as leader of his party in succession to Grimond, but resigned when he became involved in a scandal which led to a series of court cases.

[See also: Grimond]

Tindemans, Léo

Prime Minister of Belgium 1974–78 and a leading European christian democrat. Tindemans was born in 1922 in Zwijndrecht and studied at the University of Ghent and the Catholic University of Louvain. He became national Secretary-General of the Social Christian Party in 1958. He was a member of the Belgian Chamber of Deputies 1961–89. He was Minister of Community Affairs 1968–71; Minister of Agriculture and Middle Class Affairs 1972–73; Deputy Prime Minister and Minister for the Budget and Institutional Problems 1973–74. Named Prime Minister in 1974, he formed a Social Christian–Liberal minority government and introduced an austerity programme to counter the country's economic problems, a plan which was endorsed by the electorate in the elections of 1977. He resigned in October 1978 when the Flemish faction of his own party refused to support his plan to divide Belgium into three linguistic regions. He served as Minister of Foreign Affairs 1981–89; and Minister of State in 1992. He was President of his party, the Belgian Christian People's Party (CVP) from 1979 to 1981. From the mid-1970s onwards he also played a very active role in European politics. He was President of the European People's Party (EPP) 1976–85 and a Member of the European Parliament 1979–81 and again from 1989, acting as President of the EPP party group from 1992.

Trimble, David

Leader of the Ulster Unionist Party (UUP). Trimble was born in Bangor (Northern Ireland) in 1944. He studied law at Queen's University, Belfast, and then became a lecturer in law. He became a Member of the House of Commons in 1990. Trimble was elected leader of the UUP in 1995, and in that capacity was a central figure in the negotiations leading to the Good Friday Agreement and the institutional and political arrangements which followed from that. He was awarded the Nobel Peace Prize jointly with John Hume in 1998 for his efforts in producing a peace settlement in Northern Ireland. He was elected to the Northern Ireland Assembly in 1998, and, as leader of the largest party, became First Minister (Prime Minister) that same year. Because of continued violence in Northern Ireland by extremist Protestant and Catholic groups, the refusal of the IRA satisfactorily to commence abolishing its arsenals of weapons, and the concessions demanded of Unionists in relation to changes in the Royal Ulster Constabulary and various other matters, Trimble has been hard put to retain the support of a majority within his own party. In July 2001 he resigned as First Minister of the Northern Ireland government in protest at the failure of progress on arms decommissioning by the IRA, but was re-elected to that post later the same year, following negotiations relating to arms decommissioning.

[See also: Hume; Good Friday Agreement*; Irish Republican Army*]

Ulbricht, Walter

Leader of the German Democratic Republic (GDR) 1949–71. Ulbricht was born in 1893 in Leipzig. He became a qualified carpenter. He joined the Social

Democratic Party in 1912, fought in the First World War, and joined the Communist Party (KPD) in 1919. He quickly rose within the party to become a member of its Central Committee in 1923. He was elected first to the Saxony Land Parliament, then to the Reichstag in 1928. When Hitler took power, Ulbricht emigrated first to France, then to the Soviet Union. Here he was trained to assume power after the defeat of Hitler. He was sent to Berlin in April 1945, and established the authority of the refounded Communist party in the Soviet occupation zone, working closely as political adviser with the Soviet Union occupation authorities. As leader of the KPD, Ulbricht played a major role in compelling the fusion of the KPD and SPD in 1946. Ulbricht became General Secretary (and therefore leader) of the SED in 1950 and in 1960 became head of state. He was generally a loyal follower of the policies of the Soviet Union, though this meant severe disadvantages for the economy of the GDR, and was responsible for agreeing to the violent suppression of the workers' uprising in Berlin in 1953 and the erection of the Berlin Wall in 1961. In 1971 he resigned as party leader on grounds of age (but also under pressure from the USSR) and was succeeded by Honecker. Ulbricht remained head of state until his death in 1973.

[See also: Hitler; Honecker; Berlin uprising*; Berlin Wall*; German question*]

de Valera, Eammon

President of the Irish Republic 1959–73. De Valera was born in 1882 in New York but moved to Ireland as a child. Trained as a teacher, he became involved with groups which espoused republicanism for Ireland. He was one of the leaders of the 1916 Easter Rising in Dublin and imprisoned afterwards, but released under an amnesty. He

became leader of the nationalist organisation: Sinn Féin. Escaping from another prison term in 1919, he went to the USA. Though he opposed the 1921 Treaty between the United Kingdom and the Irish nationalists and for a time promoted direct action against the British, he became founder and leader of Fianna Fail in 1926, and became leader of the Irish government in 1932, a post he held until 1948 and then twice more (1951–54, 1957–59). He died in 1975.

Waldheim, Kurt

General Secretary of the UN 1971–82 and Austrian President 1986–92. Waldheim was born near Vienna in 1918. After service in the German army, he entered the diplomatic service, holding a number of posts, including that of Foreign Minister (1968–70), before becoming UN General Secretary. He was nominated as candidate of the Austrian People's Party for the presidency of Austria in 1986. During the campaign, allegations surfaced that Waldheim, as a young officer, had been involved in atrocities in the Balkans during the Second World War. Several countries refused to have dealings with Waldheim during his presidency because of these allegations. Though an investigation cleared Waldheim of the more serious allegations made against him, it did confirm that he had knowledge of the atrocities and that he had not made full admissions of such knowledge when questioned. He decided not to seek a second term as President because of this affair.

Wehner, Herbert

Leading member of the Social Democratic Party (SPD) in the Federal Republic of Germany. Wehner was born in Dresden in 1906. He joined the Communist Party of Germany in 1927, and went into exile from 1935.

Returning to Germany after the Second World War, he joined the SPD in 1946. He was elected to the Bundestag in 1949, and became a deputy chairman of the SPD in 1958. He was a supporter of the idea of a grand coalition in the 1960s, and when that coalition was created in 1966 he became a minister in Kiesinger's government. He was leader of the SPD parliamentary party in the Bundestag from 1969 until his resignation in 1983. Wehner is considered to have played a major role in securing the resignation of Chancellor Brandt in 1974, following revelations about the espionage activities of Guillaume. Wehner died in 1990.

[See also: Brandt; grand coalition*; Guillaume Affair*]

von Weizsäcker, Richard

President of the Federal Republic of Germany 1984–94. Von Weizsäcker was born in 1920 in Stuttgart. After military service in the Second World War and a period as prisoner-of-war, he trained as a lawyer. He joined the Christian Democratic Union (CDU) in 1954, and was a Member of the Bundestag 1969–81. He was an unsuccessful candidate for the office of federal president in 1974. He became lord mayor of West Berlin from 1981 until his election as federal President. He was federal President during the events leading to German reunification. As President, he became respected, especially outside the Federal Republic, for the measured statements he made concerning Germany's past and its responsibilities in the future, such as his speech on the 40th anniversary of the end of the Second World War, which he called a 'day of liberation' for Germany. He gave a controversial press interview in 1992 in which he criticised the way in which political parties in the Federal Republic seemed to have neglected their representative role in favour of their own institutional interests. He moved the

presidential offices and his private residence to Berlin in 1993.

[See also: reunification of Germany*; Vergangenheitsbewältigung*]

Wilson, Harold

James Harold Wilson was leader of the British Labour Party from 1963 to 1976 and Prime Minister from 1964–70 and 1974 until he resigned in 1976. He was knighted in 1976 and entered the House of Lords in 1983. He was born in Huddersfield in 1916. After studies at Oxford University, and a brief period as a lecturer in economics, Wilson became a civil servant. He became an MP in 1945, and held various ministerial offices, including that of President of the Board of Trade from 1947 until he resigned in 1951 (along with Bevan) over the issue of charges being imposed within the National Health Service. When Gaitskell died in 1963, Wilson was elected as leader of the Labour Party. He won the 1964 general election with a majority of only 4 seats, but called an election in 1966, which gave Labour a comfortable overall majority. In 1970 Wilson was replaced as Prime Minister by Edward Heath after unexpectedly losing the 1970 general election. He became Prime Minister again in 1974, first heading a minority government, then after a second general election that year in charge of a government with a small overall majority. He tried, unavailingly, to take Britain into the EEC in 1967. In 1975 he instituted the first official national referendum in British politics, on the issue of the terms of British membership of the European Community which Heath had accepted for British entry in 1973.

[See also: Bevan; Callaghan; Gaitskell; Heath]

Wörner, Manfred

Defence Minister of the Federal Republic of Germany 1982–88 and

Secretary-General of the North Atlantic Treaty Organisation (NATO) from 1988–94. Wörner was born in Stuttgart in 1934, and studied law at university. First elected to the Bundestag in 1965, he soon developed a reputation for expertise on military matters within the Christian Democratic (CDU) parliamentary party. In 1983 Wörner took decisive action in dismissing General Kiessling (a highly placed German officer within NATO) on grounds of homosexual behaviour, but as this action was based on false intelligence information Wörner had to make a public apology to the Bundestag. As NATO Secretary-General he had to guide NATO through the period leading up to German reunification and the collapse of the Soviet bloc, including NATO's East European counterpart, the Warsaw Pact. He died in 1994.

[See also: Kiessling Affair*]

Section 3
Abbreviations

General abbreviations

AMS Additional Member System
APO Extra-parliamentary opposition in Germany/Ausserparlamentarische Opposition
AV Alternative Vote System
DM Deutschmark
FPTP First-past-the-post (system of election)
FRG Federal Republic of Germany
GDR German Democratic Republic
GG Basic Law (Germany)/Grundgesetz
MdB Member of the Bundestag (Germany)/Mitglied des Bundestages
MP Member of Parliament
MSP Member of the Scottish Parliament
PR Proportional Representation
STV Single Transferable Vote
USA United States of America
USSR Union of Soviet Socialist Republics

Political parties

ADR/CADJ Action Committee for Democracy and Justice (Luxembourg)/Aktiounskomitee fir Demokratie a Gerechtegkeet; Comité d'Action pour la Démocratie et la Justice
AGALEV Ecology Party – 'Live Differently' (Belgium: Flemish-speaking)/Anders Gaan Leven
AN National Alliance (Italy)/Alleanza Nazionale
B '90/Die Grünen Alliance '90–The Greens (known as 'the Greens') (Germany)/Bündnis '90/Die Grünen
BNP British National Party
BSP Belgian Socialist Party (Flemish-speaking)/Belgische Socialistische Partij
C Centre Party (Sweden)/Centerpartiet
CADJ (Luxembourg) see: ADR/CADJ

CCD Christian Democratic Centre (Italy)/Centro Cristiano Democratico
CD Centre Democratic Party (Denmark)/Centrum-Demokraterne
CDA Christian Democratic Party (Netherlands)/Christen Demokratisch Appel
CDS Democratic and Social Centre (Spain)/Centro Democratico y Social
CDU Christian Democratic Union (Germany)/Christlich Demokratische Union
CDU United Christian Democrats (Italy)/Cristiani Democratici Uniti
CDU United Democratic Coalition (Portugal)/Coligação Democrático Unitária
CDV–PDC Christian Democratic People's Party (Switzerland)/Christlich-demokratische Volkspartie–Parti Démocrate-Chrétien
CiU Convergence and Union (Catalan party, Spain)/Convergencia y Unio
CP Centre Party (Sweden)/Centerpartiet
CSU Christian Social Union (Germany)/Christlich Soziale Union
CSV–PCS Christian Social People's Party (Luxembourg)/Chrëschtlech–Sozial Vollekspartei-Parti Chrétien Social
CU United Communists (Italy)/Communisti Unitari
CVP Christian Democratic People's Party (Switzerland)/Christlich-demokratische Volkspartei
CVP Christian People's Party (Belgium: Flemish-speaking)/Christelijke Volkspartij
D '66 Democrats '66 (Netherlands)/Democraten '66
DC Christian Democratic Party (Italy)/Democrazia Cristiana
DF Danish People's Party/Dansk Folkeparti
DF Freedom Movement (Austria)/Die Freiheitlichen

DIKKI Democratic Social Movement
(Greece)/Dimokratiko Kinoniko Kinema

DL Democratic Left (Ireland)

DL Liberal Democrats
(France)/Démocratie Libérale

DNA Norwegian Labour Party/Det
Norske Arbeiderparti

DP/PD Democratic Party
(Luxembourg)/Demokratesch
Partei-Parti Démocratique

DS Left Democrats (Italy)/Democratici
di Sinistra

DUP Democratic Unionist Party (N.
Ireland)

DVU German People's Union/Deutsche
Volksunion

EAJ/PNV Basque Nationalist Party
(Spain)/Eusko Alderdi Jeltzalea-Partido
Nacionalista Vasco

ECOLO Ecologist Party (Belgium:
French-speaking)/Écologistes
confédérés pour l'organisation de
luttes originales

EE Basque Left/Eusko Equerra

EH 'We Basques' (Spain)/Euskal
Herritarrok

ELRG Red–Green Unity List
(Denmark)/Einheidslisten-de
Roed-Groenne

Falange The radical right-wing party of
Franco and his military regime (Spain
1939–75)

FDF Democratic Front of
French-speakers (Belgium)/Front
Démocratique des Francophones

FDP Free Democratic Party
(Germany)/Freie Demokratische
Partei

FDP/PRD Radical Democratic Party
(Switzerland)/Freisinnige-Demokratische
Partei-Parti Radical-Democratique

FI Conservative Party (Italy)/Forza Italia
('Come on, Italy!')

Fianna Fáil Republican party ('Soldiers
of destiny') (Ireland)

Fine Gael Centre-right party ('United
Ireland') (Ireland)

FN National Front (Belgium)/Front
National

FN National Front (France)/Front
National

FP Progress Party
(Denmark)/Fremkridtspartiet

FPL People's Party – the Liberals
(Sweden)/Folkpartiet Liberalerna

FPÖ Austrian Freedom
Party/Freiheitliche Partei Österreichs

FRP Progress Party
(Norway)/Fremskrittpartiet

GA The Greens – Green Alternative
(Austria)/Die Grünen–Die Grüne
Alternativen

GL Green Left (Netherlands)/Groen
Links

GPEW Green Party of England and
Wales

GPV Reformed Political Association
(Netherlands)/Gereformeerd Politiek
Verbond

Green Federation Green Party
(Italy)/Federazione dei Verdi

Greens French Green Party/Les Verts

Greens Luxembourg Green Party/Déi
Gréng–Les Verts

H Conservative Party (Norway)/Høyre

HB United Basque People's Party
(Spain)/Herri Batasuna

IU United Left (Spain)/Izquierda Unida

KdS Christian Democratic Community
Party (Sweden)/Kristdemokratiska
Samhällspartiet

KESK Centre Party (Finland)/Suomen
Keskusta

KFP Conservative People's Party
(Denmark)/Konservative Folkeparti

KK National Coalition
(Finland)/Kansallinen Kokoomus

KKE Communist Party of
Greece/Kommounistiko Komma
Ellados

KPD Communist Party of
Germany/Kommunistische Partei
Deutschlands

KRF Christian People's Party
(Norway)/Kristelig Folkeparti

KRFP Christian People's Party
(Denmark)/Kristelig Folkeparti

KVP Catholic People's Party
(Netherlands)/Katholieke
Volkspartij

LIF Liberal Forum (Austria)/Liberales
Forum

LKP Liberal People's Party
(Finland)/Liberaalinen Kansanpuolue
LN-IF Northern League (Italy)/La Lega
Nord
LSAP–POSL Luxembourg Socialist
Workers' Party/Lëtzebuerger
Sozialistesch Arbechterpartei–Parti
Ouvrier Socialiste Luxembourgeois
Miljöpartiet de Gröna Ecology Green
Party (Sweden)
MNR National Republican Movement
(France)/Mouvement National
Républicain
MpD–La Rete Network Movement for
Democracy (Italy)/Movimento per la
Democrazia La Rete
MpU Olive Tree Movement
(Italy)/Movimento per l'Ulivo
MRG Left Radical Movement (France)
(now PRG)/Mouvement Radical de
Gauche
MSI Italian Social Movement/Movimento
Sociale Italiano
MSP Moderate Unity Party
(Sweden)/Moderate Samlingspartiet
ND New Democracy (Greece)/Nea
Demokratia
ND New Democrats (Sweden)/Ny
Demokrati
NPD National Democratic Party of
Germany/Nationaldemokratische
Partei Deutschlands
NUDF New Union for French
Democracy (France)/Nouvelle Union
pour la Démocratie Française
ÖVP Austrian People's
Party/Österreische Volkspartei
PASOK Pan-Hellenic Socialist Movement
(Greece)/Panellinion Sosialistikon
Kinima
PCF Communist Party of France/Parti
Communiste Français
PCI Communist Party of Italy/Partito
Comunista Italiano
PCS (Luxembourg) see: CSV–PCS
PD Progressive Democrats (Ireland)
PD (Luxembourg) see: DP/PD
PDC (Switzerland) see: CDV–PDC
PdCI Party of Italian Communists/Partito
dei Comunisti Italiani
PDS Democratic Party of the Left

(Italy)/Partito Democratico della
Sinistra
PDS Party of Democratic Socialism
(Germany)/Partei der Demokratischen
Sozialismus
PEV Ecologist Party – The Greens
(Portugal)/Partido Ecologista Os Verdes
PL Right-wing alliance (Italy)/Polo della
Libertà
Plaid Cymru Welsh National Party
('Party of Wales')
PLI Liberal Party (Italy)/Partito Liberale
Italiano
PNV Basque Nationalist Party
(Spain)/Partido Nacionalista Vasco
POSL (Luxembourg) see: LSAP–POSL
PP Popular Party (Portugal)/Partido
Popular
PP Popular Party (Spain)/Partido Popular
PPI Popular Party of Italy/Partito
Popolare Italiano
PR Radical Party (Italy)/Partito Radicale
PR Republican Party (France)/Parti
Républicain
PRC Communist Refoundation Party
(Italy)/Partito della Rifindazione
Comunista
PRG Left Radical Party (France)/Parti
Radical de Gauche
PRI Italian Republican Party/Partito
Repubblicano Italiano
PRL Liberal Reform Party (Belgium:
French-speaking)/Parti Réformateur
Libéral
PRO Rule-of-Law Campaign party
(Germany)/Partei Rechtsstaatlicher
Offensive (the 'Schill party')
PS Segni Pact (Italy)/Patto Segni
PS Socialist Party (Belgium:
French-speaking)/Parti Socialiste
PS Socialist Party (France)/Parti
Socialiste
PS Socialist Party (Portugal)/Partido
Socialista
PSC Social Christian Party (Belgium:
French-speaking)/Parti Social
Chrétien
PSD Social Democratic Party
(Portugal)/Partido Social Democratico
PSI Socialist Party of Italy/Partito
Socialista Italiano

PSOE Spanish Socialist Workers'
Party/Partido Socialista Obrero Español
PvdA Labour Party (Netherlands)/Partij
van de Arbeid
PVV Party of Liberty and Progress
(Belgium: Flemish-speaking)/Partij
voor Vrijheid en Vooruitgang
RC Communist Refoundation
(Italy)/Rifondazione Comunista
Die Republikaner The Republican Party
(Germany)
RPF Reformational Political Federation
(Netherlands)/Reformatorische
Politieke Federatie
RPF-IE Rally for France and the
Independence of
Europe/Rassemblement pour la
France et l'Independence de l'Europe
RPR Rally for the Republic
(France)/Rassemblement pour la
République
RV Radical Liberals (Denmark)/Radikale
Venstre
SAS Swedish Social Democratic
Workers Party/Sveriges
Socialdemokratiska Arbetareparti
SD Social Democratic Party
(Denmark)/Socialdemokratiet
SDI Italian Democratic
Socialists/Socialisti Democratici Italiani
SDLP Social Democratic and Labour
Party (N. Ireland)
SDP Social Democratic Party
(Finland)/Soumen
Sosialidemokraatinnen Puolue
SDP Social Democratic Party (UK)
SDS Socialist German Students
Association/Sozialistische Deutsche
Studentenbund
SF Irish Republican party/Sinn Féin
('Ourselves alone')
SF Socialist People's Party
(Denmark)/Socialistisk Folkeparti
SFP Swedish People's Party
(Finland)/Svenska Folkpartiet
SGP Reformed Political Party
(Netherlands)/Staatkundig
Gereformeerde Partij
SKL Finnish Christian Union/Suomen
Kristillinen Liitto
SNP Scottish National Party

SP Centre Party (Norway)/Senterpartiet
SP Socialist Party (Belgium:
Flemish-speaking)/Socialistische Partij
SP Socialist Party (Ireland)
SP/PS Social Democratic Party
(Switzerland)/Sozialdemokratische
Partei-Parti Socialiste
SPD Social Democratic Party
(Germany)/Sozialdemokratische Partei
Deutschlands
SPÖ Austrian Social Democratic Party/
Sozialdemokratische Partei Österreichs
SRP Socialist Reich Party
(Germany)/Sozialistische Reichspartei
SSDP Finnish Social Democratic
Party/Suomen Sosiaalidemokraattinen
Puolue
Statt party The 'Instead' Party
(Germany)
SV Socialist Left Party
(Norway)/Sosialistisk Venstreparti
SVP South Tyrolean People's Party
(Italy)/Südtiroler Volkspartei
SVP Swiss People's
Party/Schweizerische Volkspartei/Parti
Suisse de l'Union Démocratique du
Centre
Synaspismos Coalition of the Left and
Progress (Greece)/Synaspismos tis
Aristeras kai tis Proodou
UDF Union for French
Democracy/Union pour la Démocratie
Française
UDR Democratic Union for the Republic
(Italy)/Unione Democratica per la
Repubblica
UKIP United Kingdom Independence
Party
UUP Ulster Unionist Party (N. Ireland)
V Liberal Party (Denmark)/Venstre
VAS Left Alliance
(Finland)/Vasemmistoliitto
VB Flemish Bloc (Belgium)/Vlaams Blok
VL Green Union (Finland)/Vihreä Liitto
VLD Flemish Liberals and Democrats –
Citizens' Party (Belgium)/Vlaamse
Liberalen en Demokraten – Partij van
de Burger
VP Left Party (Sweden)/Vänsterpartiet
VU People's Union (Belgium:
Flemish-speaking)/Volksunie

VVD People's Party for Freedom and Democracy (Netherlands)/Volkspartij voor Vrijheid en Democratie

European and cross-national organisations

ACP African, Caribbean and Pacific (states)

CFSP Common Foreign and Security Policy

COREPER Committee of Permanent Representatives

CSCE Conference on Security and Co-operation in Europe

EC European Community

ECB European Central Bank

ECJ European Court of Justice

ECOFIN Economic and Finance Council (of Ministers)

ECSC European Coal and Steel Community

ECU European Currency Unit

EDC European Defence Community

EEA European Economic Area

EEC European Economic Community

EFTA European Free Trade Area

EM European Monetary System

EMI European Monetary Institute

EMU Economic and Monetary Union

EP European Parliament

ERM Exchange Rate Mechanism

ESCB European System of Central Banks

EU European Union

EUA European Unit of Account

EURATOM European Atomic Energy Community

ESCB European System of Central Banks

G-7 Group of Seven

G-8 Group of Eight

GATT General Agreement on Tariffs and Trade

IGC Intergovernmental Conference

JHA Justice and Home Affairs (pillar of the EU)

NATO North Atlantic Treaty Organisation

OEEC Organisation for European Economic Co-operation

OPEC Organisation of Petroleum Exporting Countries

OSCE Organisation for Security and Co-operation in Europe

QMV Qualified Majority Voting

SEA Single European Act

TEU Treaty on European Union (Maastricht Treaty)

UN (see UNO)

UNO United Nations Organisation

WEU Western European Union

WTO World Trade Organisation

Miscellaneous

ACLI Christian Association of Italian Workers/Associazione Cristiana Lavoratori Italiani

BDA Federation of German Employers' Associations/Bundesvereinigung Deutscher Arbeitgeberverbände

BDI Federation of German Industry/Bundesverband der Deutschen Industrie

BR Red Brigades (Italy)/Brigate Rossi

CBI Confederation of British Industry

CFD French Democratic Confederation of Labour/Confédération Française Démocratique du Travail

CFTC French Confederation of Christian Workers/Confédération Française des Travailleurs Chrétiens

CGC General Confederation of Managers (France)/Confédération Générale des Cadres

CGT General Confederation of Labour (France)/Confédération Générale du Travail

CND Campaign for Nuclear Disarmament

CNPF National Council of French Employers/Conseil National du Patronat Française

DGB German Trade Union Confederation/Deutscher Gewerkschaftsbund

ENA National College of Administration (France)/École Nationale d'Administration

ETA Basque Nation and Liberty/Euskadi Ta Askatasuna (Basque terrorist organisation)

FLN National Liberation Front
(Algeria)/Front de Libération Nationale
FO General Confederation of Workers
(France)/Confédération Générale du
Travail – Force Ouvrière
IRA Irish Republican Army
NFU National Farmers' Union (UK)

OAS Secret Army Organisation
(France)/Organisation de l'Armée
Secrête
RAF Red Army Faction
TUC Trades Union Congress (UK)
UGT General Workers' Union
(Spain)/Unión General de Trabajadores

Section 4
Chronologies

UNITED KINGDOM

General elections and changes of government

5 July 1945 First general election after the Second World War. Unusually (to allow for votes from those doing military service overseas to be sent to the United Kingdom) the count is delayed until 26 July 1945. Labour is the largest party (47.8 per cent: majority of 147 seats). Attlee becomes Prime Minister.

23 February 1950 General election. Labour remains the largest party (46.1 per cent), but with a majority of only 6 seats. Attlee remains Prime Minister.

25 October 1951 General election. Labour remains the largest party in terms of vote-share (48.8 per cent) but the Conservative Party (48.0 per cent) has a majority of 16 seats. Churchill becomes Prime Minister.

6 April 1955 Following Churchill's resignation on grounds of ill-health, Eden becomes Prime Minister.

26 May 1955 General election. The Conservative Party has a vote-share of 49.7 per cent, and a majority of 59 seats. Eden remains Prime Minister.

10 January 1957 Following Eden's resignation due to ill-health and political responsibility for the Suez crisis, Macmillan is appointed Prime Minister.

8 October 1959 General election. The Conservatives (49.4 per cent vote-share) increase their majority to 99 seats. Macmillan remains Prime Minister.

18 October 1963 Home (formerly Lord Home) becomes Prime Minister following Macmillan's resignation on grounds of ill-health.

15 October 1964 General election. Labour becomes the largest party, having a vote-share of 44.1 per cent and a majority of 5 seats. Wilson is appointed as Prime Minister.

31 March 1966 General election. Labour remains the largest party, with a vote-share of 47.9 per cent and a majority of 97 seats. Wilson remains Prime Minister.

18 June 1970 General election. The Conservatives are the largest party. Their vote-share of 46.4 per cent gives them a majority of 31 seats. Heath is appointed as Prime Minister.

28 February 1974 General election. The Conservative Party has 37.9 per cent of the vote, but Labour (with only 37.1 per cent) wins the most seats, though no party has an overall majority. Wilson is appointed Prime Minister.

10 October 1974 General election. Labour (with 39.2 per cent of votes) has an overall majority of 4 seats. Wilson remains Prime Minister.

5 April 1976 Following Wilson's resignation, Callaghan becomes Prime Minister.

3 May 1979 General election. Conservatives obtain 43.9 per cent of the votes and have a majority of 44 seats. Thatcher is appointed Prime Minister.

9 June 1983 General election. Conservatives obtain 42.4 per cent of the votes and have a majority of 144 seats. Thatcher remains Prime Minister.

11 June 1987 General election. Conservatives obtain 43.4 per cent of the vote, giving them a majority of 102 seats. Thatcher remains Prime Minister.

28 November 1990 Following Thatcher's resignation (the consequence of a

leadership election in which she
failed to be re-elected on the first
ballot) Major becomes Prime Minister.

9 April 1992 General election.
Conservatives obtain 42.3 per cent of
the votes and have a majority of 21
seats. Major remains Prime Minister.

1 May 1997 General election. Labour are
the largest party: a vote-share of 43.2
per cent gives the party a majority of
179 seats. Blair becomes Prime Minister.

7 June 2001 General election. Labour
are again the largest party, with a
majority of 167 seats. Blair forms new
government.

General

2 August 1945 Clement Davies elected
leader of the Liberal Party following
the outcome of the general election.

16 December 1949 Parliament Act
reduces delaying power of the House
of Lords from two years to one year.

6 February 1952 Accession of Queen
Elizabeth II, following the death of
her father, King George VI, that day.
The coronation took place on 2 June
1953.

13 December 1955 Gaitskell elected
leader of the Labour Party, following
the resignation of Attlee. Gaitskell
was re-elected in leadership elections
on 3 November 1960 and 2
November 1961.

29 September 1956 Grimond elected
leader of the Liberal Party following
the resignation of Clement Davies.

30 April 1958 Life Peerages Act permits
appointment of peers whose titles are
not passed to their heirs.

31 July 1963 Peerage Act, permitting
peers to disclaim hereditary peerage
titles for life (without affecting future
successors to the title) and the
admission of female hereditary peers.

14 January 1963 de Gaulle vetoes
British entry to the EEC.

14 February 1963 Wilson elected leader
of the Labour Party, following the
death of Gaitskell.

28 July 1965 Heath elected leader of
the Conservative Party: the first time a
formal election had been held.

8 November 1965 Race Relations Act
introduced, creating the Race
Relations Board to investigate
unlawful discrimination on grounds of
race.

18 January 1967 Thorpe elected leader
of the Liberal Party following the
resignation of Grimond.

19 December 1967 de Gaulle again
vetoes British entry to the EEC.

22 January 1972 Treaty of Accession
signed by which the United Kingdom
joins the EEC.

30 January 1972 'Bloody Sunday':
soldiers fire on a procession in
Londonderry (Northern Ireland),
killing and wounding several people.

31 October 1973 Publication of the
Kilbrandon Report from the Royal
Commission on the Constitution. It
recommends a directly elected
legislature for Scotland.

11 February 1975 Thatcher becomes
Conservative leader, winning on
the second ballot (having defeated
Heath on the first ballot on 4
February 1975).

5 June 1975 Referendum on continued
membership of EEC, following
renegotiation of terms of
membership. 67.2 per cent vote in
favour of remaining a member. This
is the first national referendum in
British political history.

12 November 1975 House of Lords
passes Sex Discrimination Act, which
makes discrimination on grounds of
gender an offence in fields such as
employment, education and the
provision of certain services such as
banking and insurance. It also
includes an amended version of the
Equal Pay Act 1970, to ensure that
pay scales are not differentiated on
grounds of gender.

5 April 1976 Callaghan elected leader of
the Labour Party following the
resignation of Wilson.

7 July 1976 Steel elected leader of the Liberal Party following the resignation of Thorpe.

22 November 1976 New Race Relations Act makes discrimination unlawful in various fields (e.g. education and employment) and declares the promotion of racial hatred to be an offence.

23 March 1977 Callaghan and Steel agree on a 'Lib–Lab' pact.

25 May 1978 Steel announces termination of the 'Lib–Lab' pact.

1 March 1979 Referenda in Scotland and Wales on regional assemblies. Welsh voters reject the proposals; Scottish voters narrowly support the proposals, but on a turnout too low (67 per cent) to validate the result, so the proposals are not taken forward.

28 March 1979 Labour government defeated by one vote on motion of no confidence. This precipitates a general election.

1 October 1980 Labour Party conference votes in favour of unilateral nuclear disarmament for Britain and withdrawal of the UK from the European Community.

10 November 1980 Foot elected leader of the Labour Party following the resignation of Callaghan.

25 January 1981 'Limehouse Declaration' by four senior Labour Party politicians, a prelude to their efforts to form a new social democratic party.

2 April 1982 Argentina invades the Falkland Islands, initiating a war with the United Kingdom.

2 July 1982 Jenkins elected as leader of new Social Democratic Party (SDP).

21 June 1983 Owen elected leader of the SDP, following resignation of Jenkins on 14 June 1983.

2 October 1983 Kinnock elected as leader of the Labour Party, following Foot's resignation.

6 March 1984 Strike by National Union of Mineworkers begins, involving picketing and confrontations with the police. It ends in March 1985, after a group of mineworkers had formed a breakaway trade union. This strike was regarded as the high point of the Thatcher government's conflict with the trade unions.

9 January 1986 Heseltine resigns from Thatcher cabinet, after disagreements concerning future plans for the Westland helicopter firm.

31 March 1986 Abolition of Greater London Council and other metropolitan local authorities in six conurbations.

6 August 1987 SDP agrees to pursue merger negotiations with the Liberal Party.

28 August 1987 Following Owen's resignation as SDP leader, Maclennan is elected as new party leader.

3 March 1988 Liberal Party and SDP merge formally to form Liberal Democratic Party.

28 July 1988 Ashdown elected leader of the Liberal Party, following the resignation of Steel.

20 September 1988 Thatcher makes her 'Euro-sceptical' 'Bruges speech', warning against progress towards political and economic union in Europe.

5 December 1989 Thatcher defeats Meyer in a ballot to elect the leader of the Conservative Party. The vote is 314–33.

8 October 1990 Britain joins the Exchange Rate Mechanism (ERM).

20 November 1990 Though Thatcher is ahead of Heseltine in the first round of a ballot to elect a leader of the Conservative Party, she does not secure sufficient votes to be elected, so declines to stand in the second round. Major is elected in her place, and becomes Prime Minister.

18 July 1992 John Smith elected as leader of the Labour Party, after Kinnock resigns in the aftermath of the general election outcome.

16 September 1992 Britain forced out of the ERM because of pressure on the pound.

21 July 1994 Blair elected as leader of the Labour Party following the death of John Smith.

4 July 1995 Major defeats Redwood in a ballot for the leadership of the Conservative Party, instigated by Major's decision to resign the leadership and stand in such an election in order to obtain a vote of confidence from his MPs.

19 June 1997 Hague elected leader of the Conservative Party, after Major resigns following the general election defeat.

6 May 1999 First elections held for Scottish Parliament and Welsh Assembly.

9 August 1999 Kennedy elected leader of the Liberal Party, following the resignation of Ashdown.

16 February 2000 Political Parties, Elections and Referendums Act takes effect.

4 May 2000 Livingstone becomes first directly elected lord mayor of London.

29 January and 16 February 2001 Main provisions of the Representation of the People Act 2000 take effect.

8 June 2001 Hague announces his intention to resign as Conservative Party leader.

15 September 2001 Duncan Smith elected by party membership as new Conservative Party leader, defeating Clarke.

FRANCE

The Fourth Republic

9 September 1944 de Gaulle announces composition of provisional government following the liberation of France.

21 October 1945 In a referendum 96.4 per cent of voters reject continuation of the Third Republic. In elections to the Constituent Assembly the Communists are the largest single party, securing 26 per cent of the vote.

21 November 1945 Provisional government of National Unity formed with de Gaulle as President.

3 January 1946 Decrees establish post-war system of planning.

20 January 1946 de Gaulle resigns as head of provisional government.

26 January 1946 Gouin (Socialist) forms government.

5 May 1946 Referendum rejects proposed new constitution.

2 June 1946 Elections to renewed Constituent Assembly.

23 June 1946 Bidault (Popular Republican Movement) forms government.

13 October 1946 Fourth Republic constitution accepted in a referendum by 53 per cent of those voting (33 per cent abstain).

10 November 1946 First election to Parliament of Fourth Republic.

16 December 1946 Blum (Socialist) forms government.

24 December 1946 Fourth Republic constitution takes effect.

16 January 1947 Auriol (Socialist) elected as first President of the Fourth Republic.

22 January 1947 Ramadier (Socialist) forms government.

24 November 1947 Schuman (Popular Republican Movement) forms government.

26 July 1948 Marie (Radical Socialist) forms government.

11 September 1948 Queuille (Radical Socialist) forms government, following short-lived (two-day) government formed by Schuman.

28 October 1949 Bidault (Popular Republican Movement) forms government.

12 July 1950 Pleven (Democratic and Socialist Union of Resistance) forms government, following short-lived (two-day) government formed by Queuille.

10 March 1951 Queuille (Radical Socialist) forms government.

17 June 1951 General election: Gaullists are strongest party.

10 August 1951 Pleven (Democratic and Socialist Union of Resistance) forms new government.

20 January 1952 Faure (Radical Socialist) forms government.

8 March 1952 Pinay (Independent) forms government.

8 January 1953 Mayer (Radical Socialist) forms government.

20 May 1953 France signs Agreement with Saar territory to regulate future relations.

27 June 1953 Laniel (Conservative) forms government.

17 December 1953 Coty (Liberal) elected as President, but only on 13th ballot.

7 May 1954 Fall of French garrison at Dien Bien Phu (Indo-China).

19 June 1954 Mendès-France (Radical Socialist) forms government.

30–31 August 1954 French Parliament rejects scheme to create a European Defence Community.

1 November 1954 Algerian uprising commences.

23 February 1955 Faure (Radical Socialist) forms government.

2 January 1956 General election; Poujadists get 52 seats with 11.6 per cent of the vote.

1 February 1956 Mollet (Socialist) forms government.

12 June 1957 Bourgès-Maunoury (Radical Socialist) forms government.

5 November 1957 Gaillard (Radical Socialist) forms government.

14 May 1958 Pflimlin (Popular Republican Movement) forms government.

The transition to the Fifth Republic and the Algerian issue

2 and 20 March 1956 France recognises independence of Morocco and Tunisia.

13 May 1958 Creation of military-sponsored 'Committee of Public Safety' in Algiers.

29 May 1958 On President Coty's initiative, de Gaulle agrees to form new government.

1 June 1958 National Assembly votes 339–224 to approve appointment of de Gaulle as Prime Minister with extraordinary powers.

28 September 1958 Referendum accepts constitution of Fifth Republic: 79 per cent vote in favour of it.

8 January 1961 Referendum approves self-determination for Algeria (75 per cent vote in favour).

22–25 April 1961 Attempted military putsch in Algeria.

18 March 1962 The Évian Agreement settles terms for Algerian independence.

28 April 1962 Referendum approves Algerian independence (91 per cent vote in favour).

The Fifth Republic: general

4 October 1962 National Assembly approves censure motion, forcing resignation of government (the sole instance of this device being utilised under the Fifth Republic constitution).

28 October 1962 Referendum approves direct election of president (62 per cent vote in favour).

22 January 1963 Franco-German Treaty signed.

1 July 1966 de Gaulle withdraws French troops from NATO command.

2 May 1968 Violent clashes occur between students and police in Paris.

17 May 1968 Protest marches of students and workers in Paris and elsewhere in France; occupation of factories by workers.

12 June 1968 French government prohibits demonstrations and dissolves several student organisations.

27 April 1969 Referendum rejects reform package affecting the Senate and the regions (53 per cent vote against).

9 November 1970 Death of de Gaulle.

27 June 1972 Socialist and Communist parties agree on a 'Common Programme for Government'.

21 September 1977 Socialists and Communists fail to renew 'Common Programme for Government', but agree to a pact for the general election in March 1978 whereby the parties would co-ordinate candidacies on the second ballot.

9 September 1981 Government announces far-reaching programme of nationalisation, affecting banks and many other businesses.

2 March 1982 Extensive package of measures concerning regional reform adopted (the 'Loi Deferre').

16 March 1986 National Assembly election held using proportional representation electoral system based on the Departments. (The two-ballot electoral system was reinstated from November 1986.) First direct elections to regional councils held.

20 September 1992 Referendum narrowly approves Maastricht Treaty (51 per cent vote in favour).

24 January 1999 National Front splits (mainly concerning strategies relating to alliances with other parties). Mégret leads splinter group: National Front – National Movement, later called the National Republican Movement.

24 September 2000 Referendum approves reduction in term of president from seven years to five years, but only 31 per cent participate.

11 and 18 March 2001 Local elections in France; a Socialist becomes mayor of Paris for the first time since 1871.

The Fifth Republic: elections and changes of government

23 and 30 November 1958 First National Assembly election under the new constitution.

21 December 1958 de Gaulle elected as first President of the Fifth Republic.

8 January 1959 Debré (Gaullist)
appointed Prime Minister by de Gaulle.

15 April 1962 Pompidou (Gaullist) appointed Prime Minister. He is appointed again on 4 December 1962 and on 9 January 1966 following formation of new governments.

18 and 25 November 1962 National Assembly election (held early following censure motion forcing resignation of government).

19 December 1965 de Gaulle re-elected as President on second ballot, defeating Mitterrand.

5 and 12 March 1967 National Assembly election.

6 April 1967 Pompidou again appointed Prime Minister (and reappointed 1 June 1968).

23 and 30 June 1968 New National Assembly election following wave of student and left-wing protests.

9 July 1968 Couve de Mourville (Gaullist) appointed Prime Minister.

28 April 1969 de Gaulle resigns as President following defeat in a referendum of his Senate and regional reforms. Poher, as President of the Senate, becomes interim President that day.

15 June 1969 Pompidou (Gaullist) elected as President; 56 per cent voted for him in the second ballot.

24 June 1969 Chaban-Delmas (Gaullist) appointed Prime Minister.

5 July 1972 Messmer (Gaullist) appointed Prime Minister.

4 and 11 March 1973 National Assembly elections.

2 April 1973 Messmer re-appointed as Prime Minister; he is again re-appointed on 1 March 1974 following a government reshuffle.

2 April 1974 Pompidou dies; Poher again becomes interim President.

19 May 1974 Giscard (Independent Republican) defeats Mitterrand on second ballot of presidential election by 50.6 per cent to 49.4 per cent.

27 May 1974 Chirac (Gaullist) appointed Prime Minister.

25 August 1976 Barre (UDF) appointed Prime Minister and re-appointed on 29 March 1977 following a government reshuffle.

12 and 19 March 1978 National Assembly elections.

31 March 1978 Barre re-appointed as Prime Minister.

10 May 1981 Mitterrand (Socialist) elected President, defeating Giscard on the second ballot.

21 May 1981 Mauroy (Socialist) appointed Prime Minister and re-appointed on 23 June 1981 and 22 March 1983 following government reshuffles.

14 and 21 June 1981 National Assembly elections.

17 July 1984 Fabius (Socialist) appointed Prime Minister.

16 March 1986 National Assembly election based on proportional representation, so only one ballot used.

20 March 1986 Chirac (Gaullist) appointed Prime Minister (first cohabitation).

8 May 1988 Mitterrand again elected as president, defeating Chirac by 54 per cent–46 per cent.

10 May 1988 Rocard (Socialist) appointed Prime Minister and re-appointed June 1988 following National Assembly elections.

5 and 12 June 1988 National Assembly election.

15 May 1991 Cresson (Socialist) appointed as Prime Minister (the first female Prime Minister in the history of France).

2 April 1992 Bérégovoy (Socialist) appointed Prime Minister.

21 and 28 March 1993 National Assembly election.

29 March 1993 Balladur (Gaullist) appointed Prime Minister (second cohabitation).

7 May 1995 Chirac defeats Jospin on second ballot of presidential election by 52.6 per cent to 47.4 per cent.

17 May 1995 Juppé (Gaullist) appointed Prime Minister and re-appointed

7 November 1995 following a government reshuffle.

25 May and 1 June 1997 National Assembly election: victory of the left-wing and Green alliance.

2 June 1997 Jospin (Socialist) appointed as Prime Minister (third cohabitation).

5 May 2002 Chirac re-elected as President, defeating Le Pen on second ballot by 82.2 per cent to 17.8 per cent.

GERMANY

Bundestag elections, changes of government and election of federal presidents

14 August 1949 Bundestag election. CDU–CSU are largest party.

12 September 1949 Theodor Heuss (FDP) elected as first federal President.

15 September 1949 Konrad Adenauer (CDU) elected as federal Chancellor. Coalition of CDU–CSU, FDP and DP takes office.

6 September 1953 Bundestag election. CDU–CSU are largest party.

9 October 1953 Konrad Adenauer elected as federal Chancellor. Coalition of CDU–CSU, FDP and DP continues in office.

17 July 1954 Theodor Heuss re-elected as federal President.

25 February 1956 FDP leaves the coalition, but its ministers, calling themselves the Free People's Party (FVP: Freie Volkspartei), continue in office.

15 September 1957 Bundestag election. CDU–CSU obtain overall majority of seats.

22 October 1957 Konrad Adenauer elected as federal Chancellor. Coalition consists of CDU–CSU and DP. The DP ministers later join the CDU, leaving Adenauer effectively with a single-party government.

1 July 1959 Heinrich Lübke (CDU) elected as federal President.

17 September 1961 Bundestag election. CDU–CSU are largest party.

7 November 1961 Konrad Adenauer elected as federal Chancellor. Coalition of CDU–CSU and FDP takes office.

16 October 1963 Following resignation of Adenauer as federal Chancellor, Ludwig Erhard is elected as his successor. The coalition remains unchanged, though ministerial posts are redistributed.

1 July 1959 Heinrich Lübke re-elected as federal President.

19 September 1965 Bundestag election. CDU–CSU are largest party.

20 October 1965 Ludwig Erhard elected as federal Chancellor. Coalition of CDU–CSU and FDP continues in office.

1 December 1966 Kurt Georg Kiesinger elected as federal Chancellor, following termination of coalition by the FDP, resignation of Erhard as federal Chancellor and the construction of a 'grand coalition' consisting of CDU–CSU and SPD.

5 March 1969 Gustav Heinemann (SPD) elected as federal President.

28 September 1969 Bundestag election. CDU–CSU are largest party.

21 October 1969 Election of Willy Brandt as federal Chancellor. Coalition of SPD and FDP takes office.

19 November 1972 Bundestag election (the first to be held following a premature dissolution of the Bundestag). SPD are largest party.

14 December 1972 Willy Brandt elected as federal Chancellor. Coalition of SPD and FDP continues in office.

15 May 1974 Walter Scheel (FDP) elected as federal President.

16 May 1974 Helmut Schmidt elected as federal Chancellor, following resignation of Willy Brandt as federal Chancellor. Coalition of SPD and FDP continues in office.

3 October 1976 Bundestag election. CDU–CSU are largest party.

15 December 1976 Helmut Schmidt elected as federal Chancellor.

Coalition of SPD and FDP continues in office.

23 May 1979 Karl Carstens (CDU) elected as federal President.

5 October 1980 Bundestag election. CDU–CSU are largest party.

5 November 1980 Helmut Schmidt elected as federal Chancellor. Coalition of SPD and FDP continues in office.

1 October 1980 Helmut Kohl elected as federal Chancellor by means of constructive vote of no confidence (its first successful use) following termination of the SPD–FDP coalition by the FDP. Coalition of CDU–CSU and FDP takes office.

6 March 1983 Bundestag election, following constructive vote of no confidence on 1 October 1982 and premature dissolution of Bundestag. CDU–CSU are largest party.

29 March 1983 Helmut Kohl elected as federal Chancellor. Coalition of CDU–CSU and FDP continues in office.

23 May 1984 Richard von Weizsäcker (CDU) elected as federal President.

25 January 1987 Bundestag election. CDU–CSU are largest party.

23 May 1989 Richard von Weizsäcker (CDU) re-elected as federal President.

2 December 1990 Bundestag election (the first for reunified Germany). CDU–CSU largest party.

17 January 1991 Helmut Kohl elected as federal Chancellor. Coalition of CDU–CSU and FDP continues in office.

23 May 1994 Rainer Herzog elected as federal President.

16 October 1994 Bundestag election. CDU–CSU are largest party.

15 November 1994 Helmut Kohl elected as federal Chancellor. Coalition of CDU–CSU and FDP continues in office.

27 September 1998 Bundestag election. SPD are largest party.

27 October 1998 Gerhard Schröder elected as federal Chancellor. SPD and Green Party coalition takes office.

23 May 1999 Johannes Rau (SPD) elected as federal President.

22 September 2002 Bundestag election. SPD and Greens continue as governing coalition.

The division and reunification of Germany

8 May 1945 Unconditional surrender of Germany ends Second World War.

5 June 1945 Berlin Declaration: occupation regime commences. Germany divided into four zones of occupation.

15 December 1947 London Conference of Foreign Ministers of Allies terminates without agreement on future of Germany being reached.

6 March 1948 London Six-Power Conference (without USSR participation) ends its first session, having decided to create a temporary West German state, pending a peace treaty.

2 June 1948 London Six-Power Conference ends its second session, having decided to require the ministers-President of the Land governments of West Germany to convene a constitutional convention to create a temporary constitution for a West German state.

20–21 June 1948 West German currency reform introduces the Deutschmark for western occupation zones.

23–28 June 1948 East German currency reform introduces Eastern Mark for the Soviet Union's zone of occupation.

1 July 1948 Western occupying powers hand to ministers-President of West German Land governments the three 'Frankfurt Documents', setting terms for the creation of a provisional West German state.

1 September 1948 Parliamentary Council of 65 delegates of Länder Parliaments begins its deliberations in Bonn.

23 May 1949 Basic Law is promulgated.

24 May 1949 Basic Law takes effect. Founding date of Federal Republic of Germany.

30 May 1949 East German People's Congress (delegates from political parties and other organisations, such as the trade union) adopts a constitution for an East German state.

7 October 1949 Founding of the German Democratic Republic (GDR).

10 March 1952 'Stalin Note' offers German reunification under certain conditions, including the neutrality of the German state.

17 June 1953 After strikes and protests on 15 and 16 June by building workers in East Berlin against new working conditions imposed by the GDR government, large numbers of workers strike and demonstrate throughout the GDR. The demonstration is suppressed by the Soviet military and by the GDR security services.

25 March 1954 USSR recognises full sovereignty of GDR.

5 May 1955 End of occupation rights in FRG. Federal Republic acquires full sovereignty.

23 September 1955 Announcement by government of the FRG of 'Hallstein Doctrine', whereby states offering diplomatic recognition of the GDR could not enjoy diplomatic relations with the FRG.

27 January 1956 GDR becomes a member of the Warsaw Pact defence organisation.

13 August 1961 Erection of Berlin Wall.

17 December 1963 Signing of first Berlin Visa Agreement, allowing citizens of West Berlin to visit relatives in East Berlin over the Christmas period: the first such opportunity since the erection of the Berlin Wall. Further such Agreements follow in 1964–66.

19 March 1970 Chancellor Brandt and GDR Prime Minister Stoph meet in Erfurt for talks. A second meeting in Kassel follows on 21 May 1970.

157 CHRONOLOGIES

12 August 1970 FRG and USSR sign Moscow Treaty, which affects the policy of the FRG towards the GDR and is a main plank in the Ostpolitik of Brandt's government.

3 September 1971 Four-Power Agreement on Berlin regulates the situation concerning the divided city.

21 December 1972 Agreement signed between GDR and FRG concerning their future relations.

7–11 September 1987 Official visit of Honecker (leader of the GDR) to the Federal Republic.

15 January 1989 Demonstration in Leipzig for freedom of expression and freedom to travel, on occasion of 70th anniversary of murder of Rosa Luxemburg and Karl Liebknecht.

2 May 1989 The Hungarian government announces it is to demolish the 'iron curtain' border apparatus between Hungary and Austria. This later enables GDR visitors to Hungary to flee easily to the West.

7 May 1989 Local elections in the GDR. Observation of polling stations by dissidents results in challenges to the accuracy of the official results and the turnout figures. Rejection of challenges to the result leads to monthly demonstrations.

19 September 1989 'New Forum', a group of GDR dissidents wanting to foster free political discussion and reform, applies for official recognition as an association. The Interior Minister rejects the application on 21 September 1989.

2 October 1989 One of a regular series of Monday evening demonstrations in Leipzig of citizens demanding reform is broken up by police using violent methods.

7 October 1989 Fortieth anniversary celebration of founding of GDR. Gorbachev, attending as a guest, emphasises the need for reform in the GDR. A new Social Democratic party is founded in the GDR.

18 October 1989 Resignation of Honecker as leader of GDR on 'health grounds'. Krenz replaces him.

9 November 1989 Opening of the Berlin Wall following press conference where it was announced that travel restrictions for GDR citizens were to be diminished.

13 November 1989 Hans Modrow, known as a reformer in the GDR Communist party, becomes head of the GDR government.

28 November 1989 Kohl sets out a Ten-Point Plan which could lead to German reunification.

3 December 1989 Krenz and the Politburo of the GDR Communist party resign en bloc.

7 December 1989 First meeting of the GDR 'Round Table': a forum for representatives of new parties and political organisations, as well as from the Communist party and the former bloc parties and other organisations previously associated with it.

8 December 1989 A special congress of the GDR Communist party (continued on 9, 16 and 17 December) decides to change its organisational structure, adopt new policies and change its name from Socialist Unity Party (SED) to Socialist Unity Party–Party of Democratic Socialism (SED–PDS).

18 March 1990 First democratic election for the Volkskammer (the legislature of the GDR). Victory for the Christian Democratic-led 'Alliance for Germany' which favours swift reunification. Lothar de Maizière (CDU) forms a coalition government, and is elected as Prime Minister by the Volkskammer on 12 April 1990.

5 May 1990 First meeting of the Foreign Ministers of the four former Allied occupation powers (USA, United Kingdom, France and USSR) and of the two German states: the so-called 'Two Plus Four' talks, to regulate international aspects of the reunification of Germany. This takes place in Bonn. Other meetings take place on 22 June (East Berlin),

17 July (Paris) and 12 September (Moscow). At the Moscow meeting a Treaty was signed which was, in effect, a peace treaty ending the Second World War and regulating the international aspects of German reunification, including the borders of the reunified German state.

18 May 1990 Treaty between FRG and GDR signed, to institute an economic and currency union involving the two German states.

1 July 1990 Treaty of Economic, Monetary and Social Union comes into effect. The Deutschmark (the currency of the FRG) replaces the GDR Mark at rates of parity for some savings and for incomes, and at 1:2 for most other transactions.

31 August 1990 Signing of Treaty between GDR and FRG to unify the two German states.

3 October 1990 Treaty of Unification takes effect.

2 December 1990 First election in reunified Germany for the Bundestag.

General

30 April 1945 Hitler commits suicide in his Berlin bunker headquarters.

1 May 1945 Dönitz announces that he has been appointed successor to Hitler as German leader.

8 May 1945 Unconditional surrender of Germany in Berlin ends the Second World War in Europe.

2 August 1945 Potsdam conference of the 'Big Three' (USA, USSR and United Kingdom) which commenced on 17 July 1945 ends. Decisions made concerning the future administration of Germany, as well as other aspects of the post-war situation.

20 November 1945 Nuremberg international war-crimes tribunal commences (terminating on 1 October 1946). Twelve of the accused sentenced to death.

6 September 1946 'Stuttgart speech' of US Foreign Minister Byrnes, in

which the creation of a provisional West German state was foreshadowed.

1 January 1947 Creation of the 'Bizone': a fusion of the US and British zones of occupation.

24 June 1948 Berlin blockade commences.

26 June 1948 Commencement of Berlin airlift to relieve shortages in Berlin.

10 May 1949 Parliamentary Council votes by 33–29 for Bonn, rather than Frankfurt, as the seat of government for the FRG.

12 May 1949 Berlin blockade formally ends.

23 October 1952 Socialist Reich Party banned by the Federal Constitutional Court.

9 May 1955 Federal Republic of Germany joins NATO.

23 October 1955 Plebiscite in the Saar region, which in effect supports membership of the Saar as a Land in the FRG.

25 February 1956 The FDP withdraws from the Adenauer coalition.

17 August 1956 The Communist Party (KPD) is banned by the Federal Constitutional Court.

1 January 1957 The Saarland joins the Federal Republic of Germany, after being under French administration since the end of the Second World War.

13–15 November 1959 SPD party congress at Bad Godesberg, near Bonn, accepts the Godesberg Programme, which abandons traditional aspects of the SPD's ideology and programme, making it a more open and modern party.

26 October 1962 Police searches of offices of the news magazine *Der Spiegel* begin what becomes known as the 'Spiegel Affair'.

6 November 1966 The radical right-wing National Democratic Party (founded 28 November 1964) win seats in the Hesse Land Parliament. Later in 1966 and in the period 1967–68 they win seats in several other Land Parliaments. However, in the federal election in 1969 they only secure 4.3 per cent of the list votes, thus failing to qualify for seats in the Bundestag.

24 July 1967 Party Law comes into effect.

12–14 April 1969 German Communist Party (DKP) officially founded. This replaces the banned KPD.

12 August 1970 Treaty of Moscow signed by FRG and USSR. This establishes the basis for a series of treaties (the culmination of the Brandt government's Ostpolitik) forming the basis for improved relations between Germany and the communist bloc states.

27 April 1972 First use of the constructive vote of no confidence (Art. 67 of the Basic Law) to try to replace Chancellor Brandt by Barzel (CDU) fails by two votes.

6 May 1974 Brandt resigns as Chancellor following the arrest on 24 April of Guillaume, a GDR spy who worked on Brandt's staff. Brandt remains as SPD leader.

12–14 January 1980 Federal Green party formed at a congress in Karlsruhe.

17 September 1982 FDP ministers withdraw from Schmidt's coalition government.

1 October 1982 First successful use of the constructive vote of no confidence replaces Schmidt as Chancellor by Kohl (CDU).

20 June 1991 The Bundestag votes by 338 votes to 320 to make Berlin the seat of government, in place of Bonn. The Bundesrat votes on 5 July 1991 to remain in Bonn for the foreseeable future.

18 May 1992 Genscher (FDP) resigns as Foreign Minister, having served since 1974.

1 July 1992 A new law takes effect, speeding up the process of assessing requests for political asylum and making it more difficult to mis-use the right to political asylum.

12 July 1994 The Federal Constitutional Court decides that 'out-of-area' utilisation of German military units is constitutionally permissible, though the government must obtain prior approval by the Bundestag for such operations.

11 March 1999 Lafontaine, leader of the SPD and Minister of Finance, resigns from his party and public offices following disagreements with the decisions of Chancellor Schröder.

12 March 1999 Schröder appointed party Chairman in place of Lafontaine by SPD Executive; he is confirmed in that office by a party congress on 12 April 1999.

19 April 1999 Inaugural session of Bundestag in the Reichstag building in Berlin.

30 November 1999 Following accusations of improper and corrupt party financing involving various CDU politicians, former Chancellor Kohl admits knowledge of secret party accounts. On 29 December 1999 an announcement is made that a criminal investigation into Kohl and the CDU will be opened. Party leader Wolfgang Schäuble resigns as a result.

10 April 2000 Angela Merkel elected as CDU leader: the first female leader of a major party in Germany.

11 January 2002 Stoiber (leader of the Bavarian CSU) acknowledged as CDU–CSU Chancellor-candidate for the 2002 Bundestag elections following Merkel's announcement that she would not seek that position.

ITALY

General

25 July 1943 Mussolini deposed.

3 September 1943 Secret armistice signed by Italy with the Allies.

9 May 1946 Abdication of King Victor Emmanuel III; Umberto II succeeds as King.

2 June 1946 First post-war elections and

referendum which rejects the monarchy in favour of a republic.

18 June 1946 Proclamation of the Republic following abdication of King Umberto II on 13 June 1946.

1 January 1948 New constitution takes effect.

5 October 1954 Italy and Yugoslavia agree on status of Trieste.

15 June 1977 'Red Brigades' trial opens. Five terrorists are sentenced to terms of imprisonment on 23 June 1987.

16 March 1978 Moro kidnapped by Red Brigades terrorists.

9 May 1978 Moro murdered by Red Brigade kidnappers.

23 June 1978 Curcio, founder of Red Brigades, sentenced to 15 years' imprisonment for forming an armed association and kidnapping.

18 February 1984 New Concordat between Italian government and Holy See.

29 January 1985 Parliamentary Commission to consider political reform, under chairmanship of Bozzi, concludes its work.

11 July 1988 Trial concludes of right-wing extremists relating to bombing at Bologna railway station. Four terrorists receive life sentences.

3 February 1991 Founding conference of PDS (formed by former PCI members) approves name of new party, following official disbandment of PCI that day.

10 February 1991 Bossi creates Northern League party, linking various regional Leagues.

9 June 1991 Referendum on reform of electoral system: 95.5 per cent support proposed changes.

23 May 1992 Assassination by Mafia of Judge Falcone.

19 July 1992 Assassination by Mafia of Judge Borsellino.

18–19 April 1993 Referendum on electoral reform: 82.7 per cent vote in favour.

3–4 August 1993 Approval by Parliament of new electoral system.

12–14 February 1998 Congress of PDS approves new name: Left Democrats (DS) to accommodate other parties which joined it in forming the DS.

10 December 1999 17 Mafia members are given life sentences for the murder of Judge Borsellino in Palermo in 1992.

8 October 2001 Referendum approves greater powers for the regions (but turnout only 34 per cent).

11 October 2001 Berlusconi acquitted of corruption charges on appeal (relating to charges in 1998 of bribing tax inspectors).

Elections and changes of government

20 June 1945 Parri appointed Prime Minister.

10 December 1945 De Gasperi appointed Prime Minister.

1946 General election.

28 June 1946 de Nicola takes office as President.

13 July 1946 De Gasperi re-appointed Prime Minister.

2 February 1947 De Gasperi re-appointed Prime Minister.

31 May 1947 De Gasperi re-appointed Prime Minister.

11 May 1948 Einaudi takes office as President.

23 May 1948 De Gasperi re-appointed Prime Minister.

27 January 1950 De Gasperi re-appointed Prime Minister.

26 July 1951 De Gasperi re-appointed Prime Minister.

16 July 1953 De Gasperi re-appointed Prime Minister.

7 June 1953 General election.

17 August 1953 Pella appointed Prime Minister.

18 January 1954 Fanfani appointed Prime Minister.

10 February 1954 Scelba appointed Prime Minister.

11 May 1955 Gronchi takes office as President.

6 July 1955 Segni appointed Prime Minister.

19 May 1957 Zoli appointed Prime Minister.

25 May 1958 General election.

1 July 1958 Fanfani re-appointed Prime Minister.

15 February 1959 Segni re-appointed Prime Minister.

25 March 1960 Tambroni appointed Prime Minister.

26 July 1960 Fanfani re-appointed Prime Minister.

21 February 1962 Fanfani re-appointed Prime Minister.

6 May 1962 Segni takes office as President.

28–29 April 1963 General election.

21 June 1963 Leone appointed Prime Minister.

4 December 1963 Moro appointed Prime Minister.

22 July 1964 Moro re-appointed Prime Minister.

28 December 1964 Saragat takes office as President.

23 February 1966 Moro re-appointed Prime Minister.

19–20 May 1968 General election.

24 June 1968 Leone re-appointed Prime Minister.

12 December 1968 Rumor appointed Prime Minister.

5 June 1969 Rumor re-appointed Prime Minister.

27 March 1970 Rumor re-appointed Prime Minister.

6 August 1970 Colombo appointed Prime Minister.

29 December 1971 Leone takes office as President.

17 February 1972 Andreotti appointed Prime Minister.

7–8 May 1972 General election.

26 June 1972 Andreotti re-appointed Prime Minister.

7 July 1973 Rumor re-appointed Prime Minister.

14 March 1974 Rumor re-appointed Prime Minister.

23 November 1974 Moro appointed Prime Minister.

12 February 1976 Moro re-appointed Prime Minister.

20 June 1976 General election.

29 July 1976 Andreotti appointed Prime Minister.

11 March 1978 Andreotti appointed Prime Minister.

15 June 1978 Fanfani takes office as President.

8 July 1978 Pertini takes office as President.

20 March 1979 Andreotti re-appointed Prime Minister.

3 and 4 June 1979 General election.

4 August 1979 Cossiga appointed Prime Minister.

4 April 1980 Cossiga re-appointed Prime Minister.

18 October 1980 Forlani appointed Prime Minister.

28 June 1981 Spadolini appointed Prime Minister.

23 August 1982 Spadolini re-appointed Prime Minister.

1 December 1982 Fanfani appointed Prime Minister.

26 and 27 June 1983 General election.

4 August 1983 Craxi appointed Prime Minister.

24 June 1985 Cossiga elected President.

1 August 1986 Craxi re-appointed Prime Minister.

17 April 1987 Fanfani re-appointed Prime Minister.

29 July 1987 Goria appointed Prime Minister.

14 and 15 June 1987 General election.

13 April 1988 De Mita appointed Prime Minister.

23 July 1989 Andreotti re-appointed Prime Minister.

13 April 1991 Andreotti re-appointed Prime Minister.

5 and 6 April 1992 General election. Northern League win 55 seats.

28 May 1992 Scalfaro takes office as President.

28 June 1992 Amato appointed Prime Minister.

29 April 1993 Ciampi appointed Prime Minister.

10 May 1994 Berlusconi appointed Prime Minister.

17 January 1995 Dini appointed Prime Minister.

21 April 1996 General election.

18 May 1996 Prodi appointed Prime Minister.

21 October 1998 D'Alema appointed Prime Minister.

22 December 1999 D'Alema re-appointed Prime Minister.

25 April 2000 Amato appointed Prime Minister.

13 May 2001 General election.

11 June 2001 Berlusconi appointed Prime Minister.

SPAIN

General

5 October 1966 Spain closes border with Gibraltar.

11 January 1980 Catalan and Basque regional governments commence rule.

10 April 1980 Spain re-opens border with Gibraltar.

9 December 1981 Spain joins NATO.

12 June 1985 Spain becomes member of EEC.

12 March 1986 Referendum accepts Spain's continued membership of NATO.

The transition to democracy

22 July 1969 Franco names Juan Carlos, grandson of King Alfonso XIII, as heir to the throne and successor to Franco as head of state.

20 November 1975 Franco dies.

22 November 1975 Juan Carlos proclaimed King of Spain.

14 July 1976 Ban on political parties lifted.

16 November 1976 Cortes (Spanish legislature) passes Political Reform Law to establish democratic elections and a bicameral legislature.

15 December 1976 Referendum approves Political Reform Law, allowing transition to democracy.

9 April 1977 Communist party legalised.

23 February 1981 Attempted military coup; armed officers hold Members of the Cortes hostage.

24 February 1981 King Juan Carlos condemns attempted coup by officers; coup collapses.

Elections and changes of government

5 July 1976 Suarez appointed Prime Minister.

15 June 1977 Election of Constituent Assembly: the first democratic general election since the civil war. Union of the Democratic Centre (UDC) has largest share of the vote (34.5 per cent).

1 March 1979 General election. UDC has largest share of the vote (35.1 per cent).

26 February 1981 Calvo appointed Prime Minister.

28 October 1982 General election. Socialists win largest share of the vote (48.3 per cent).

2 December 1982 González appointed Prime Minister.

22 June 1986 General election. Socialists win largest share of the vote (44.3 per cent).

29 October 1989 General election. Socialists win largest share of the vote (39.9 per cent).

1 November 1989 González re-appointed Prime Minister.

6 June 1993 General election. Socialists win largest share of the vote (39.1 per cent).

14 July 1993 González re-appointed Prime Minister.

3 March 1996 General election. Popular Party wins largest share of the vote (39.2 per cent).

4 May 1996 Aznar appointed Prime Minister.

12 March 2000 General election. Popular Party wins largest share of the vote (44.6 per cent).

27 April 2000 Aznar re-appointed Prime Minister.

SMALLER DEMOCRACIES

4 November 1948 Queen Juliana becomes Queen of the Netherlands, following the abdication of her mother, Queen Wilhelmina.

16 July 1951 Leopold III, King of the Belgians, abdicates; the following day his son, King Baudoin, succeeds to the throne.

5 June 1953 Greenland becomes an integral part of Denmark, having previously been a colony.

15 May 1955 Austrian State Treaty signed, ending condition of occupation in Austria.

21 April 1967 Military coup in Greece commences. Military junta takes office.

1 June 1973 Greek monarchy declared abolished.

25 April 1974 Military coup overthrows dictatorship of Salazar in Portugal.

23 July 1974 Military rule in Greece terminates.

1 August 1974 Restoration of 1952 Greek constitution.

13 February 1975 Turkish Cypriots proclaim an independent republic for their part of Cyprus; Denktash becomes President.

25 April 1976 New, democratic, constitution adopted in Portugal.

1 May 1980 Queen Beatrix becomes monarch of the Netherlands, following the abdication of her mother, Queen Juliana.

21 October 1981 Papandreou forms Greece's first ever Socialist-led government.

28 February 1986 Assassination of Palme, Sweden's Prime Minister.

8 June 1986 Kurt Waldheim elected President of Austria.

3 December 1990 Mary Robinson becomes first female President of the Irish Republic.

22 July 1991 New method of choosing president of Finland by direct election (using a two-ballot system) comes into effect.

30 January 1992 Haughey resigns as Ireland's Prime Minister following allegations of wire-tapping.

13 February 1992 Prime Minister, Bildt, announces end of Sweden's neutrality status.

14 July 1993 Law passed which makes Belgium a federal state.

31 July 1993 Albert becomes King of the Belgians on the death of King Baudoin.

1 February 2000 EU commences imposition of diplomatic sanctions against Austria as protest against the inclusion of the radical right-wing party: the Austrian People's Party, in a coalition government after the general election in October 1999.

EUROPE

Integration

19 September 1946 Churchill makes speech in Zurich advocating European integration.

1 November 1947 Benelux customs union (taking effect from 1 January 1948).

5 May 1949 Statutes of the Council of Europe signed by ten West European states.

10 August 1949 First meeting of Assembly of Council of Europe in Strasbourg.

9 May 1950 Announcement of Schuman Plan which leads to foundation of ECSC.

18 April 1951 Treaty establishing ECSC signed.

23 July 1952 ECSC Treaty comes into effect.

30–31 August 1954 French Parliament rejects European Defence Community scheme, which would have provided for the rearmament of the Federal German Republic within a European defence alliance.

1–2 June 1955 Messina conference on the further development of European integration.

29 May 1956 Foreign ministers of member states of the ECSC meet in Venice and agree to proceed towards the creation of the EEC and EURATOM on the basis of decisions taken at the Messina conference (1–2 June 1955).

25 March 1957 Treaties of Rome signed to create EEC and EURATOM.

1 January 1958 Treaties of Rome come into effect.

20–21 July 1959 Seven countries including the United Kingdom agree to create EFTA.

3 May 1960 EFTA treaty comes into effect.

31 July, 9–10 August 1961 Applications made by the United Kingdom, Ireland and Denmark to join the EEC.

30 April 1962 Norway applies to join the EEC.

14 January 1963 de Gaulle in effect vetoes the British application for membership of EEC.

1 July 1965 The 'empty chair crisis': France withdraws from meetings of the Council of Ministers following disputes about the future financing of the CAP.

4 August 1965 Treaty signed by EEC, ECSC and EURATOM merging the executive organs of those institutions.

29 January 1966 The 'Luxembourg compromise' permitting national vetoes on certain matters means that France returns to meetings of the Council of Ministers.

10–11 May 1967 Renewed applications for membership of EC received from United Kingdom, Ireland and Denmark.

1 July 1967 Executives of EC, ECSC and EURATOM merged.

25 July 1967 Norway renews application to become a member of the EC.

28 July 1967 Sweden applies for membership of EC.

19 December 1967 de Gaulle again rejects EC membership of United Kingdom.

1–2 December 1968 Summit meeting of EC leaders at the Hague at which (a) agreement is reached to open negotiations with prospective member states; (b) it is confirmed that a European Economic and Monetary Union would be created by 1980; and (c) it is agreed that a foreign policy co-operation process will be developed.

27 October 1970 Luxembourg Report on European Political Co-operation (EPC) issued to develop foreign policy co-operation.

19 November 1970 First ministerial meeting under EPC procedures.

16 November 1971 House of Commons votes 356–244 to accept membership of EC.

22 January 1972 Accession treaties for new member states of EC signed.

23 April 1972 Referendum in France approves EEC enlargement (68 per cent vote in favour).

10 May 1972 Referendum in Ireland approves EC membership: 83 per cent vote in favour.

24 September 1972 Norwegian voters in a referendum reject EC membership by 53.5 per cent to 46.5 per cent.

1 October 1972 Danish referendum on EC membership: 63 per cent approve.

1 January 1973 First enlargement of EC takes effect by addition of United Kingdom, Ireland and Denmark as members.

9–10 December 1974 Paris meeting of heads of governments of EC member states agree (a) to hold such meetings (to be referred to as the 'European council') at regular intervals in future and (b) to permit direct elections to the European Parliament.

10–11 March 1975 European Council in Dublin discusses renegotiation of terms of British membership.

9 April 1975 British House of Commons votes in favour of EC membership: 396 in favour, 170 against.

5 June 1975 United Kingdom holds its first ever nationwide referendum: by 67.2 per cent to 32.8 per cent it approves continued membership of the EC on the basis of renegotiated terms.

13 March 1979 European Monetary System (EMS) is established.

28 May 1979 Agreement is reached on terms of membership of EC for Greece.

7–10 June 1979 First direct elections to European Parliament.

1 January 1981 Greece becomes the tenth member of the EC.

23 February 1982 Greenland voters decide in a referendum to withdraw from the EC. This takes effect from February 1985.

12 June 1985 A decision is taken that Spain and Portugal can become members of the EC.

1 January 1986 Spain and Portugal become members of the EC.

17 February 1986 Single European Act signed, as a comprehensive reform of the European Treaties.

1 July 1987 Single European Act takes effect.

20 September 1988 Mrs Thatcher's controversial 'Bruges speech', criticising what she perceives to be centralising trends of the EC.

26–27 June 1989 Delors Report on Economic and Monetary Union approved by European Council meeting in Madrid.

17 July 1989 Austria applies for membership of EC.

3 October 1990 Reunification of Germany adds large amount of territory, but not an additional member, to the EC.

8 October 1990 The pound sterling is included in the ERM.

1 July 1991 Sweden applies for EC membership.

9–10 December 1991 Meeting of European Council in Maastricht agrees content of Maastricht Treaty on European Union.

7 February 1992 Foreign and Finance Ministers sign Maastricht Treaty.

18 March 1992 Finland applies for EC membership.

3 May 1992 European Economic Area agreement signed, linking EC and EFTA.

2 June 1992 First referendum in Denmark on the Maastricht Treaty: 50.7 per cent vote to reject acceptance.

16 September 1992 'Black Wednesday': United Kingdom and Italy leave the Exchange Rate Mechanism which links EU currency rates.

20 September 1992 Referendum in France approves Maastricht Treaty (but only 51 per cent vote in favour).

6 December 1992 Swiss voters reject Switzerland's membership of EEA.

18 May 1993 Second Danish referendum on Maastricht Treaty: 56.8 per cent vote for acceptance.

21–22 June 1993 European Council, meeting in Copenhagen, agrees criteria for acceptance of new member states.

2 August 1993 Currency speculation against the French franc and other currencies forces the effective suspension of the Exchange Rate Mechanism.

1 November 1993 Maastricht Treaty comes into effect, involving introduction of the name: European Union to apply to the structure of European integration involving the EC and other integrative procedures.

1 January 1994 The EEA takes effect, introducing closer economic relations between EU and EFTA states (except for Switzerland).

12 June 1994 Austrian voters agree to membership of EU: 67 per cent vote in favour of EU membership.

16 October 1994 Referendum in Finland approves EU membership: 57 per cent vote in favour.

13 November 1994 Swedish voters agree to EU membership by a 52 per cent–48 per cent majority.

28 November 1994 Referendum in Norway on EU membership: 52 per cent vote against membership.

1 January 1995 Austria, Finland and Sweden become member states in the EU.

26 March 1995 Schengen Agreement comes into force, removing most border checks and controls between signatory states.

2 October 1997 Treaty of Amsterdam signed, expanding upon and clarifying aspects of the Rome and Maastricht Treaties.

1–2 May 1998 European Council meeting in Brussels agrees that 11 members meet the convergence criteria which are conditions for qualification for membership of the single currency project. It appoints Wim Duisenberg as head of the European Central Bank, which will be located in Frankfurt.

1 January 1999 Eleven member states commence use of the 'euro' as the single currency, alongside national currencies, but with unchangeable fixed rates of exchange within the group of eleven states.

14 January 1999 Motion of censure on EU Commissioners by European Parliament, on basis of allegations of corruption and other behaviour unsuited to the office of

Commissioner. The motion is rejected by 293–232.

16 March 1999 EU Commission resigns en bloc following publication of an independent report detailing cases of corruption and mismanagement.

10–13 June 1999 European Parliament elections; turnout in most member states declines.

28 September 2000 Danish voters reject membership of the European single currency project: 53 per cent vote against Danish membership.

1 January 2001 Greece joins European single currency.

1 January 2002 'Euro' replaces national currencies as means of exchange.

General

5 June 1947 Marshall, in a speech at Harvard University, proposes what becomes the European Recovery Programme (the 'Marshall Plan').

4 April 1949 North Atlantic Treaty Organisation founded by treaty signed by 12 original member states.

5 May 1949 Statute signed to establish the Council of Europe.

30 September 1961 Organisation for European Economic Co-operation and Development (OECD) replaces Organisation for European Economic Co-operation (OEEC).

Section 5
Data relating to political systems

THE COUNTRIES OF WESTERN EUROPE

Austria

Population 8.1 million (2000)
Capital Vienna
Territory 83,857 sq. km
GDP per capita US$25,788 (2000)
Unemployment 3.7 per cent of
   workforce (2000)
State form Republic. The Austrian
   constitution of 1920, as amended in
   1929, was restored on 1 May 1945. On
   15 May 1955, the four Allied Powers
   signed the State Treaty with Austria,
   ending the occupation and
   recognising Austrian independence.
   Current head of state President
   Thomas Klestil (took office 8 July
   1992, re-elected 1998).
State structure A federation with nine
   provinces (Länder), each with its own
   constitution, legislature and
   government.
Government The president appoints the
   prime minister (chancellor), and, on
   the chancellor's recommendation, a
   cabinet (Council of Ministers) of
   around fifteen members. The Council
   of Ministers is responsible to the
   lower chamber of Parliament, the
   183-member National Council
   (Nationalrat). The second chamber,
   the 64-member Federal Council
   (Bundesrat), is elected by the
   Parliaments of the Länder. The
   government, or individual ministers,
   can be removed from office by a vote
   of no confidence in the National
   Council. The Federal Council has the
   power to delay legislation, but not to
   veto it. For certain important matters,
   the two chambers meet together as
   the Bundesversammlung. Certain
   matters may be subject to a
   referendum. The constitutional court
   (Verfassungsgerichtshof) determines
   the constitutionality of legislation and
   executive acts.
Current government The 1999
   election brought to an end the
   13-year government coalition
   between the Social Democratic Party
   of Austria (SPÖ) and Austrian
   People's Party (ÖVP), which had
   been under considerable strain. When
   the two parties failed to reach a
   coalition agreement, Austria found
   itself short of viable alternatives. The
   record gains of the radical right
   Freedom Party of Austria (FPÖ) had
   changed the balance of power within
   the party system. The other two
   numerically viable coalitions –
   SPÖ/FPÖ or ÖVP/FPÖ – had been
   ruled out in advance by the two
   mainstream parties. An attempt by the
   SPÖ to form a minority government
   failed. Finally, a coalition was formed
   between the ÖVP and FPÖ under
   Wolfgang Schüssel (ÖVP) and
   reluctantly sworn in by President
   Klestil on 5 February 2000. The
   decision to form a government
   including a party of the far right –
   six of the 12-member cabinet were
   FPÖ members – provoked
   international outrage and a period of
   sanctions imposed by the European
   Union.
Electoral systems The president is
   elected by direct universal suffrage for
   a term of six years and may not serve
   more than two terms.
   Elections to the Nationalrat are based
   on a system of proportional
   representation, the 'enforced'
   preference voting system, with a 4 per
   cent threshold. Term of office: four
   years.

Austrian presidential elections, 19 April 1998

	Votes (%)
Thomas Klestil (independent, backed by ÖVP and FPÖ)	63.4
Gertraud Knoll (SPÖ)	13.6
Heide Schmidt (LF)	11.1
Richard Lugner (independent)	9.9
Nowak	1.9

Election to the Austrian Nationalrat, 3 October 1999

	Votes (%)	Seats
Social Democratic Party (SPÖ)	33.1	65
People's Party (ÖVP)	26.9	52
Freedom Party (FPÖ)	26.9	52
Greens	7.4	14
Liberal Forum (LF)	3.6	0
Others	2.1	0
Total		183

Party system Since the Second World War, the Austrian party system has been dominated by the SPÖ and ÖVP, which, until the general election of 1990, together took 90 per cent of the vote. The Greens emerged in the early 1980s, and, in 1986, the FPÖ became a serious electoral force under the charismatic leadership of Jörg Haider. A controversial figure, Haider has in the past expressed approval of the National Socialist (Nazi) regime in Germany. On 28 February 2000, Haider unexpectedly resigned as party leader of the FPÖ, ostensibly as a conciliatory gesture to its coalition partner the ÖVP, but he remains acknowledged as the *de facto* leader of his party.

Belgium

Population 10.3 million (2000)
Capital Brussels
Territory 30,519 sq. km
GDP per capita US$26,570 (2000)
Unemployment 7.0 per cent of workforce (2000)
State form Constitutional monarchy. Belgium seceded from the Netherlands in 1830, and the constitution of 1831 established Belgium as a 'unitary decentralised state'. Between 1970 and 1993 a four-stage process of constitutional reform transformed the country into a federation and culminated in the new Belgian constitution of 1994.
Current head of state King Albert II (sworn in 9 August 1993).
State structure A federation characterised by three linguistic communities (French-, Flemish- and German-speaking), three regions (Walloon, Flemish and Brussels) and four linguistic regions (French-speaking, Flemish-speaking, German-speaking and the bilingual region of Brussels-Capital). The unusually complex federal arrangements are designed to contain the conflicts between the country's linguistic communities.
Government The monarch appoints a formateur to negotiate the formation of a new government. The monarch appoints the prime minister, and, on the prime minister's advice, a cabinet of up to fifteen members comprising an equal number of Flemish and French speakers. Executive power is nominally held by the monarch, but in practice is exercised by the cabinet. The cabinet is responsible to the lower chamber of Parliament, the Chamber of Representatives. Since the constitutional reform of 1993, the upper chamber of Parliament, the Senate, has had only limited legislative powers.
Current government The outgoing christian–social four-party coalition of CVP/PSC/PS/SP under Jean-Luc Dehaene (CVP) had been in government since 1988 but had made losses at each subsequent election. Its heavy defeat in June 1999 was seen as a public response to a range of scandals including an ongoing health-related scandal concerning contaminated feed for livestock and the earlier paedophile scandal of 1996. The series of scandals had

rocked the establishment and had provoked calls for a democratic renewal in Belgium. A new 'purple-green' (ie, red, blue and green) coalition comprising six parties (VLD/PRL–FDF–MCC/SP/PS/AGALEV/ ECOLO) was formed on 12 July 1999 led by Guy Verhofstadt (VLD). It was the first government to exclude the christian democratic parties since 1958.

Electoral systems A constitutional amendment of 1993 altered the membership of the two chambers of Parliament. The Chamber of Representatives formerly had 212 members and now has 150; the Senate formerly had 182 members and now has 71.

Elections to both chambers are by a system of proportional representation for a four-year term. However, only forty of the Senate's seventy-one members are directly elected; the remaining thirty-one are co-opted from the councils of the linguistic communities. In May 1995 elections were held for the first time to the new assemblies for the regional/linguistic communities and to the Brussels assembly. These assemblies each have a term of office of five years.

Elections to the Belgian Chamber of Representatives, 13 June 1999

	Votes (%)	Seats
Flemish Liberals and Democrats (VLD)	14.3	23
Christian People's Party (CVP)	14.1	22
Walloon Socialist Party (PS)	10.1	19
Liberal Reform Party (PRL–FDF–MCC)	10.1	18
Flemish Bloc	9.9	15
Flemish Socialist Party (SP)	9.6	14
ECOLO (Walloon Greens)	7.3	11
AGALEV (Flemish Greens)	7.0	9
Social Christian Party (PSC)	5.9	10
People's Union	5.6	8
National Front (FN)	1.5	1
Others	4.6	0
Total		150

Elections to the Belgian Senate, 13 June 1999

	Votes (%)	Seats
Flemish Liberals and Democrats (VLD)	15.4	6
Christian People's Party (CVP)	14.8	6
Liberal Reform Party (PRL–FDF–MCC)	10.6	5
Walloon Socialist Party (PS)	9.7	4
Flemish Bloc	9.4	4
Flemish Socialist Party (SP)	8.9	4
ECOLO (Walloon Greens)	7.4	3
AGALEV (Flemish Greens)	7.1	3
Social Christian Party (PSC)	6.1	3
People's Union	5.1	2
National Front (FN)	1.5	0
Others	4.0	0
Total		40

Party system Reflecting Belgium's linguistic divide, each of the main ideological families in Belgium is represented by two separate parties: the christian democrats by the Flemish CVP and Walloon PSC; the socialists by the Flemish SP and Walloon PS; the liberals by two recently 'renovated' groupings, the Flemish VLD (formerly PVV) and Walloon PRL–FDF; and the Greens by the Flemish AGALEV and Walloon ECOLO. In addition, there are many protest and fringe groups, of which the most significant are the extreme right-wing Flemish Bloc, the more moderate Flemish Nationalist People's Union, and the extreme right Walloon National Front. With the electorate's rejection of the christian–social coalition in June 1999, the liberal parties emerged as the largest 'political family' for the first time since 1883. For the first time since the 1920s, the christian and socialist families no longer held a combined majority in Parliament. The Green family gained ground while the far right family's standing was eroded overall. New parties demanding a complete overhaul of the political system failed to gain a seat in the federal Parliament.

Denmark

Population 5.3 million (2000)

Capital Copenhagen

Territory 43,075 sq. km

GDP per capita US$28,448 (2000)

Unemployment 4.7 per cent of workforce (2000)

State form Constitutional monarchy, based on the constitution of 5 June 1953.

Current head of state Queen Margrethe II (succeeded to the throne 14 January 1972).

State structure Unitary. Home rule was granted to the Faroe Islands in 1948 and to Greenland in 1979.

Government The monarch appoints the prime minister and, on the advice of the prime minister, the cabinet of around twenty members, which is responsible to the unicameral Parliament (Folketing). Legislative authority rests jointly with the monarch and Parliament. A bill adopted by the Folketing may be submitted to referendum on the request of one-third of the members of the Folketing. The bill is invalid if it is rejected by a majority of the votes cast, provided this represents at least 30 per cent of the electorate.

Current government On 31 October 2001 Prime Minister Poul Nyrup Rasmussen (SDP) called an early general election in what critics saw as an attempt to capitalise on the popularity of his support for the US-led campaign against Afghanistan. The gamble backfired and the SDP suffered losses which cost the party its customary position as the largest party in the Folketing. The defeat led to the transfer of government to the former opposition centre-right. Helped by the parliamentary votes of the right-wing DF, a new minority government was formed comprising the liberals (V) and conservatives (KF), led by Anders Fogh Rasmussen (V).

Electoral systems The Folketing has a maximum of 179 members, two of whom are elected in the Faroe Islands and two in Greenland. The Folketing is elected by a system of proportional representation for a term of office of four years.

Election to the Danish Folketing, 20 November 2001 (excluding representatives from the Faroes and Greenland)

	Votes (%)	Seats
Liberal Party (V)	31.3	56
Social Democratic Party (SDP)	29.1	52
Danish People's Party (DF)	12.0	22
Conservative People's Party (KF)	9.1	16
Socialist People's Party (SF)	6.4	12
Social Liberals (RV)	5.2	9
Red-Green Unity List (ELRG)	2.4	4
Christian People's Party (KrF)	2.3	4
Total		175

Party system The main parties currently fall into two broad groupings of centre-right (V, KF, KrF) and centre-left (SDP, RV, SF and ELRG). The far-right DF was founded in 1995 following a split within the Progress Party (FP). Since the centre-right government depends on its support for a parliamentary majority, the DF now holds a key position within the party system.

Finland

Population 5.2 million (2000)

Capital Helsinki

Territory 338,145 sq. km

GDP per capita US$24,414 (2000)

Unemployment 9.7 per cent of workforce (2000)

State form Republic. Finland was part of the Kingdom of Sweden until 1809 when it became an autonomous Grand Duchy under the Russian Empire. During the Russian Revolution of 1917 Finland claimed its independence and, after a brief civil war, the republic was founded in 1919. Finland's founding republican constitution of 17 July 1919 was replaced with a new constitution on 1 March 2000.

Current head of state President Tarja Halonen (took office 1 March 2000).

State structure Unitary

Government In Finland, the president has traditionally enjoyed a more prominent executive and legislative role than most Western European heads of state. However, the new constitution of 1 March 2000 restricted the president's role, effectively formalising recent practical steps towards institutional relationships more typical of a parliamentary democracy. In future, the president's role will be largely ceremonial. Whereas the president formerly held supreme executive power, this is now shared with the cabinet (Council of State) of around fifteen ministers, headed by the prime minister. Whereas the president used to play a key role in the formation of governments, his or her role is now reactive: to appoint the prime minister selected by the unicameral Parliament (Eduskunta) and those ministers of the Council of State nominated by the prime minister. The prime minister directs the activities of the government. Legislative proposals are introduced in Parliament either by the government or by a private member. The Parliament appoints a parliamentary ombudsman to serve for a term of four years. The president still has a leading role in foreign policy, but must exercise this in co-operation with the Council of State. In other areas, the president must work to proposals submitted by the Council of State. On the request of the prime minister, the president may call an early election to the Eduskunta. The president may be impeached on grounds of treason or of crimes against humanity.

Current government For the first time since independence in 1917, Finland saw a continuation of precisely the same governing coalition following the elections of March 1999. Prime Minister Paavo Lipponen (SSDP) restored his five-party 'rainbow' coalition comprising SSDP/KOK/SFP/VAS/VIHR, arguing that a solid base of co-operation and ministerial experience would be needed for Finland's forthcoming EU presidency.

Electoral systems Following constitutional amendments from 1987, the president is elected by direct universal suffrage for a term of six years and may not serve more than two consecutive terms. If no presidential candidate obtains more than 50 per cent of the vote, a second ballot is held to determine the winner, in which only the two leading candidates of the first ballot may compete.

The 200-member Eduskunta is elected by a system of proportional representation for a four-year term.

Finnish presidential elections, 16 January and 6 February 2000

	First ballot (%)	Second ballot (%)
Tarja Halonen (SSDP)	40.0	51.6
Esko Aho (KESK)	34.4	48.4
Riitta Uosukainen (KOK)	12.8	
Elisabeth Rehn (SFP)	7.9	
Heidi Hautala (VIHR)	3.3	
Ilkka Hakalehto (True Finns)	1.0	
Risto Kuisma (Independent)	0.6	

Elections to the Finnish Eduskunta, 21 March 1999

	Votes (%)	Seats
Finnish Social Democratic Party (SSDP)	22.9	51
Centre Party (KESK)	22.4	48
National Coalition Party (KOK)	21.0	46
Left-Wing Alliance (VAS)	10.9	20
Greens (VIHR)	7.3	11
Swedish People's Party (SFP)	5.1	11
Finnish Christian League (SKL)	4.2	10
Others	6.2	3
Total		200

Party system In common with other Western European countries, Finland's parties are largely divided by the class

173 DATA RELATING TO POLITICAL SYSTEMS

cleavage, with the VAS, SSDP and VIHR on the left, and KESK, KOK, SFP and SKL on the right. (The SKL changed its name to the Christian Democratic Party of Finland on 25 May 2001.) Unlike the practice in other countries, it has been common in Finland for the parties to co-operate across the class divide in broad-based coalition governments.

France

Population 58.9 million (2000)
Capital Paris
Territory 543,965 sq. km
GDP per capita US$23,276 (2000) (overseas territories excluded)
Unemployment 9.5 per cent of workforce (2000)
State form Republic, based on the constitution of 1958 establishing the Fifth French Republic. Following the liberation of France from German occupation in 1944 and a brief provisional government led by General Charles de Gaulle, the Fourth French Republic was founded in 1946. This regime, which proved unstable, was replaced in 1958 by the current one.
Current head of state President Jacques Chirac (took office 17 May 1995, re-elected May 2002).
State structure Unitary, comprising 96 metropolitan departments and 10 overseas departments. Corsica has its own directly elected legislative assembly.
Government The president appoints the prime minister and a cabinet (Council of Ministers) of around twenty members, which is responsible to the bicameral Parliament. Executive power is vested in the president, who is in practice the most politically powerful head of state in Western Europe. The president 'presides' over the Council of Ministers and may, under specified circumstances, dismiss the government ministers and

accept the resignation of the prime minister; submit a bill to a referendum; declare emergency powers; and dissolve the lower chamber of Parliament, the National Assembly (Assemblée Nationale) once in a twelve-month period. The president makes appointments to senior civil and military posts. Throughout most of the Fifth Republic, the electorate has returned a majority supporting the party or coalition of the president to the National Assembly. This has enabled the president to be the effective executive leader of France. Exceptionally, the electorate has instead returned a majority from the opposing 'bloc'. During these periods of 'cohabitation' (1986–88; 1993–95; 1997–2002), executive power has been shared between the president and the prime minister, with the latter commanding the support of the majority in the National Assembly. The constitutionality of bills is determined by the Constitutional Council.
Current government The first ballot of the French presidential election, held on 21 April 2002, shocked the nation when the candidate of the far-right FN took second place from the socialist leader and Prime Minister Lionel Jospin (PS). After this crushing defeat, Jospin stood down as head of the left-radical coalition government. In his place, President Jacques Chirac (RPR) named Jean-Pierre Raffarin (DL) as interim Prime Minister. After the parliamentary elections, Raffarin was confirmed as Prime Minister and on 18 June 2002 took office at the head of a government comprising RPR and DL. These parties had campaigned together during the parliamentary elections as the Union for the Presidential Majority (UMP).
Electoral systems From 1962 to 1995, the president of France was elected

by direct universal suffrage for a term of office of seven years. In September 2000 a referendum approved the reduction of the term of office to five years with effect from the presidential elections of 2002. If no presidential candidate obtains more than 50 per cent of the vote, a second ballot is held to determine the winner, in which only the two leading candidates of the first ballot may compete.

The National Assembly has 577 members: 555 for metropolitan France and 22 for the overseas departments. Members are elected by a single-member constituency system of direct election, using a second ballot if the first fails to produce an absolute majority for any one candidate. The term of office is five years.

The upper chamber of Parliament, the Senate, has 321 members, 296 for metropolitan France, 13 for the overseas territories and 12 for French nationals abroad. It is elected by an electoral college composed of members of the National Assembly and delegates from the councils of the departments and municipal authorities. Senators are elected for a nine-year term of office, but the Senate is not elected as a single body. Instead, one-third of the senators is elected every three years.

French presidential elections, 21 April and 5 May 2002

	First ballot (%)	Second ballot (%)
Jacques Chirac (RPR)	19.9	82.2
Jean-Marie Le Pen (FN)	16.9	17.8
Lionel Jospin (PS)	16.2	
Francois Bayrou (UDF)	6.8	
Arlette Laguiller (Workers' Struggle)	5.7	
Jean-Pièrre Chevènement (Citizen's Movement, MdC)	5.3	
Noel Mamere (Green)	5.3	
Alain Madelin (DL)	3.9	
Robert Hue (PCF)	3.4	
Others	16.6	

Elections to the French National Assembly, 9 and 16 June 2002

	Second ballot (%)	Seats
Union for the Presidential Majority (UMP (RPR and DL))	33.4	355
Socialist Party (PS)	23.8	140
National Front (FN)	11.1	–
French Communist Party (PCF)	4.9	21
Union for French Democracy (UDF)	4.8	29
Greens (les Verts)	4.4	3
Radical Socialist Party (PRG)	1.5	7
Others	16.1	22
Total		577

Elections to the French Senate, 23 September 2001 (resulting total distribution of seats in the Senate)

	Seats
Rally for the Republic (RPR) and allies	96
Socialist Party (PS) and allies	83
Union of the Centre*	53
Republicans and Independents †	40
French Communist Party (PCF) and allies	23
Democratic and Social European Rally*	19
Independents (non-aligned)	6
Vacant	1
Total	321

* mostly UDF   † various right-wing groups

Party system During the years of the Fifth Republic, an initially fragmented party system has developed into a bipolar system of two main 'blocs' of parties on the centre-right and centre-left. Each bloc comprises many parties which frequently splinter and merge. For a time, these blocs were almost balanced in terms of electoral support, but recent elections show that their support is very unpredictable. The landslide defeat of the Socialist Party (PS), the main party of the centre-left, in the 1993 general election was followed by an impressive recovery in the first round of the presidential elections of 1995. In the general election of 1997, a collapse in the vote of the centre-right, whose main parties are the RPR and UDF, was accompanied by a surge in support for the far right National Front (FN). In 2002, the FN's success in entering the second round of the presidential elections prompted a 'pro-republican' cross-party initiative to secure the centre-right candidate Chirac's election in the second round. Finally, in the parliamentary elections of 2002, the parties of the left (socialists, communists and greens) saw their vote share fall dramatically from 318 seats to 171 seats. This ensured the end of the period of 'cohabitation' between a centre-left government and the centre-right President Chirac which had begun in 1997. In spite of the evidence of growing support for the FN, the party lost its only parliamentary seat in the election of 2002.

Germany

Population 82.1 million (2000)
Capital Berlin
Territory 356,959 sq. km
GDP per capita US$24,931 (2000)
Unemployment 7.9 per cent of
  workforce (2000)
State form Republic, based on the
  Basic Law of 1949, with subsequent
  amendments. The Federal Republic of
  Germany (FRG) was founded in 1949
  from the three western zones of
  occupied Germany. On 3 October
  1990, the territories of the former
  German Democratic Republic (GDR)
  and Berlin joined the federation and
  accepted the authority of the Basic
  Law.
Current head of state President
  Johannes Rau (took office 1 July
  1999).
State structure Federation of 16 Länder,
  each of which has its own
  constitution, legislature and
  government.
Government The federal prime minister
  (chancellor) is elected by an absolute
  majority of the Parliament
  (Bundestag) and can only be
  dismissed if a successor is elected on
  the same occasion (a 'constructive

vote of no confidence'). The chancellor selects a cabinet of around twenty members and the president formally appoints the chancellor and cabinet ministers. Executive authority rests with the federal government, which is responsible to the Bundestag. The Federal Council (Bundesrat) is composed of representatives of the governments of the Länder. Each Land sends between three and six delegates according to the size of its population, and may only vote en bloc. The Bundesrat may veto certain legislation. The president's activities are strictly defined and observed and include, under specified circumstances, the dissolution of the Bundestag. The Federal Constitutional Court (Bundesverfassungsgericht) determines the constitutionality of legislation and executive acts.
Current government A centre-left coalition of SPD and Alliance 90/Greens led by Gerhard Schröder of the SPD.
Electoral systems The president is elected by the Federal Convention (Bundesversammlung), comprising the members of the Bundestag and an equal number of delegates elected by the Parliaments of the Länder. The candidate who wins an absolute majority of votes is elected. If no candidate secures an absolute majority in two ballots, a third ballot is held in which a relative majority is sufficient to win. The term of office is five years. A president may not serve more than two successive terms. The Bundestag is elected by direct universal suffrage. Since September 2002 the Bundestag has a standard complement of 598 seats, but the electoral system sometimes allocates surplus mandates. Half of the 598 seats are allocated to constituency candidates on the simple majority plurality ('first past the post') principle

and the remainder by proportional representation based on party lists. Parties receive a share of seats in the Bundestag proportional to their share of party list votes, so that the electoral system is effectively one of proportional representation. The term of office is four years.

Election to the German Bundestag, 22 September 2002

	Votes (%)	Seats
Social Democratic Party (SPD)	38.5	251
Christian Democratic Union (CDU)	29.5	190
Christian Social Union (CSU)	9.0	58
Alliance 90/Greens	8.6	55
Free Democratic Party (FDP)	7.4	47
Party of Democratic Socialism (PDS)	4.3	2
Others	3.0	0
Total		603

Party system From 1961, only three parties won seats in the Bundestag: the CDU–CSU, the SPD and the small liberal FDP. The Greens entered the Bundestag in 1983 and the former GDR reformed communists, the PDS, followed after German re-unification in 1990. The formation of a red–green coalition under Schröder ended Helmut Kohl's 16-year incumbency as Chancellor for the CDU–CSU.

Greece

Population 10.6 million (2000)
Capital Athens
Territory 131,957 sq. km
GDP per capita US$16,244 (2000)
Unemployment 10.9 per cent of workforce (2001)
State form Republic, based on the constitution of 1975. The liberation of Greece from German occupation in 1944 was followed by a civil war which lasted until 1949, when the communist forces were defeated and the constitutional monarchy restored. In 1967, a coup led by right-wing army officers took over the government and set up a façade democracy. The King went into exile,

and, in 1973, Greece was declared a republic. In 1974, after a period of violent instability, former Prime Minister Konstantinos Karamanlis was invited to form a civilian government. A return to constitutional monarchy was rejected by referendum in December 1974. In June 1975, a new republican constitution was introduced, establishing a parliamentary democracy.
Current head of state President Konstantinos Stefanopoulos (took office 10 March 1995).
State structure Unitary, with 10 regions.
Government The president appoints the prime minister, and, on the prime minister's recommendation, the cabinet of around twenty members. In 1986, constitutional amendments reduced the office of president to a largely ceremonial one and transferred many of the president's former executive powers to the unicameral Parliament (Vouli ton Ellinon). The amendments restricted the president's right to call a referendum, transferred the right to call a state of emergency to Parliament, and removed the president's right to dismiss the prime minister. In addition, the president may now dissolve Parliament only if the resignation of two governments in rapid succession demonstrates a lack of political stability. The president may still ask Parliament to reconsider legislation, or to pass it with an enhanced majority.
Current government The incumbent PASOK, led by Kostas Simitis, narrowly won a third successive term in office at the election of April 2000. Simitis had called the election five months ahead of schedule to benefit from his government's good economic record.
Electoral systems The president is elected by Parliament for a term of five years.
The Vouli ton Ellinon has 300

DATA RELATING TO POLITICAL SYSTEMS

members and is elected by direct
universal suffrage for a term of four
years.

Election to the Greek Vouli ton Ellinon, 9 April 2000

	Votes (%)	Seats
Panhellenic Socialist Movement (PASOK)	43.8	158
New Democracy (ND)	42.7	125
Communist Party of Greece (KKE)	5.5	11
Alliance of Left and Progressive Forces (Synaspismos)	3.2	6
Democratic Social Movement (DHKKI)	2.7	0
Others	2.1	0
Total		300

Party system The main parties are
PASOK and the centre-right ND. The
communist KKE has maintained a
small presence in the party system.

Iceland

Population 281,000 (2000)
Capital Reykjavik
Territory 102,820 sq. km
GDP per capita US$27,608 (2000)
Unemployment 2.3 per cent of
workforce (2000)
State form Republic, based on the
constitution of 17 June 1944, when
Iceland declared its independence
from Denmark.
  Current head of state President Ólafur
  Ragnar Grímsson (first took office 1
  August 1996, re-elected 2000).
State structure Unitary
Government The president appoints the
prime minister and a cabinet of
around ten members. Executive
power is vested in the president and
the cabinet, but in practice is
exercised by the cabinet. The cabinet
is responsible to the Parliament
(Althingi), unicameral since 1991.
Ministers may be impeached by the
Althingi and tried by a court of
impeachment. The president may
dissolve the Althingi. In turn, the
president may be dismissed by the

Althingi by a resolution supported by
three-quarters of its members and
confirmed by a referendum. If the
president disapproves a law passed
by the Althingi, it must be confirmed
by referendum.
  Current government The incumbent
  centre-right coalition of the
  Independence Party and Progressive
  party continued under the leadership
  of Prime Minister Davíd Oddsson
  (Independence Party).
Electoral systems The president is
  elected by direct universal suffrage for
  a term of four years.
  The 63-member Althingi is elected by
  a system of proportional
  representation in eight constituencies.
  The term of office is four years.

Election to the Icelandic Althingi, 8 May 1999

	Votes (%)	Seats
Independence Party	40.8	26
United Left	26.8	17
Progressive Party	18.4	12
Left–Green Alliance	9.1	6
Liberals	4.2	2
Others	0.7	0
Total		63

Party system With the parliamentary
election of May 1999, the Icelandic
party system underwent its most
radical restructuring since the Second
World War. Only two parties gaining
seats in the 1995 election competed
in 1999 in the same form: the
centre-right Independence Party and
the centrist Progressive Party. The
Social Democratic Party (including the
People's Movement, which had
broken away from the Social
Democratic Party in 1994) joined
forces with the radical Women's
Alliance to contest the election under
the umbrella of the United Left. Two
further parties, the Left–Green Alliance
and the Liberals, managed to win
seats. The Left–Greens, a splinter
group from the former left–socialist
People's Alliance, formed to represent

the increasing concerns for the environment from a leftist platform. The Liberals formed to contest the 1999 election essentially as a single-issue protest party concerned with fisheries policy.

Ireland

Population 3.8 million (2000)
Capital Dublin
Territory 70,283 sq. km
GDP per capita US$28,895 (2000)
Unemployment 4.2 per cent of
   workforce (2000)
State form Republic, based on the
   constitution of 29 December 1937.
   Ireland was formerly part of the
   United Kingdom. In 1920 the island
   was partitioned, the six north-eastern
   counties remaining part of the UK. In
   1922 the twenty-six southern counties
   achieved dominion status, under the
   British Crown, as the Irish Free State.
   In 1937, the new constitution was
   adopted by referendum, giving the
   Irish Free State full sovereignty within
   the Commonwealth. Formal ties with
   the Commonwealth were ended in
   1949, when the twenty-six southern
   counties became the Republic of
   Ireland (Eire).
Current head of state President Mary
   McAleese (took office 11 November
   1997).
State structure Unitary
Government The president summons
   and dissolves the bicameral
   Parliament on the advice of the
   government or prime minister
   (Taoiseach). On the nomination of
   the lower chamber of Parliament
   (Dáil Éireann), the president appoints
   the prime minister, and, on the
   advice of the prime minister and the
   Dáil, the cabinet of around fifteen
   members. The president is advised by
   a Council of State. The president may
   refer certain bills to the Supreme
   Court for a ruling on their
   constitutionality. With the support of a

prescribed proportion of members of both chambers of Parliament, the president may refer certain bills to a referendum.
Current government Following the
   parliamentary elections of May 2002,
   the outgoing prime minister Bertie
   Ahern (FF) was confirmed at the
   head of his Fianna Fáil/Progressive
   Democrat coalition with the support
   of independents to secure the
   required vote of investiture. As before,
   the government programme featured
   the promotion of a lasting peace
   settlement in Northern Ireland and
   measures to ensure a strong economy.
Electoral systems The president is
   elected by direct universal suffrage for
   a term of office of seven years.
   The Dáil Éireann has 166 members
   and is elected by STV for a term of
   five years.
   The upper chamber of parliament, the
   Seanad Éireann, has sixty members.
   Eleven are nominated by the prime
   minister, six are elected by the
   universities and forty-three by a
   broad-based electoral college. The
   term of office is five years.

Irish presidential election, 30 October 1997

	First count (%)	Second count (%)
Mary McAleese (FF)	45.2	58.7
Mary Banotti (FG)	29.3	41.3
Rosemary Scallon (independent)	13.8	
Adi Roche (LP)	7.0	
Derek Nally (independent)	5.0	

Election to the Irish Dáil Éireann, 17 May 2002

	First preference votes (%)	Seats
Fianna Fáil (FF)	41.5	80
Fine Gael (FG)	22.5	31
Labour (LP)	10.8	21
Sinn Féin	6.5	5
Progressive Democrats	4.0	8
Green Party (GP)	3.8	6
Others/Independents	11.0	14
Speaker		1
Total		166

Party system The two main parties, FF and FG, are both right of centre. Their differences stem from their positions on the Anglo-Irish Treaty establishing the Irish Free State (1921). This cleavage remains as a largely latent but significant cleavage in Irish politics. The anti-Treaty FF formed in 1926; the pro-Treaty FG in 1933. In 2001, the small Democratic Left (DL) joined with the larger left party LP. The other significant parties in the party system are the radical left–nationalist Sinn Féin and the conservative–liberal Progressive Democrats. In 2002, the Progressive Democrats renewed their alliance with FF to form the new government.

Italy

Population 57.2 million (2000)
Capital Rome
Territory 301,277 sq. km
GDP per capita US$24,395 (2000)
Unemployment 10.5 per cent of workforce (2000)
State form Republic, based on the constitution of 1948. The constitutional framework of the previous regime, a constitutional monarchy, had remained in place throughout Mussolini's fascist dictatorship (1922–43) and was terminated by a national referendum held in June 1946.
Current head of state President Carlo Azeglio Ciampi (took office May 1999).
State structure Unitary, with twenty regions, five with a special status. The regions each have an elected legislature and regional executive and enjoy a large degree of autonomy.
Government The president appoints the prime minister, and, on the prime minister's advice, the other members of the cabinet (Council of Ministers). The cabinet has around fifteen full ministers and is responsible to Parliament. The bicameral Parliament has a lower chamber, the Chamber of Deputies (Camera dei Deputati), of

630 members and an upper chamber, the Senate (Senato), of 315 elected members plus ten life senators, appointed by the president of the republic. The two houses of Parliament have equal powers. A constitutional court carries out the judicial review of legislation and judges accusations brought against the president of the republic or government ministers. For many years, a crisis of legitimacy had been building up in the Italian republic, centring on the endemic corruption of the traditional Italian political parties and their consequent failure to work within the institutions to provide strong, democratic government. In 1993, a series of scandals thoroughly discredited Italy's political elite. The crisis set in motion a meltdown and realignment of the party system and an ongoing attempt to bring about a fundamental reform of the country's political system. The project is hoped to lead to a speculative, improved 'Second Republic', but there are fears that the setbacks suffered may have cost the reform movement its impetus. A reform package introduced by the former centre-left government in June 1998 was blocked in the Chamber of Deputies by FI leader Silvio Berlusconi.
Current government A radical right populist coalition led by Prime Minister Silvio Berlusconi (FI) and comprising the FI/AN/LN/CCD–UCD and allied small groupings.
Electoral systems The president of the republic is elected for a seven-year term of office by an electoral college made up of both chambers of Parliament and fifty-eight regional representatives.
New electoral systems for elections to the Chamber of Deputies and the Senate were introduced in 1993. These symbolised the reform process in Italy and were hailed by some as the start of a new Republic. The

Chamber of Deputies has 630 members. Three-quarters (475) are elected on the single-member, single-ballot, plurality principle, as in the UK. The remaining 155 members are elected on a system of proportional representation based on twenty-seven districts, with a 4 per cent threshold.

The Senate has 315 elected members. Three-quarters (238) are elected by a majority vote in regional constituencies and the rest by proportional representation on a regional basis. The term of office for both the Chamber of Deputies and the Senate is five years.

At the 1996 elections, these new electoral arrangements proved so unsatisfactory that they were expected to be replaced with another alternative. However, on 18 April 1999, a referendum proposing new electoral systems failed as the turnout fell just short of the required 50 per cent plus one of the electorate.

Election to the Italian Chamber of Deputies, 13 May 2001

	Votes (%)	Seats
House of Freedoms	49.6	368
Olive Tree Alliance	35.0	250
Refounded Communist Party (PRC)	5.0	11
Others	10.4	1
Total		630

Election to the Italian Senate, 13 May 2001

	Votes (%)	Seats
House of Freedoms	42.5	177
Olive Tree Alliance	38.7	125
Refounded Communist Party (PRC)	5.0	3
Others	11.6	10
Total		315

Party system Italy's party system is currently in a state of flux. Widely discredited by the corruption scandals of 1993, the traditional parties found it impossible to continue under their old names and identities and were forced to reinvent themselves. In spite of this dramatic upheaval, there are strong elements of continuity in the emerging party system. Currently, the powerful House of Freedoms alliance represents a broad spectrum of parties of the right. It comprises Berlusconi's populist, pro-market and right-wing Forza Italia (the party name sounds like a football chant), the far-right National Alliance, the radical right separatist Northern League, the Christian Democratic Centre, the Christian Democratic Union and the New Italian Socialist Party. A similar grouping won the 1994 general election under the banner of the Freedom Alliance. House of Freedoms is opposed by an equally broad range of leftist and Green parties. It includes the Democratic Party of the Left (PDS); the La Margherita alliance (Italian People's Party, Democrats, Italian Renovation, South Tyrolean People's Party (SVP)); the Italian Communist Party; the Greens and the Italian Democratic Socialists.

Luxembourg

Population 439,000 (2000)
Capital Luxembourg-Ville
Territory 2,586 sq. km
GDP per capita US$46,502 (2000)
Unemployment 2.4 per cent of workforce (2000)
State form Constitutional monarchy, based on the constitution of 17 October 1868, as revised in 1919. The last subsequent amendment was on 12 January 1998.
Current head of state Grand Duke Henri (acceded April 2001).
State structure Unitary
Government After consulting the parliamentary party leaders, the Grand Duke nominates the prime minister (President of the Council) who must receive a vote of confidence from Parliament. The prime minister heads a cabinet (Council of Ministers) of around ten ministers, who must not simultaneously hold seats in

Parliament. In theory, Parliament may dismiss the cabinet, but early dissolution is not now seen as a realistic option. The unicameral Parliament (Chamber of Deputies) has sixty members (since 1989). An advisory body of twenty-one members, the Council of State, reviews legislative proposals before they can be adopted by Parliament. The Council of State may delay legislation for up to three months and require Parliament to vote on it a second time.

Current government A coalition of the CSV/PCS and DP/PD under Prime Minister Jean-Claude Juncker was approved by the Grand Duke on 7 August 1999.

Electoral system The Chamber of Deputies is elected on a system of proportional representation based on four districts. The parties put forward lists of candidates and voters may choose to vote for a party list *en bloc*, or for individual candidates across party lists. Voting is compulsory. The term of office is five years (since 1959).

Elections to the Luxembourg Chamber of Deputies, 13 June 1999

	Votes (%)	Seats
Social Christians (CSV/PCS)	30.4	19
Democratic Party (DP/PD)	24.0	15
Socialist Party (LSAP/POSL)	22.6	13
Action for Democracy and Pension Justice (ADR)	9.4	7
Greens (déi Gréng)	8.5	5
The Left (déi Lénk)	1.7	1
Total		60

Party system The three main parties date from the turn of the twentieth century. The CSV/PCS have been in almost every government since 1945, with either the liberal DP/PD or the LSAP/POSL. Other parties include the Green Party (déi Gréng) formed in December 1994 from a merger of existing green groupings, and a single-issue party which campaigns for pension reform (ADR). With the elections of June 1999 there was a significant swing away from the LSAP/POSL and Green Party to the DP/PD, leaving the liberals – in opposition since 1984 – the second strongest party in the Chamber of Deputies and the chance of a return to government.

Malta

Population 379,000 (2000, estimate)
Capital Valletta
Territory 316 sq. km
GDP per capita US$ 8,793 (1995)
Unemployment 5.3 per cent of workforce (2000)
State form Republic, based on the constitution of 1964, subsequently amended. Malta was a Crown Colony of the United Kingdom from 1814. In 1964 it adopted the Independence Constitution, becoming an independent sovereign state within the British Commonwealth. The constitution was amended in 1974, establishing Malta as a democratic republic within the Commonwealth. Further amendments in January 1987 protect Malta's neutrality and ensure that the party with the majority of votes forms the government.
Current head of state President Guido de Marco (selected 4 April 1999).
State structure Unitary
Government The president appoints the prime minister, and, on the prime minister's advice, a cabinet of ten to fifteen ministers, the chief justice, the judges and the attorney-general. The cabinet can be dismissed by the unicameral, 65-member Parliament (House of Representatives).
Current government The majority Nationalist Party (NP) government under Edward Fenech Adami took office on 6 September 1998.
Electoral systems The president is elected by the House of

Representatives for a term of five years.

The House of Representatives is elected by STV, based on thirteen constituencies. The term of office is five years.

Elections to the Maltese House of Representatives, 5 September 1998

	Votes (%)	Seats
Nationalist Party (NP)	51.8	35
Malta Labour Party (PLM)	47.0	30
Democratic Alternative (AD)	1.2	0
Others	0.1	0
Total		65

Party system The major parties are the NP and the PLM. Minor parties include the AD and the Malta Democratic Party (PDM). In 1998, the ousting of the PLM government under Alfred Sant put Malta back on course to join the EU. Malta's application for EU membership had been frozen by the PLM government.

The Netherlands

Population 15.9 million (2000)
Capital The Hague
Territory 33,937 sq. km (land only)
GDP per capita US$27,662 (2000)
Unemployment 2.9 per cent of workforce (2000)
State form Constitutional monarchy, based on the constitution of 1814 and later revisions of 1848 and 1983.
  Current head of state Queen Beatrix (took the throne 30 May 1980).
State structure Unitary. The twelve provinces are each administered by a directly elected council, provincial executive and a sovereign commissioner, who is appointed by royal decree.
Government The monarch appoints a senior politician (informateur) to identify a potential prime minister, who, as a formateur, will form a coalition government. The monarch appoints the prime minister, and, on the advice of the prime minister, the other members of the cabinet. There is no formal vote of investiture for the cabinet, which has some fifteen members. Government ministers must not simultaneously hold seats in Parliament, but may attend Parliament and take part in debates there. The cabinet, under the prime minister, is responsible to Parliament. The Parliament (States-General) is bicameral. The lower chamber, confusingly termed the Second Chamber, has 150 members; the upper house (First Chamber) has 75. Legislation may be proposed by the Crown (as advised by a Council of State) and the lower chamber of Parliament. The Council of State must be consulted on all bills and draft general administrative orders. The First Chamber may approve or reject legislation, but not amend it.
Current government Until shortly before the May 2002 parliamentary election, the left-liberal PvdA/VVD/D66 government of the outgoing Prime Minister Wim Kok (PvdA) had been expected to be endorsed on the strength of a sound economic performance over the previous eight years. However, the assassination on 6 May 2002 of Pim Fortuyn, the controversial leader of the populist LPF, turned the campaign from economic issues to those of immigration, crime and anti-establishment issues. In a dramatic shift to the right, the CDA emerged as the largest party in Parliament with the LPF in second place, ahead of the PvdA. Support for the PvdA fell by almost half to return the party with just 23 seats. It was the party's worst defeat since the Second World War. The CDA's new leader, Jan Peter Balkenende, was expected to form a government coalition of the right, possibly with the LPF and VVD.
Electoral systems The Second Chamber is elected by a system of proportional

representation based on national party lists. Its term of office is four years. The First Chamber is elected by members of the twelve provincial councils. Its term of office is six years, with half its members retiring every three years.

Elections to the Netherlands Second Chamber, 15 May 2002

	Votes (%)	Seats
Christian Democratic Appeal (CDA)	27.9	43
Pim Fortuyn's List (LPF)	17.0	26
People's Party for Freedom and Democracy (VVD)	15.4	24
Labour Party (PvdA)	15.1	23
Green Left (GL)	7.0	10
Socialist Party (SP)	5.9	9
Democrats '66 (D66)	5.1	7
Christian Union (CU) (christian fundamentalist)	2.5	4
SGV (christian fundamentalist)	1.7	2
Livable Netherlands (populist)	1.6	2
Others	0.8	0
Total		150

Party system The electoral landslide of 2002 rocked a party system which had been settling into one of four main parties: the PvdA, CDA, VVD and D66; and numerous small parties including the Green Left and the protestant fundamentalist parties, SGP and CU. The 2002 election brought two new populist parties into Parliament, with LPF, only three months old on election, likely to play a significant role in the party system at least for the current electoral period. The new parties represent anti-establishment as well as populist elements.

Norway

Population 4.5 million (2000)
Capital Oslo
Territory 323,878 sq. km
GDP per capita US$29,311 (2000)
Unemployment 3.5 per cent of workforce (2000)
State form Constitutional monarchy, based on the constitution of 17 May

1814. Norway was formerly linked to the Swedish throne, but declared its independence in 1905 and elected its own monarchy.
Current head of state King Harald V (acceded on 17 January 1991).
State structure Unitary, with nineteen counties (Fylker)
Government The king appoints the prime minister, and, on the prime minister's advice, the cabinet (Council of Ministers) of around twenty members. The cabinet is responsible to Parliament. Ministers must not be members of Parliament, but they may attend and speak there. The unicameral Parliament (Storting) has 165 members. The Storting is elected as a single institution, but then chooses one-quarter of its members to form the upper chamber (Lagting) while the remainder form the lower chamber (Odelsting). Legislation is proposed in the Odelsting and requires the consent of both houses, but, if the houses disagree, can be passed by a joint session of the Storting by a two-thirds majority. Constitutional amendments must be passed by a two-thirds majority of a joint session. The king may veto legislation, but his veto may be overturned by three successively elected Stortings.
Current government A minority centre-right coalition of the Christian People's Party (KrF), the Conservative Party (H), and the Liberal Party (V) won sufficient support in Parliament to form a government under Prime Minister Kjelle Magne Bondevik (KrF), which took office on 19 October 2001.
Electoral systems The Storting is elected by proportional representation based on district party lists; 157 members of the total 165 are constituency representatives, while the remaining eight are elected so as to achieve a greater degree of proportionality among the parties. The four-year term

of office is fixed by the constitution and cannot be terminated early.

Election to the Norwegian Storting, 10 September 2001

	Votes (%)	Seats
Labour Party (AP)	24.4	43
Conservative Party (H)	21.2	38
Progress Party	14.7	26
Christian People's Party (KrF)	12.5	22
Socialist Left Party (SV)	12.4	23
Centre Party (Sp)	5.6	10
Liberal Party (V)	3.9	2
Coastal Party (TF)	1.7	1
Others	3.6	0
Total		165

Party system The main parties are AP, the agrarian Sp, conservative H, christian democratic KrF, the Progress Party, liberal V and the hard left SV. Since the early 1960s, government has usually fallen either to a coalition of centre-right parties or to a Labour minority government. After the elections of September 2001, the incumbent left-of-centre coalition was replaced by the opposition centre-right.

Portugal

Population 10.0 million (2000)
Capital Lisbon
Territory 92,072 sq. km
GDP per capita US$17,556 (2000)
Unemployment 4.1 per cent of workforce (2000)
State form Republic (since 1976). Portugal's First Republic was declared in 1910, but in 1926 fell to a military takeover. This had given way by 1932 to the right-wing dictatorship of Antonio de Oliveira Salazar, led by Marcello Caetano after 1968. In April 1974, this regime was overthrown by the military group, the Armed Forces Movement (MFA). A liberal democratic regime was established with the constitution of 1976. The substantial constitutional revision of 1982 removed the direct political influence of the military and reduced the president's powers; a further

revision of 1989 removed the constitutional commitment to Marxist principles.
Current head of state President Jorge Sampaio (took office 9 March 1996).
State structure Unitary; the Azores and Madeira are autonomous regions.
Government The president appoints the prime minister, and, on the prime minister's advice, a cabinet (Council of Ministers) of around fifteen members. The cabinet's programme must win a vote of confidence from Parliament within ten days of taking office. The cabinet may be dismissed by the Parliament following a vote of no confidence. The unicameral Parliament, the Assembly of the Republic (Assembléia da República) has 230 members. The president may dissolve the Parliament. Legislation passed by Parliament is subject to judicial review by the Constitutional Court. The president may veto legislation. Parliament can overturn a presidential veto with an absolute majority of all its members. The Council of State is the political advisory body of the president.
Current government After the elections of March 2002, the PSD formed a coalition government with the CDS/PP under PSD leader José Mañuel Durao Barroso, who became Prime Minister elect on 22 March 2002.
Electoral systems Presidential elections are by direct universal suffrage. The candidate who wins more than one half of the valid votes is elected. If no candidate achieves an absolute majority, a second ballot is held to decide between the two leading candidates of the first ballot. The term of office is five years. The president may not be re-elected for a third consecutive term of office. The Assembly is elected by a system of proportional representation, with a term of office of four years.

Portuguese presidential elections, 14 January 2001

	Votes (%)
Jorge Sampaio (PS)	55.8
Ferreira do Amaral (PSD)	34.5
António Abreu (PCP)	5.1
Fernando Rosas (BE)	3.0
Garcia Pereira (MRPP)	1.6

Elections to the Portuguese Assembly, 17 March 2002 (excluding the autonomous regions*)

	Votes (%)	Seats
Social Democratic Party (PSD)	40.1	102
Socialist Party (PS)	37.8	95
Democratic Social Centre/People's Party (CDS/PP)	8.7	14
Communist Party (PCP)	7.0	12
Left Bloc (BE)	2.7	3
Others	1.6	0
Total		226

* At the time of writing, the outcome for the autonomous regions (4 seats) was not known.

Party system Despite the revolutionary rhetoric of the 1976 constitution, party competition has been dominated by the centre-left PS and the centre-right PSD. On the radical left are the Portuguese Communist Party (PCP) and the Greens. The small CDS/PP is a conservative grouping. After the elections of October 1999, the incumbent Socialist Party (PS) remained in power under Prime Minister António Guterres. The PS was one seat short of an absolute majority, but was able to form a government with the parliamentary support of other parties of the left. With the election of 2002 the PSD overtook its rival the PS and was expected to form a government with the CDS/PP.

Spain

Population 39.5 million (2000)
Capital Madrid
Territory 504,782 sq. km
GDP per capita US$19,194 (2000)
Unemployment 14.1 per cent of workforce (2000)
State form Constitutional monarchy. The constitution was adopted by national referendum in December 1978. The previous dictatorship of General Franco, established in 1939 following the three-year civil war, effectively ended on Franco's death in 1975.
Current head of state King Juan Carlos I de Borbón (sworn in 22 November 1975).
State structure Unitary, but with considerable devolution of executive and administrative powers to seventeen elected regional assemblies.
Government After consultation with the parliamentary party groups, the king appoints the prime minister (President of the Government), who must win a vote of confidence on his proposed government programme in the lower house of Parliament, the Congress of Deputies (Congreso de los Diputados). On the prime minister's advice, the king appoints a cabinet (Council of Ministers) of fifteen to twenty members. The cabinet is responsible to, and may be dismissed by, the Congress of Deputies. The Parliament (Cortes Generales) is bicameral, consisting of the 350-member Congress of Deputies and an upper chamber, the Senate (Senado) of 256 members. The prime minister may dissolve either or both houses of Parliament once in a twelve-month period. Legislation passed by the Cortes Generales is subject to judicial review by a constitutional court.
Current government A majority government under the centre-right Popular Party (PP) led by Prime Minister José María Aznar.
Electoral systems The Congress of Deputies is elected by proportional representation for a four-year term. The electoral district is the province. 208 members of the Senate are elected by a majority system on a provincial basis, with four senators for every mainland province. The remaining senators, currently 48, are chosen by the assemblies of the

autonomous regions. The term of office is four years.

Elections to the Spanish Congress of Deputies, 12 March 2000

	Votes (%)	Seats
Popular Party (PP)	44.5	183
Spanish Socialist Party (PSOE)	34.1	125
Convergence and Union (CiU)	4.2	15
United Left (IU)	5.5	8
Basque Nationalist Party (PNV)	1.5	7
Others	10.2	12
Total		350

Elections to the Spanish Senate, 12 March 2000, elected members only

	Seats
Popular Party (PP)	127
Spanish Socialist Party (PSOE)	61
Convergence and Union (CiU)	8
Basque Nationalist Party (PNV)	6
Canary Islands Coalition (CC)	5
Independent Party of Lanzarote (PIL)	1
Total	208

Party system The main parties are the PP and the PSOE. Also significant is the far-left coalition, the United Left (IU), which includes the Communists. The main regionalist parties are the CiU and PNV. Numerous other small parties contest elections, many representing regional positions. In the election of March 2000 the PP scored the first majority victory for a centre-right party in contemporary democratic Spain. The party had previously been in a government coalition with CiU and PNV.

Sweden

Population 8.9 million (2000)
Capital Stockholm
Territory 449,964 sq. km
GDP per capita US$24,309 (2000)
Unemployment 5.9 per cent of workforce (2000)
State form Constitutional monarchy. The constitution of 1975 replaced the outmoded version of 1809. It was revised in 1979 to incorporate a new bill of rights.
Current head of state King Carl XVI Gustaf (took the throne 15 September 1973).
State structure Unitary
Government After consultation with the parties represented in Parliament (Riksdag), the Speaker of the Riksdag proposes a candidate prime minister. The prime minister must receive a vote of confidence in the Riksdag before taking office. The prime minister appoints a cabinet (Council of State) of around twenty ministers, which is responsible to Parliament. Individual ministers may also be dismissed by Parliament. The Riksdag has been unicameral since 1969 and has 349 members.
Current government A minority government of the Social Democratic Labour Party (SAP) under Prime Minister Göran Persson (SAP), with parliamentary support from the Left Party (VP) and the Greens (MP), formed on 6 October 1998.

Election to the Swedish Riksdag, 20 September 1998

	Votes (%)	Seats
Swedish Social Democratic Labour Party (SAP)	36.4	131
Moderate Unity Party (M)	22.9	82
Left Party (VP)	12.0	43
Christian Democrats (KD)	11.8	42
Centre Party (C)	5.1	18
Liberals (Fp)	4.7	17
Green Party (MP)	4.5	16
Others	2.6	0
Total		349

Electoral system The Riksdag is elected by a system of proportional representation based on districts. In order to win seats, parties must secure 4 per cent of the total vote or 12 per cent in one district. Of the 349 seats, 310 are permanent constituency seats and 39 are 'adjustment' seats, allocated to ensure that the distribution of seats in the Riksdag is proportionate to the total votes cast for each party. The term of office is four years (since 1994).

Party system The main parties are SAP, M, the Fp, C and KD. Also significant are the Left Party (VP) (the former Communist Party, which changed its name in 1990), and the MP. The right-wing ND lost all of its twenty-five parliamentary seats in the 1994 election. The outcome of the 1998 election was a blow for the SAP, which received its worst share of the vote since 1928. It nevertheless managed to negotiate sufficient parliamentary support to take office as a minority government.

Switzerland

Population 7.2 million (2000)
Capital Bern
Territory 41,293 sq. km
GDP per capita US$29,892 (2000)
Unemployment 3.0 per cent of workforce (1999)
State form Republic, based on the constitution of 29 May 1874. A new constitution was accepted by popular referendum on 18 April 1999 and came into force on 1 January 2000. Although seen as a fundamental review, the new constitution did not substantially change the institutional framework of government in Switzerland. Amongst other measures, it abolished Switzerland's gold-standard status and enshrined the right to strike.
Current head of state President Kaspar Villiger (2002). The president and vice-president of the federation hold office for one year only and are chosen from the seven members of the Federal Council of the Swiss executive. They are elected by the Parliament, the Federal Assembly. The president's role is not comparable with any other Western European presidency. The Swiss president has no special political privileges, but performs the formal

duties of a head of state together with formally chairing the Federal Council.
State structure Confederation of twenty cantons and six half-cantons.
Government The executive body, the Federal Council, consists of seven members, each from a different canton, who act as government ministers. These members represent a coalition of four parties which has been in power since 1959. The members of the Federal Council are elected by a joint session of the bicameral Parliament (United Federal Assembly) for a term of office of four years. Although the Federal Council is held 'responsible' to the Federal Assembly, the Federal Council may not be dismissed before the end of its term of office. The Federal Council is a collegiate body: there is no prime minister and most decisions are agreed by the Federal Council as a whole. The lower chamber of Parliament (National Council) has 200 members and represents the Swiss people. The upper chamber (Council of States), representing the cantons, has forty-six members, two from each canton and one from each half-canton. The lower and upper chambers have equal powers. Referenda are crucial to the legislative process in Switzerland. On 4 March 2002 the electorate approved a referendum to join the UN, ending Switzerland's traditional stance of isolation. A formal application will be submitted at the UN General Assembly in September 2002.
Current government The government does not hinge directly on election results, as in other Western European countries, but comprises the formula coalition, noted above, of the Christian Democratic Party of Switzerland (CVP), Social Democratic Party (SPS), the liberal Radical Democratic Party (FDP) and the agrarian right Swiss People's Party (SVP).

Electoral systems Elections to the National Council are by proportional representation based on party lists. Each canton or half-canton forms one electoral district. The term of office is four years.

The method of election to the Council of States varies from canton to canton.

Elections to the Swiss National Council, 24 October 1999

	Votes (%)	Seats
Social Democratic Party (SPS)	22.5	51
Swiss People's Party (SVP)	22.5	44
Radical Democratic Party (FDP)	19.9	43
Christian Democratic Party (CVP)	15.9	35
Green Party (GPS)	5.0	9
Liberal Party (LPS)	2.3	6
Others	11.9	12
Total		200

Party system In addition to the four main parties which make up the government coalition (CVP, SPS, FDP and SVP), a number of other parties contest general elections. These include the liberal LPS, Green GPS, Swiss Democrats (SD) (formerly known as National Action against Foreign Infiltration of the People and Homeland) and the evangelical EVP.

United Kingdom

Population 59.5 million (1999)
Capital London
Territory 244,103 sq. km
GDP per capita US$ 22,882 (1999)
Unemployment 6.6 per cent of workforce (2000)
State form Constitutional monarchy, without a written constitution.
   Current head of state Queen Elizabeth II (acceded 6 February 1952).
State structure Unitary, with differential devolution of powers to Scotland, Wales and Northern Ireland.
Government The monarch appoints the prime minister, usually the leader of the largest party in the lower house of Parliament, the House of Commons. The prime minister chooses a cabinet of around twenty members, who are appointed by the monarch. The House of Commons has 659 members. The incumbent Labour government is currently attempting a piecemeal reform of the upper house, the House of Lords. Traditionally, the House of Lords has had a variable membership of around 1,200. It was a non-elected body with three categories of member: hereditary and non-hereditary peers appointed by the monarch; archbishops and senior bishops of the Church of England; and law lords, who, within the House of Lords, performed the function of a final court of appeal. Reforms to date have concentrated on reducing the proportion of hereditary peers with automatic membership: 90 peers were elected in October 1999 and it is proposed that an increasing proportion of peers are to be appointed or elected to their seats or positions. The reform proposals are controversial and their outcome remains uncertain. As before, legislation must be passed by both houses and obtain royal assent. The House of Lords may delay legislation by up to a year. The prime minister may ask the monarch to dissolve Parliament at any time. Following legislation enacted in 1998, a system of devolution was introduced to the UK with the election of two new chambers in May 1999: the Scottish Parliament and the National Assembly for Wales. UK devolution is open-ended and is expected later to encompass the English regions. Although intended to incorporate the Northern Ireland Assembly, the status of devolution has in practice remained uncertain in Northern Ireland with the imposition of temporary suspensions. UK devolution is asymmetric in that the powers awarded to each of the devolved authorities differ in nature and in scope.

Current government A majority Labour Party government under Prime Minister Tony Blair.

Electoral systems The House of Commons is elected for a five-year term of office by a simple majority system of voting in single-member constituencies (first-past-the-post system). The Scottish Parliament and the National Assembly for Wales are elected on a system of proportional representation in which voters have two votes, one for a constituency contest and one for party lists, designed to ensure proportionality. Members of the Scottish Parliament are elected by a mixed system: 73 members represent single-member constituencies and are elected by a simple-majority vote and the remaining 56 are allocated according to an additional member system (AMS) so as to enhance proportionality in the Scottish Parliament. Members of the National Assembly for Wales are elected on similar principles: 40 members representing single-member constituencies are elected by simple-majority vote and 20 members by AMS on regional party lists. The Northern Ireland Assembly has 108 members elected on a proportional basis, with six members from each of the 18 constituencies of the central Westminster Parliament.

Party system The main parties are the Labour and Conservative Parties. The Liberal Democrats are the third national force. The Scottish National Party (SNP) and the Welsh nationalist Plaid Cymru attract regional support in Scotland and Wales respectively. Within Northern Ireland, the main parties are the Protestant Unionist parties (OUP, DUP, PUP and the Alliance Party) and the mainly Catholic Social Democratic and Labour Party (SDLP). The extreme nationalist Sinn Féin also contests elections.

Election to the UK House of Commons, 7 June 2001

	Votes (%)	Seats
National parties		
Labour Party	42.0	412
Conservative Party	32.7	166
Liberal Democrats	18.8	52
Regionally significant parties		
Scottish National Party (SNP)	1.8 (20.1*)	5
Plaid Cymru	0.7 (14.3†)	4
Ulster Unionist Party (UUP)	0.8 (26.8‡)	6
Democratic Unionist Party (DUP)	0.7 (22.5‡)	5
Sinn Féin	0.7 (21.7‡)	4
Social Democratic and Labour Party (SDLP)	0.6 (21.0‡)	3
Independent		1
Speaker		1
Total		659

* of votes cast in Scotland † of votes cast in Wales ‡ of votes cast in Northern Ireland

Election to the Scottish Parliament, 6 May 1999

	First vote (%)	Second vote (%)	Seats (total)
Labour Party	38.8	33.8	56
Scottish National Party (SNP)	28.7	27.0	35
Conservative Party	15.6	15.4	18
Liberal Democrats	14.2	12.5	17
Others	2.7	11.4	3
Total			129

Election to the National Assembly for Wales, 6 May 1999

	First vote (%)	Second vote (%)	Seats (total)
Labour Party	37.6	35.4	28
Plaid Cymru	28.4	30.5	17
Conservative Party	15.9	16.5	9
Liberal Democrats	13.4	12.6	6
Others	4.7	5.1	0
Total			60

Election to the Northern Ireland Assembly, 25 June 1998

	Votes (%)	Seats
Social Democratic and Labour Party (SDLP)	22.0	24
Ulster Unionist Party (UUP)	21.3	28
Democratic Unionist Party (DUP)	18.0	20
Sinn Féin	17.6	18
Alliance Party of Northern Ireland	6.5	6
United Kingdom Unionist Party	4.5	5
Others	10.1	7
Total		108

INTERNATIONAL ORGANISATIONS IN WESTERN EUROPE

Council of Europe

Established in 1949 in Strasbourg to promote unity between its members, to encourage their economic and social progress and to uphold the principles of parliamentary democracy and respect for human rights. The ten founding members were: Belgium, Denmark, France, Ireland, Italy, Luxembourg, the Netherlands, Norway, Sweden and the United Kingdom. There are now forty-one members including all the countries of Western Europe and a number of Eastern European countries. Other countries of Eastern Europe have applied to join.

The Council of Europe has an intergovernmental Committee of Ministers, whose members are usually the foreign minister of their respective member state, and which makes decisions unanimously. It usually meets twice a year. The consultative Parliamentary Assembly has 236 members and meets four times a year. The current Secretary-General of the Council of Europe is Dr Walter Schwimmer (Austria).

The European Convention for the Protection of Human Rights and Fundamental Freedoms was drawn up in 1950 on the recommendation of the Assembly and came into force in 1953. Under the Convention, the European Commission of Human Rights was established in 1954 to investigate alleged violations of human rights, and the European Court of Human Rights was set up in 1959.

European Union (EU)

The European Union has fifteen member states. Its institutions are in three sites: Brussels, Luxembourg and Strasbourg. The EU is regulated by the Treaty of Rome (1957), the later accession agreements for new member states, the Treaty on European Union (1993) and the Treaty of Amsterdam (1999).

The decision-making process within the EU is as follows: proposals originate in the Commission or European Parliament (EP) and are passed to the Council of Ministers (representing the member states), which must agree the proposals before they can come into effect. Once passed by the Council of Ministers, the Commission oversees the implementation of decisions. The EP debates issues, questions Commissioners and ministers, may amend parts of the budget and accept or reject the budget as a whole. It can dismiss the Commission *en bloc*. The Treaty of Amsterdam, which came into force in 1999, expanded and simplified the Parliament's legislative role. The current President of the Commission is Romano Prodi (Italy), who took office in July 1999.

Direct elections to the EP were introduced in 1979. Each member state uses its own electoral system to elect representatives on a five-year term. In 1995 the EP was expanded from a chamber of 567 members to one of 626 to encompass new members with the accession of Austria (21 MEPs), Finland (16) and Sweden (22). Similar to the development in the member state Parliaments, 'party groups' have formed within the EP. The main groupings are: christian democrats (European People's Party), Socialists, Liberal Group, Green/European Free Alliance, Confederal Group of the United Left, Union for a Europe of the Nations, Independents, the Europe of Democracies and Diversities and non-attached members.

191 DATA RELATING TO POLITICAL SYSTEMS

North Atlantic Treaty Organisation (NATO)

The Atlantic Alliance was established on the basis of the 1949 North Atlantic Treaty to provide common security for its members through co-operation in military, political and economic matters. The objectives of the Alliance are implemented by NATO, based in Brussels. The twelve founding members in 1949 were: Belgium, Canada, Denmark, France, Iceland, Italy, Luxembourg, the Netherlands, Norway, Portugal, the United Kingdom and the United States of America. Greece, Spain, Turkey and (West) Germany joined subsequently. Spain remained outside the Alliance's military structure until 1999. The status of France is somewhat unusual. It is a member of the Atlantic Alliance but opted out of the integrated military structure of NATO in 1966 and does not attend these meetings. In 1996, France resumed participation in some but not all of the military organs of NATO. Since the dissolution of the Soviet-led Warsaw Pact in 1991, formerly regarded as the main adversary of the Atlantic Alliance, NATO has undergone radical restructuring in an attempt to meet the new security challenges in Europe. The Czech Republic, Hungary and Poland were formally admitted as members of NATO in March 1999, bringing membership to a total of nineteen members.

NATO has an intergovernmental North Atlantic Council. It is attended on a weekly basis by permanent representatives of the member states, and at least twice a year by member state foreign ministers or their heads of government and state. At all levels, it has effective decision-making authority and decisions are taken by common consent. NATO's Defence Planning Committee is convened twice a year at ministerial level and is attended by member state ministers of defence (although France does not send a representative). The current Secretary-General of NATO is Lord Robertson of Port Ellen (UK).

Selected references*

Books

D. S. Bell, D. Johnson and P. Morris (eds), *Biographical Dictionary of French Political Leaders since 1870* (New York and London: Harvester Wheatsheaf, 1990).

A. Briggs and P. Clavin, *Modern Europe 1789–1989* (London and New York: Longman, 1997).

D. Butler and G. Butler, *British Political Facts, 1900–1994* (Basingstoke: Macmillan, 7th edn, 1994).

D. Butler and G. Butler, *Twentieth Century British Political Facts 1900–2000* (Basingstoke: Macmillan, 8th edn, 2000).

C. Cook and J. Paxton, *European Political Facts, 1918–1990* (Basingstoke: Macmillan, 3rd edn, 1992).

C. Cook and J. Stevenson, *The Longman Handbook of Modern European History 1763–1985* (London and New York: Longman, 1987).

C. Cook and J. Stevenson, *The Longman Handbook of the Modern World: International History and Politics since 1945* (Harlow: Longman, 1998).

A. J. Day (ed.), *Directory of European Union Political Parties* (London: John Harper, 2000).

D. Dinan (ed.), *Encyclopedia of the European Union* (Basingstoke: Macmillan, updated edn, 2000).

Electoral Studies (Guildford: Butterworths, Vols 15 (1996) to 21 (2002)).

European Commission, *Glossary: Institutions, Policies and Enlargement of the European Union* (Luxembourg: Office for Official Publications of the European Communities, 2000).

M. Gilbert, *A History of the Twentieth Century. Volume III, 1952–1999: Challenge to Civilisation* (London: Harper Collins, 1999).

M. Howard and W. R. Louis (eds), *The Oxford History of the Twentieth Century* (Oxford and New York: Oxford University Press, 1998).

R. S. Katz and P. Mair (eds), *Party Organizations: A Data Handbook on Party Organizations in Western Democracies, 1960–1990* (London: Sage, 1992).

Keesing's Record of World Events (Harlow: Longman, Vols 1 (1931 to 48 (2002)). (Titled *Keesing's Contemporary Archives* until 1986.)

P. Legrain (ed.), *Le Dictionnaire des Belges* (Brussels: Paul Legrain, 1981).

I. McLean, *Oxford Concise Dictionary of Politics* (Oxford: Oxford University Press, 1996).

F. Nicholson (ed.), *Political and Economic Encyclopaedia of Western Europe* (Harlow: Longman, for Cambridge International Reference on Current Affairs (CIRCA) Ltd, 1990).

W. Nicoll and T. Salmon, *Understanding the European Union* (Harlow: Longman, 2001).

Organisation for Economic Co-operation and Development (OECD), *Main Economic Indicators* (Paris: OECD, January 2002).

J. Palmowski, *Dictionary of Twentieth Century World History* (Oxford and New York: Oxford University Press, 1997).

---

* This listing has been selected from the sources used in preparing this book. The titles have been chosen as those most likely to help students who wish to pursue a specific interest or field of research. Whereas the listing gives the most recent edition available at the time of writing, students should note that earlier editions are often an invaluable source of historical material.

M. Parry, *Chambers Biographical Dictionary* (Edinburgh: Chambers, 6th edn, 1997).

A. Roney, *EC/EU Fact Book. A Complete Guide* (London: Kogan Page, 6th edn, 2000). *The Europa World Yearbook 2001* (London, Europa Publications Ltd, 12th edn, 2000). *The International Who's Who 2001* (London, Europa Publications Ltd, 64th edn, 2001). *The International Who's Who 2002* (London, Europa Publications Ltd, 65th edn, 2002).

B. Turner (ed.), *The Statesman's Yearbook 2001. The Politics, Cultures and Economies of the World* (Basingstoke: Macmillan, 2000).

D. W. Urwin, *A Dictionary of European History and Politics, 1945–1995* (London: Longman, 1996).

Western Europe 2000 (London: Europa Publications Ltd, Taylor and Francis Group, 3rd edn, 1999).

Who's Who in European Politics (London: Bowker Saur, 3rd edn, 1997).

Who's Who in France/Qui est Qui en France 2000 (Paris: Éditions Jacques Lafitte, Levallais-Perret 31st edn, 1999).

Internet sources

www.politicalresources.net/europe.htm
www.ifes.org/eguide/elecguide.htm
www.magnet.mt/home/cos/(re Malta)
www.statistics.gr/netscape/English/MainPa ge/index_eng.html (National Statistical Service of Greece)